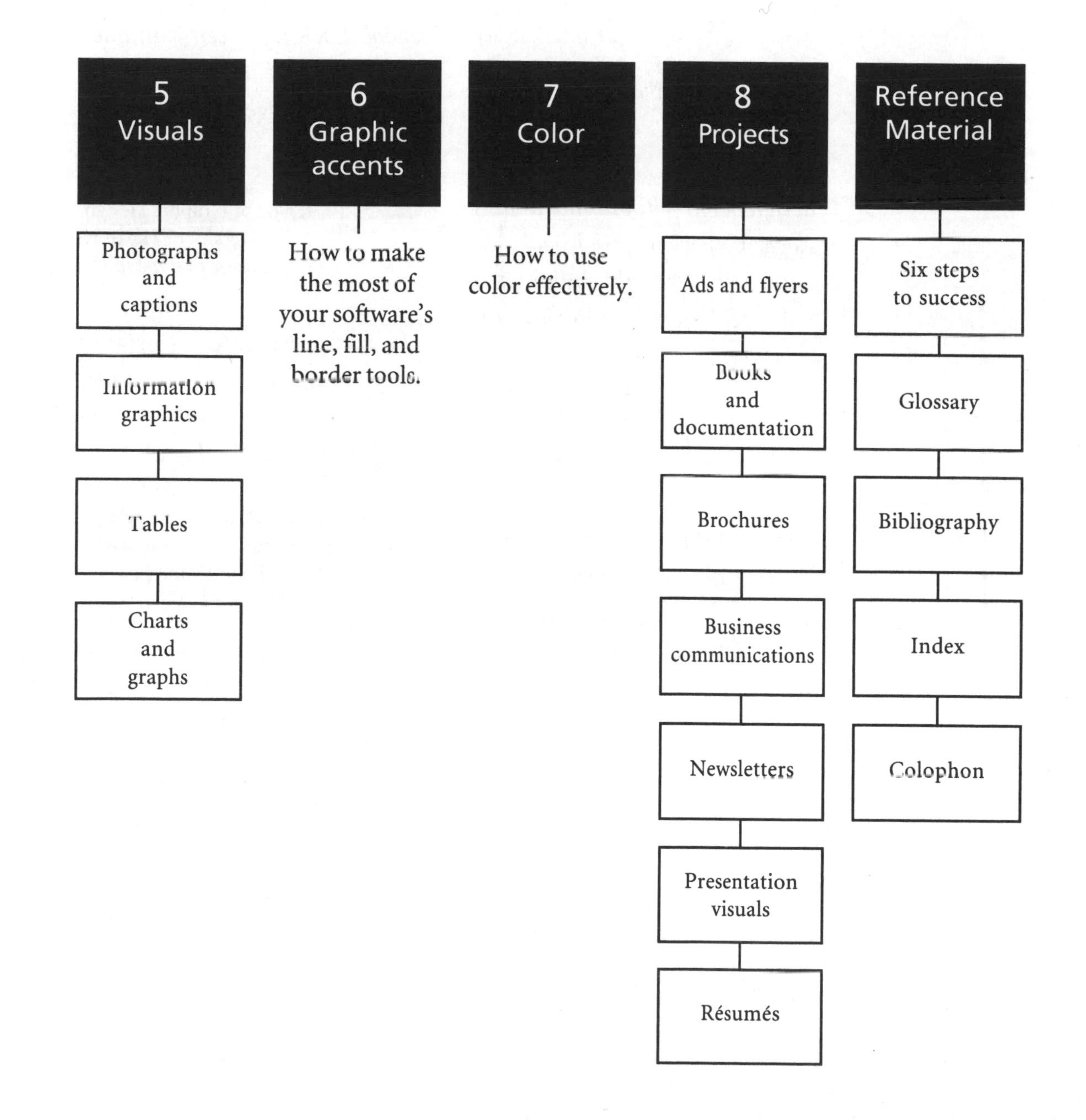
5
Visuals
Photographs and captions
Information graphics
Tables
Charts and graphs
6
Graphic accents
How to make the most of your software's line, fill, and border tools.
7
Color
How to use color effectively.
8
Projects
Ads and flyers
Books and documentation
Brochures
Business communications
Newsletters
Presentation visuals
Résumés
Reference Material
Six steps to success
Glossary
Bibliography
Index
Colophon

Praise for the *One-Minute Designer*

Sets a new standard for easy-to-design publications that get results.

Mark Beach
Author, *Editing Your Newsletter and Getting It Printed*

It's impossible to talk about design books without mentioning Roger C. Parker. [His] books are eminently readable and deal with real-world problems and solutions.

Instant and Small Commercial Printer,
May 1993

One percent of the DTP world doesn't need it. But it will give 99% of the people using desktop publishing programs ideas that will make their work easier to read, which means more effective.

Arthur Einstein
Founder/President,
Lord Geller Frederico and Einstein

The One-Minute Designer *is essential for students of design, whether practicing or still in school. Each tip is self-contained and described as an easy-to-digest idea nugget, making reference effortless.*

Alex White
Professor of Graphic Design,
University of Hartford
author of *Type in Use*

The One-Minute Designer *brings to the surface details that are usually inaccessible or submerged in specialized books.*

Elizabeth Keyes
Professor, Department of Language,
Literature, and Communication,
Rensellaer Polytechnic Institute

Should be required reading for every PageMaker, Quark, WordPerfect, and Microsoft Word for Windows user.

David Field
Desktop Publishing Leader,
Boston Computer Society

Beginners as well as pros will benefit from the wealth of illustrations that show at a glance what works and what doesn't. If readers apply just a few of the ideas in this unique book, their printed messages will create easy-to-read pages with visual allure. In the end, desktop publishing—and its millions of readers—will be the winners.

Frank Grazian
Executive Editor
Communication Briefings

I've created various newsletters for years and immediately absorbed five new ideas from the book I want to try.

Duncan H. Brown
PC Help

Helps PageMaker users take a fresh look at their work.

Olev Kvern
PageMaker 5
Engineering Team,
Columnist, *Aldus* magazine,
author, *Real World Freehand*

Whether you're the writer, photographer, art director, or printer, Parker's One-Minute Designer *has something valuable for you.*

Howard Penn Hudson,
Newsletter Clearing House,
Publisher, *Newsletter on Newsletters*

The One-Minute Designer *is full of strategic ways that people like myself, fledgling designers, can solve real-world problems, resulting in better-looking, easier-to-read publications.*

Stefan Wennik
Bitstream, Inc.

ONE-MINUTE DESIGNER

Revised Edition

MIS:Press
A Division of Henry Holt and Company, Inc.
115 West 18th Street
New York, New York 10011
http://www.mispress.com

Printed in the United States of America

Library of Congress Cataloging-in-Publication Data

Parker, Roger, C.
[One minute designer]
Roger C. Parker's one minute designer / by Roger C. Parker. --Rev. ed.
p. cm.
ISBN 1-55828-593-8
1. Graphic design (Typography) 2. Desktop publishing. I. Title. II. Title: One minute designer.
Z246.P37 1997 97-37145
686.2'252--DC21 CIP

MIS:Press and M&T Books are available at special discounts for bulk purchases for sales promotions, premiums, and fundraising.

For details contact: Special Sales Director
MIS:Press and M&T Books
Divisions of Henry Holt and Company, Inc.
115 West 18th Street
New York, New York 10011

10 9 8 7 6 5 4 3

Associate Publisher: *Paul Farrell*

Editor: *Rebekah Young*
Managing Editor: *Shari Chappell*
Production Editor: *Kitty May*
Copy Edit Manager: *Karen Tongish*

About the Author

Roger C. Parker is the president of The Write Word, a design, training, and consulting firm located in Dover, NH.

Through his books, seminars, and Web presence (http://www.rcparker.com), Roger has helped over one million users create better-looking pages.

Roger is the author of 24 books, including *Roger C. Parker's Guide to Web Content and Design* (MIS:Press, 1997) and the best-selling *Looking Good in Print* and *Desktop Publishing with WordPerfect for Windows.* He can be reached at:

The Write Word
P.O. Box 697
Dover, NH 03820
http://www.rcparker.com

Contents

Foreword

People don't read books any more. They want it all on CD-ROM with music and fun and maybe a bit of animation. Gotta keep 'em hopping, because attention span is down to a minute-and-a-half.

Nonsense! Of course people read, and people will continue to read because print media is still the handiest, cheapest, and most concise way to transmit information.

There's nothing wrong with a good read. You know, the sort of story you get lost in. It could be literature, some silly mystery, or a romance. The text flows from a beginning to a middle and an end, and characters develop in a plot that twists and turns. That is reading for pleasure.

At the opposite end of the reading spectrum is the telephone directory. It, too, contains words set in type in book form, but nobody actually *reads* it. People look things up in it. Nobody would set the telephone directory as running copy because it would be impossible to find anything in it.

Consider a pro-and-con article in a magazine, in which one writer is for and the other against something. It is logical to place the opposing viewpoints side by side. These kinds of stories have a distinctive shape that resembles neither running text nor a directory.

How about interviews? Why do we automatically set the question first and the answer beneath it? The story represents interaction between two people, so it would be more logical to place the question alongside the answer (like the usual pro-and-con make-up), right? Then the format would reveal the *structure of the material.*

The Form Reveals the Structure of the Material

The form should give the reader a clue to what kind of material it being presented. Is it a story because it looks like running text, a directory that is broken up into little bits, or two opposing points of view?

The form represents the function and exposes it to view. That is where design comes in. It used to be thought that Design's contribution to the product was to make it look nice. Of course it must do that, but pleasing the eye is no longer enough. Too many things are competing for readers' attention. Now we must please the brain as well as the eye.

Design must be raised to a higher, more valuable plane; it must become a partner in the communication process. What we say and how we say it must become fully integrated so that the message jumps up off the page and hits the unsuspecting skimmer/glancer/scanner/page riffler right between the eyes. It is not simply a matter of shortening the text using big, dramatic photos or lots of wild colors, or breaking up the text with incidental drop caps. That's all window dressing. It is counterproductive because it assumes that reading is a bore and that people have to be bamboozled into doing it. It denigrates the value of the words, which carry the message itself. Instead of camouflaging the message, we must do all in our power to reveal it.

Reading is Not Changing

What is changing is the method of transmitting printed information, and this is where the *One-Minute Designer* comes in. First, it is a compendium of fundamental insights vital to anyone using words in print. On a more subtle level, it practices what it preaches. No wonder it was such a success when it was first published in 1993. I welcome its second edition, which is even better than the first. Here's why:

- *Organization.* Its accessible, one-idea-per-page format is ideal.
- *Speed.* It distills each point to 25 or so concise lines—and soundbites work.
- *Clarity.* Before and after illustrations present each point clearly.
- *Accessibility.* The material is grouped logically and intuitively. Just glance at the roadmap inside the front cover. It's a visual index.

—Jan V. White

Publication consultant,
art director, and author of
Editing by Design, Color for Impact, and *Graphic Design for the Electronic Age.*

Introduction

Do parents have favorite children?

You're holding the revised edition of my favorite book, a timeless guide to graphic design without an abundance of theory—just simple tips and ideas, reinforced with short explanations and before-and-after examples.

I think *One-Minute Designer* is my best graphic design book to date. It's my masterpiece, my carefully-crafted attempt to dissect graphic design into the hundreds of tiny elements that spell the difference between success and failure. I enjoyed writing it, and judging from its reviews and comments I've received from satisfied readers, others have enjoyed it just as much.

Origin

The *One-Minute Designer's* originated from Ludwig Mies van der Rohe's statement: "God is in the details." Although spoken by an architect whose work and influence have transformed the skylines of cities around the world, these wise words also apply to graphic design.

The more I analyze the thousands of newsletters, brochures, and advertisements that cross my desk each year, the more I'm convinced that overall design is less important than the details. All too often, pages lose their impact—their appearance is boring and they are hard to read—not because of poor overall design, but because relatively simple details were executed poorly. Conversely, mediocre designs often appear acceptable and readable because the details were executed competently.

In many ways, this book is also an outgrowth of the frustration I experience at the seminars and workshops I conduct around the world. Often, participants are familiar with the tools of design yet fail to apply them consistently. Just about everyone knows what kerning is, for example, yet how many newsletters do we encounter with unkerned headlines?

Premise and Purpose

Design is not an all-or-nothing skill nor is it a talent bestowed upon a lucky few. Rather, effective design results from consistently making the right decisions. This is achieved by incremental fine-tuning, or fixing problems one at a time until the result best serves the reader's needs.

Accordingly, the purpose of this book is to provide a framework to help you make the right decisions, by evaluating and improving your work as you do it. A secondary purpose is to help you take a more critical look at the work of others.

Just One Minute?

Don't quit your day job yet. You aren't going to become a designer in a minute. On the other hand, any of the ideas inside this book can be read in less than a minute and implemented in less than a minute.

Cumulatively, the ideas described in this book will greatly improve the quality of your print communications by helping you to:

- Develop a new perspective on the purpose of design
- Add visual impact to your pages and increase their readability by helping you use white space and typographic contrast as tools
- Fine-tune your pages to eliminate visual distractions and misleading reader cues

My goal in writing this book was to make as much information as possible both accessible and easy to read, hence the one-idea-per-page format.

Who Should Read this Book?

This book is for anyone who is interested in creating better-looking pages as quickly as possible. This book is for you regardless of your experience level and regardless of the hardware and software you use.

You can create great-looking, easy-to-read pages with inexpensive software by using white space and proper typographic techniques. You can also use extremely expensive, dedicated page-layout software to produce ugly, hard-to-read pages. *The power is in the user, not the software!*

Indeed, as you gain experience and your design skills improve, you need this book more than ever—that is, the better you get, the more visible your mistakes will become. As your skills improve, details will become more important, and it will be more important than ever to make incremental improvements so details don't undermine the excellence of your designs.

How to Use this Book

This is not a book that must be read from cover to cover in one sitting. Read it and digest it a page at a time, as time and interest permit. Feel free to open the book to topic you're currently experiencing difficulties with and read forward from there. This is not a "bookshelf" book. Keep it by your computer, where it will always be available for reference.

Notice that some ideas appear to contradict each other. This is not to say that one idea is better than another is, only that there is a time and a place for each idea. It is up to you, as a designer- or writer-turned-designer, to try out various alternatives and learn when to employ each approach.

How this Book is Organized

This book is loosely organized in terms of the major elements of page design. Topics are indexed to make it easy to locate information as it is needed.

A Word About Tone

In the interest of brevity, headlines have been edited to the bone, and qualifiers have been deliberately omitted. Thus most headlines begin with an imperative verb. This is not to imply that you must do what the headline says. In graphic design there are few, if any, absolutes—only "appropriates" and "inappropriates." Feel free to add your own qualifiers to soften the tone.

The Economics of Good Design

Effective design costs no more than ineffective design. Indeed, ineffective design *costs more* through wasted postage, production, and media dollars.

The days of the pure writer or the pure designer are disappearing. To survive in today's competitive job market, communicators must be both writers and designers. At the same time, the reduced costs of hardware, software, and fonts (i.e., typeface designs) is also raising reader expectations. More and more readers want more than the typical Times Roman/Helvetica look of so many documents.

In the final analysis, this book isn't about design as much as it is about surviving and advancing in a competitive world. By developing your design skills, you increase your job security and can develop increased opportunities for creative self-expression.

I hope you enjoy reading the revised edition of my favorite desktop publishing design book as much as I enjoyed preparing it!

—Roger C. Parker

Dover, New Hampshire
August 1997

Free Updates

As a buyer of the One-Minute Designer, *you're entitled to free updates, additional examples, and a list of valuable resources. These resources include a downloadable PreFlight Checklist as well as a Reader Response Form (we want to know what additional topics you'd like covered in future versions of the* One-Minute Designer*).*

To take advantage of this valuable resource, visit the One-Minute Designer *Reader Website at:*

http://www.rcparker.com

Section 1

Planning for Success

You make most of your important design decisions before you start work. These involve seeking the right "fit" between message and reader. No computer hardware or new typeface can provide direction or substitute for solid planning.

Think of yourself as a competitive designer. 1

Design is marketing made visual. Your goal is not to "make pretty pages" as much as it is to "market ideas," to present your ideas – or those of your client or employer – in a way that makes the ideas appealing and accessible to your readers.

Success begins with planning. Each time you begin work on a project, regardless of its size or complexity, take the time to answer the following six questions. Your answers will help you remain on target and help you apply the test of appropriateness to every decision you make as you work on your project.

1. What is the purpose of your publication?

Inform, motivate, persuade?

2. Who are your readers?

Young or old? (Older readers will appreciate a larger type size.)

3. How motivated are they?

4. What action do you want your readers to take?

How much of a "selling job" do you have to do?

5. Are there any production or printing limitations?

Consider the resolution of your output device and the paper your publication will be printed on.

6. Where will readers encounter your publication?

Does your message have to compete with other print communications?

2 Inventory your project's contents.

Document design is similar to solving a jigsaw puzzle. When working with a jigsaw puzzle, the first step is typically to place all pieces face up on the table top. Then you separate border pieces (identified by straight edges) and isolate other pieces likely to be used together, such as blue and white pieces used in the sky.

Page design is similar. You start by identifying the text and visual elements you have to work with and then choose the structure that best accommodates them. *Ask yourself questions like those below.*

A publication, like a novel, containing long extended text passages requires a totally different architecture than a newsletter containing numerous short articles.

What text elements must be accommodated?

A few long articles? ____________________

Many short text elements? ____________________

A mixture of both? ____________________

In general, five- and seven-column grids offer the most flexibility for a variety of visuals of different size, type, and importance.

What types of visuals will you include?

Charts? ____________________

Photographs? ____________________

Graphs? ____________________

Illustrations? ____________________

Clip art? ____________________

Decide on the hierarchy of ideas before design begins.

3

Successful design is based on determining the relative importance and sequence of ideas. Before you can add emphasis through size or typographic contrast, you must be able to identify those elements which tell the greatest story. Ask yourself questions like the ones below.

Idea: Use a thick-tipped, yellow felt-tip marker to establish the hierarchy of ideas at the word processing or manuscript stage. Each time you encounter an important new idea, draw a line between the new paragraph and the preceding paragraph. *This identifies possible subhead locations.* Each time you encounter a few words that summarize adjacent material, highlight them. *This helps you identify pull-quotes.*

Exercise restraint, however. Clutter quickly results when too many text elements are emphasized. Too much emphasis leads to no emphasis!

Have you thoroughly organized your ideas?

What is the most important idea you're trying to communicate? ______________________

What is the *next* most important idea, and the important ideas that follow? ______________________

Which ideas are merely supportive or illustrative? ______________________

Can you identify key words and short phrases that summarize adjacent material? ______________________

Can you tell at a glance where new ideas are introduced? ______________________

Also analyze the content of your visuals. If you do not have access to a scanner, photocopy your photographs and use a marker to draw boxes around the parts that contain the most storytelling power. This crops out unessential details.

4 Determine your publication's image and the type of reader you want to attract.

Analyze your own and your audience's attitudes and expectations. Before you begin working, ask yourself: "What image do you want to project – what type of reader do you want to attract?"

Idea: As a starting point, analyze your options by choosing from "opposites" like the ones below. Choosing from opposites makes it easy to determine the image you want to project and the desired attitudes of your target market.

Your answers to the questions below will influence later design decisions like typeface, the number and symmetrical or asymetrical arrangement of columns and the text inside them, the amount and placement of white space, plus appropriate colors.

Your readers will respond to your choice of typeface, column placement, and page borders on an immediate, nonverbal level, quickly making "read" or "not-read" decisions before they even begin to notice your words.

What atmosphere do you want to project?

Conservative or elegant? ______________________

Affordable or expensive? ______________________

Casual or formal? ______________________

Tolerant or precise? ______________________

Friendly or exclusive? ______________________

Describe your reader. ______________________

Design with your computer turned off. 5

Start by trying out possible solutions with a pencil and paper. Computers are "miracle machines" as far as producing documents, but computer technology is too limiting to permit you to "brainstorm" new ideas.

Part of the problem is that computers are too literal: you're apt to focus on words to the exclusion of shapes and spatial relationships. In addition, typing, pulling down menus, and clicking with a mouse inhibit the creative flow of ideas.

In the examples below, notice how even the roughest illustrations are enough to suggest the appearance of the final, produced pages. By using thick and thin squiggles to indicate type and rough outlines of photos, you can easily try out different page layouts.

Hint: Instead of working on an unstructured, blank page, work at reduced sizes on grid sheets with suggested column layouts, as described on the next page.

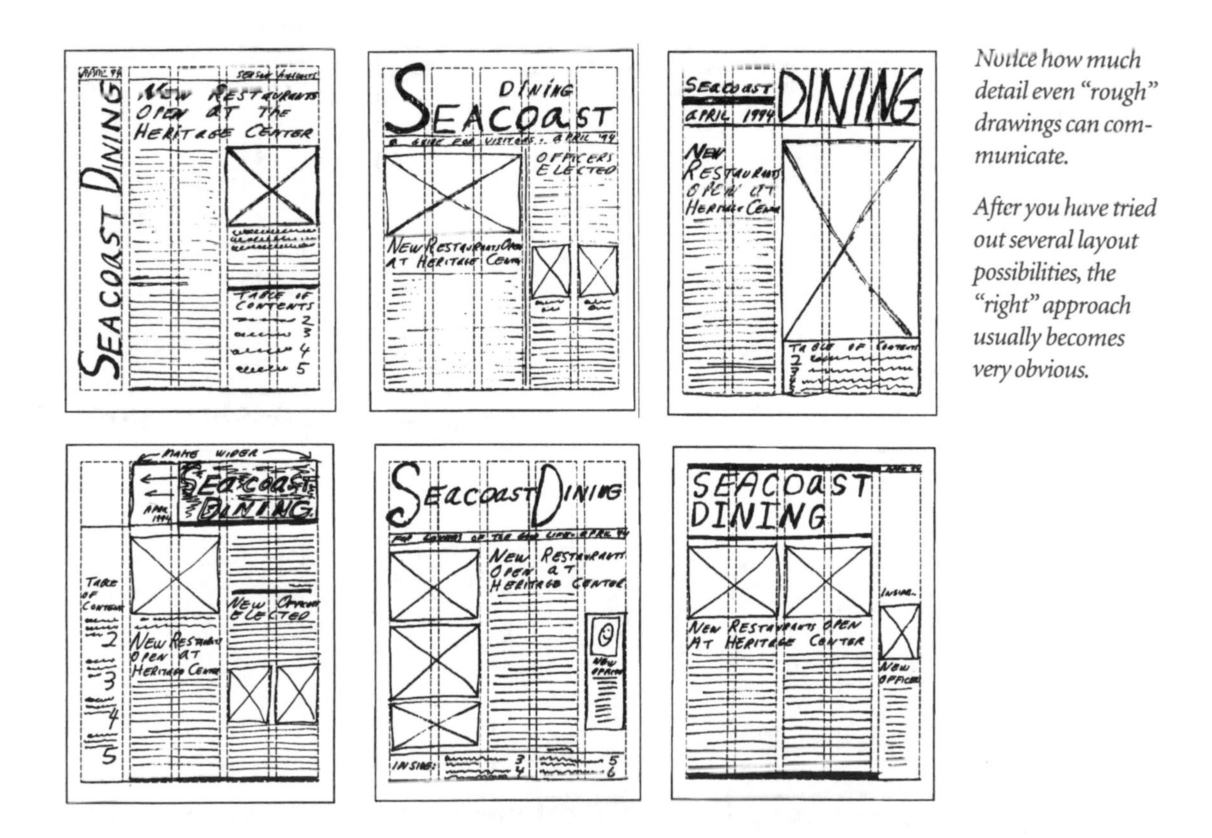

Notice how much detail even "rough" drawings can communicate.

After you have tried out several layout possibilities, the "right" approach usually becomes very obvious.

6 Use your software program's drawing tools to create a framework for experimentation.

Use your software program's box-drawing tools to create reduced-size layout sheets with grids containing varying numbers of columns. Grids consist of nonprinting horizontal and vertical lines that appear on your computer screen to help you align text and visual elements and build consistent amounts of white space into your publication. Grids provide a foundation for your pencil and eraser trial layouts.

Note that the underlying grid provides a framework for combining columns. In most cases, text and visuals will extend over two, or more, columns in the underlying grid.

Grids prepared with your software program's box drawing tool make it easy for you to try out various layout ideas using a pencil and eraser.

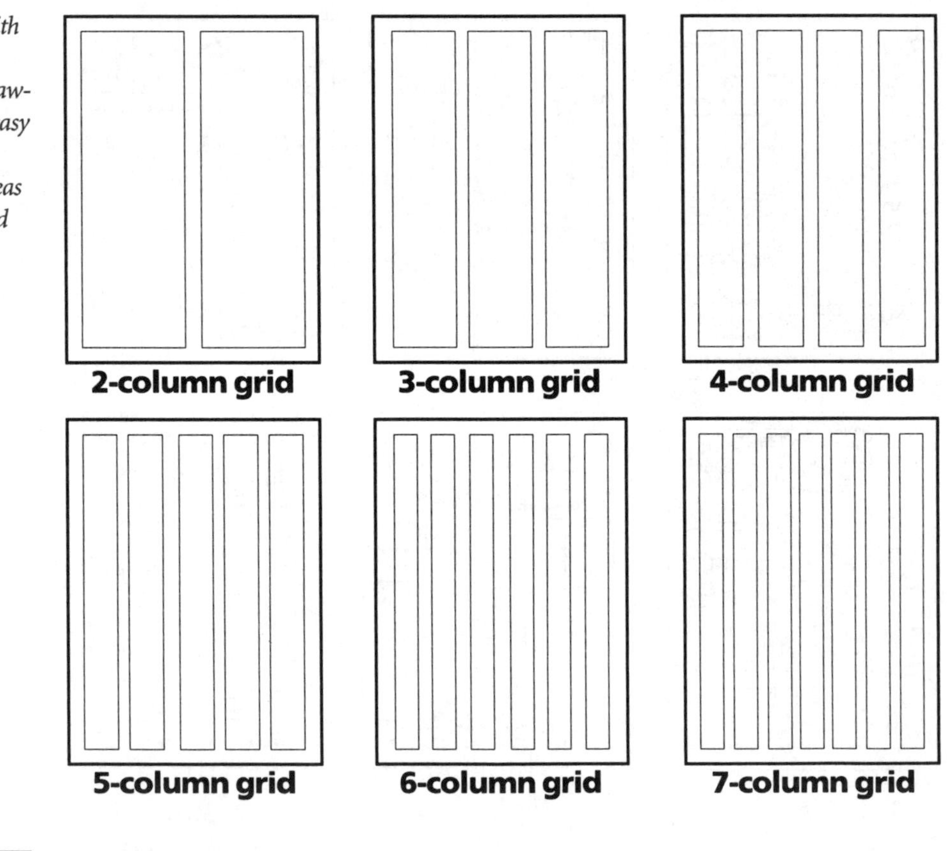

Establish realistic budgets and schedules before work begins.

7

Budgets and schedules help you determine the design options available for you. Budgets influence paper-choice options, publication size, and whether you can use techniques like multicolor printing and bleeds (images that extend to the edges of a page).

Schedules help you prioritize your work and avoid "deadline madness" caused by unrealistic expectations (your own, or your client's or co-worker's). Remember: Last-minute work rarely turns out right; *errors increase as deadlines approach!*

The following planning lists provide some sample questons.

Schedule Planner

Delivery To Reader ________

Mailing Date ________

Final Approval of Proofs ________

Page Layout Ends ________

Page Layout Begins ________

Final Manuscript ________

Budget Planner

Layout and Production $ ________

Service Bureau $ ________

Printing Costs $ ________

Preparing and Applying Mailing Labels $ ________

Postage $ ________

Schedules and budgets like these will help you and your co-workers establish realistic deadlines and budgets.

8 Think of publications as physical products.

Avoid the myopia which results from paying too much attention to the single pages – or portions of a page – that appear on the computer screen. Readers encounter your publication as a *tangible physical object* with a beginning, middle, and end. In addition, readers usually see left- and right-hand pages together.

Your perspective changes when you view your publication as a *tangible physical object* intended to be held in your readers' hands. You are more likely to include sufficient margins for holding the publication, for example.

Likewise, by designing a flyer or poster to be easily read from four or five feet away, you're likely to choose a shorter headline and a larger type size than if you view it simply from the perspective of your computer screen. *Ask yourself questions like those below.*

Will readers hold your project in their hands, or view it hanging on a wall or projected on a screen?

A brochure or newsletter dominates the reader's visual attention, but an ad in a newspaper must compete with adjacent advertisements and editorial material.

How and where will your publication be read?

Where will readers encounter your project? ______________________

Will readers see single pages or two-page spreads? ______________________

What other print communications must your publication compete with? ______________________

Section 2

Page Layout

Page layout involves creating the "container" for text and graphics and determines the way text and graphic elements are placed on the page, particularly elements repeated on all pages.

Let publication content determine column size and placement.

9

The complexity of your document's unique mix of text and graphics should determine the underlying column grid. A simple one- or two-column format with generous top, bottom, and side margins is appropriate if your document consists of extended text with few subheads or visuals. These layouts are appropriate when the emphasis is on words, rather than visuals.

Choose more sophisticated column layouts as the content of your publication grows in complexity. If your publication contains both long and short text features and differently sized visuals, choose grids with columns of varying widths. These offer you the most flexibility to incorporate visuals of varying sizes.

1

Lawrence Learns of Arabia

LOREM IPSUM dolor sit amet, consectetuer adipiscing elit, sed diam nonummy nibh euismod tincidunt ut laoreet dolore magna ali quam erat volutpat. Ut wisi enim ad minim veniam, quis nostrud exerci tation ullamcorper suscipit lobortis nisl ut aliquip ex ea commodo consequat. Duis autem vel eum iriure dolor in hendrerit in vulputate velit esse molestie consequat, vel illum dolore eu feugiat nulla facilisis at vero eros et accumsan et iusto odio dignis sim qui blandit praesent luptatum zzril delenit augue duis dolore te feugait nulla facilisi. Lorem ipsum dolor sit amet, cons ectetuer ad ipiscing elit, sed diam nonummy nibh euismod tincidunt ut laoreet dolore magna aliquam erat volutpat. Ut wisi enim ad minim veni am, quis nostrud exerci tation ullamcorper suscipit lobortis nisl ut aliquip ex ea commodo consequat.

Duis autem vel eum iriure dolor in hendrerit in vulputate velit esse molestie consequat, vel illum dolore eu feugiat nulla facilisis at vero eros et accumsan et iusto odio dignissim qui blandit praesent luptatum zzril delenit augue duis dolore te feugait nulla facilisi. Nam liber tempor cum soluta nobis eleifend option congue nihil imperdiet doming id quod mazim placerat facer possim assum.

Lorem ipsum dolor sit amet, consectetuer adipiscing elit, sed diam nonummy nibh euismod tincidunt ut laoreet dolore magna aliquam erat volutpat. Ut wisi enim ad minim veniam, quis nostrud exerci tation ullamcorper suscipit lobortis nisl ut aliquip ex ea commodo consequat. Duis autem vel eum iriure dolor in hendrerit in vulputate velit esse molestie consequat, vel illum dolore eu feugiat nulla facilisis at vero eros et accumsan et iusto odio

7

Lestie consequat, vel illum dolore vero eros et accumsan et iusto odio dignissim qui blandit praesent lu

Duis autem vel eum iriure dolor in hendrerit in vulputate velit esse molestie consequat, vel illum dolore vero eros et accumsan et iusto odio dignissim qui blandit praesent luptatum zzril delenit augue duis dolore te feugait nulla facilisi. Lorem ipsum dolor sit Amet, consectetuer adipiscing elit, sed diam nonummy nibh euismod tincidunt ut laoreet dolore magna aliquam erat volutpat. Ut wisi enim ad minim qui blandit praesent luptatum zzril delenit augue duis dolore te feugait nulla facilisi. Lorem ipsum dolor sit Amet, autem vel eum iriure dolor in hendrerit in vulputate velit esse molestie consequat, vel illum dolore eu feugiat nulla facilisis at vero eros et accumsan et iusto odio dignissim qui blandit praesent luptatum zzril delenit augue duis dolore te feugait nulla facilisi. Lorem ipsum dolor sit amet, consectetuer adipiscing elit, sed diam nonummy nibh euismod tincidunt ut laoreet dolore magna aliquam erat volutpat.

Ut wisi enim ad minim veniam, quis nostrud exerci tation ullamcorper suscipit lobortis nisl consequat. Duis autem vel eum iriure dolor in hendrerit in vulputate velit esse molestie.

Consequat, vel illum dolore eu feugiat nulla facilisis at vero eros et accumsan et iusto odio dignissim qui blandit praesent luptatum zzril delenit augue duis dolore te feugait nulla facilisi. Lorem ipsum dolor sit amet, consectetuer adipiscing elit, sed diam Lorem ipsum dolor sit amet, consectetuer adipiscing elit, sed diam nonummy nibh euismod tincidunt ut laoreet dolore magna aliquam erat.

Ut wisi enim ad minim veniam, quis nostrud exerci tation ullamcorper suscipit lobortis nisl ut aliquip ex ea commodo consequat. Duis autem vel eum iriure dolor in hendrerit in vulputate velit esse molestie consequat, vel illum dolore eu feugiat nulla facilisis at vero eros et

Inside

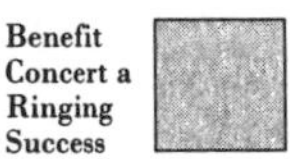

Hendrerit in vulputate velit esse molestie consequat, vel illum dolore eu feugiat nulla facilisis at vero eros et accumsan et iusto odio dignissim qui blandit praesent luptatum zzril delenit augue duis dolore te feugait nulla facilisi.

Single-column formats are ideal for linear publications containing a single level of text, such as novels and mysteries.

Multicolumn layouts, using differently sized columns, can accommodate a more complex mix of text and graphics.

10 Organize pages along an invisible vertical spine.

One of the easiest ways to improve all categories of documents, even simple letterheads and business cards, is to use two columns of unequal width, with text and visuals organized along a single vertical axis. Place this axis at approximately one-quarter to one-fifth of the width of the page, measured from the left-hand border of the page (depending on the size of your firm's logo).

Text and graphics in the left-hand column should be aligned flush right. Objects in the right-hand column should be organized flush left.

This approach presents a more orderly appearance than documents with centered logos, addresses, and headlines. Centering often creates pages with an apparently random design. *Your readers will sense the underlying presence of the vertical axis and be subtly impressed by your attention to detail.*

The vertical white space in the example at right provides organization and presents a more "open" appearance. The white space also allows the firm's logo, address, and phone information to emerge with added clarity.

Note, also, how flush-right alignment of the "to" and "from" fax information makes this information easier to locate.

Glacial Transport

FAX Transmission

To: A-1 Customer
From: Jane
Re: Delivery Contract
Date: June 9, 2010
Pages: 4

Lorem ipsum dolor sit amet, consectetuer adipiscing elit, sed diam nonummy nibh euismod tincidunt ut laoreet dolore magna aliquam erat volutpat. Ut wisi enim ad minim veniam, quis nostrud exerci tation ullamcorper suscipit lobortis nisl ut aliquip ex ea commodo consequat.

Duis autem vel eum iriure dolor in hendrerit in vulputate velit esse molestie consequat, vel illum dolore eu feugiat nulla facilisis at vero eros et accumsan et iusto odio dignissim qui blandit praesent luptatum zzril delenit augue duis dolore te feugait nulla facilisi. Lorem ipsum dolor sit amet, consectetuer adipiscing elit, sed diam nonummy nibh euismod tincidunt ut laoreet dolore magna aliquam erat volutpat. Ut wisi enim ad minim veniam, quis nostrud exerci tation ullamcorper suscipit lobortis nisl ut aliquip ex ea commodo consequat.

Duis autem vel eum iriure dolor in hendrerit in vulputate velit esse molestie consequat, vel illum dolore eu feugiat nulla facilisis at vero eros et accumsan et iusto odio dignissim qui blandit praesent luptatum zzril delenit augue duis dolore te feugait nulla facilisi. Nam liber tempor cum soluta nobis eleifend option congue nihil imperdiet doming id quod mazim placerat facer possim assum.

123 Vertical Street Thistown, NH 12345

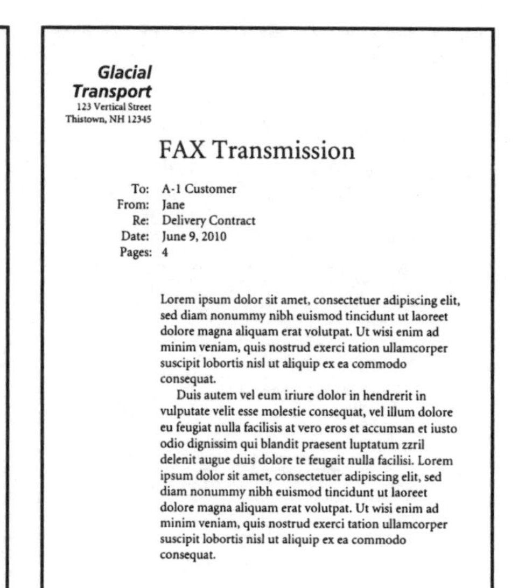

Glacial Transport
123 Vertical Street
Thistown, NH 12345

FAX Transmission

To: A-1 Customer
From: Jane
Re: Delivery Contract
Date: June 9, 2010
Pages: 4

Lorem ipsum dolor sit amet, consectetuer adipiscing elit, sed diam nonummy nibh euismod tincidunt ut laoreet dolore magna aliquam erat volutpat. Ut wisi enim ad minim veniam, quis nostrud exerci tation ullamcorper suscipit lobortis nisl ut aliquip ex ea commodo consequat.

Duis autem vel eum iriure dolor in hendrerit in vulputate velit esse molestie consequat, vel illum dolore eu feugiat nulla facilisis at vero eros et accumsan et iusto odio dignissim qui blandit praesent luptatum zzril delenit augue duis dolore te feugait nulla facilisi. Lorem ipsum dolor sit amet, consectetuer adipiscing elit, sed diam nonummy nibh euismod tincidunt ut laoreet dolore magna aliquam erat volutpat. Ut wisi enim ad minim veniam, quis nostrud exerci tation ullamcorper suscipit lobortis nisl ut aliquip ex ea commodo consequat.

Add white space to the top of each page. 11

The easiest way to improve the appearance of most documents is to add a consistent amount of white space to the top of each page. You can create this white space using your word processing program's header feature or build it into your page layout program's templates or master pages.

Apply a consistent amount of white space on each page between the top of the page and the header text (or header rule), as well as between the header and the beginning of text columns. This white space builds page-to-page continuity and provides space to emphasize headlines.

After readers become accustomed to seeing a consistent amount of white space at the top of each page, you can add impact to your pages by surprising them with a headline or photograph that breaks into the white space.

Concerned citizens urged to speak out

Lorem ipsum dolor sit amet, consectetuer adipiscing elit, sed diam nonummy nibh euismod tincidunt ut laoreet dolore magna aliquam erat volutpat. Ut wisi enim ad minim veniam, quis nostrud exerci tation ullamcorper suscipit lobortis nisl ut aliquip ex ea commodo consequat. Duis autem vel eum iriure dolor in hendrerit in vulputate velit esse molestie consequat, vel illum dolore eu feugiat nulla facilisis at vero eros et accumsan et iusto odio dignissim qui blandit praesent luptatum zzril delenit augue duis dolore te feugait nulla facilisi. Lorem ipsum dolor sit amet, consectetuer adipiscing elit, sed diam nonummy nibh euismod tincidunt ut laoreet dolore magna aliquam erat volutpat.

Ut wisi enim ad minim veniam, quis nostrud exerci tation ullamcoit lobortis nisl ut aliquip ex ea commodo consequat.

Duis autem vel eum iriure dolor in hendrerit in vulputate velit esse molestie consequat, vel illum dolore eu feugiat facilisis at vero eros et accumsan et iusto odio dignissim qui blandit praesent luptatum zzril delenit augue duis dolore te feugait nulla facilisi. Nam liber tempor cum soluta nobis eleifend option congue nihil imperdiet doming id adipiscing elit, sed diam nonummy nibh euismod tincidunt ut laoreet dolore magna aliquam erat volutpat. Ut wisi enim ad minim veniam, quis nostrud exerci tation ullamcorper suscipit lobortis nisl ut aliquip ex ea commodo consequat.

Duis autem vel eum iriure dolor in hendrerit in vulputate velit esse molestie consequat, vel illum dolore eu feugiat nulla facilisis at vero eros et accumsan et iusto odio dignissim qui blandit praesent luptatum zzril delenit augue duis dolore te feugait nulla facilisi. Nam liber tempor cum soluta nobis eleifend option congue nihil imperdiet doming id quod mazim placerat facer possim assum.

Lorem ipsum dolor sit amet, consectetuer adipiscing elit, sed diam nonummy nibh euismod tincidunt ut laoreet dolore magna aliquam erat volutpat. Ut wisi enim ad minim veniam, quis nostrud exerci tation ullamcorper suscipit lobortis nisl ut aliquip ex ea commodo consequat. Duis autem vel eum iriure dolor in hendrerit in vulputate velit esse molestie consequat, vel illum dolore eu feugiat nulla facilisis at vero eros et accumsan et iusto odio dignissim qui blandit praesent luptatum zzril delenit augue duis dolore te feugait nulla facilisi. Lorem ipsum dolor sit amet, consectetuer adipiscing elit, sed diam nonummy nibh euismod tincidunt ut laoreet dolore magna aliquam erat volutpat.

Ut wisi enim ad minim veniam, quis nostrud exerci tation ullamcorper suscipit lobortis nisl ut aliquip ex ea commodo consequat. Duis autem vel eum iriure dolor in hendrerit in vulputate velit esse molestie consequat, vel illum dolore eu feugiat nulla facilisis at vero eros et accumsan et iusto odio dignissim qui blandit praesent luptatum zzril delenit augue duis dolore te feugait nulla facilisi. Lorem ipsum dolor sit amet, consectetuer adipiscing elit, sed diam nonummy nibh euismod tincidunt ut laoreet dolore magna aliquam erat volutpat.

Concerned citizens urged to speak out

Lorem ipsum dolor sit amet, consectetuer adipiscing elit, sed diam nonummy nibh euismod tincidunt ut laoreet dolore magna aliquam erat volutpat. Ut wisi enim ad minim veniam, quis nostrud exerci tation ullamcorper suscipit lobortis nisl ut aliquip ex ea commodo consequat. Duis autem vel eum iriure dolor in hendrerit in vulputate velit esse molestie consequat, vel illum dolore eu feugiat nulla facilisis at vero eros et accumsan et iusto odio dignissim qui blandit praesent luptatum zzril delenit augue duis dolore te feugait nulla facilisi. Lorem ipsum dolor sit amet, consectetuer adipiscing elit, sed diam nonummy nibh euismod tincidunt ut laoreet dolore magna aliquam erat volutpat.

Ut wisi enim ad minim veniam, quis nostrud exerci tation ullamcoit lobortis nisl ut aliquip ex ea commodo consequat.

Duis autem vel eum iriure dolor in hendrerit in vulputate velit esse molestie consequat, vel illum dolore eu feugiat facilisis at vero eros et accumsan et iusto odio dignissim qui blandit praesent luptatum zzril delenit augue duis dolore te feugait nulla facilisi. Nam liber tempor cum soluta nobis eleifend option congue nihil imperdiet doming id adipiscing elit, sed diam nonummy nibh euismod tincidunt ut laoreet dolore magna aliquam erat volutpat. Ut wisi enim ad minim veniam, quis nostrud exerci tation ullamcorper suscipit lobortis nisl ut aliquip ex ea commodo consequat.

Duis autem vel eum iriure dolor in hendrerit in vulputate velit esse molestie consequat, vel illum dolore eu feugiat nulla facilisis at vero eros et accumsan et iusto odio dignissim qui blandit praesent luptatum zzril delenit augue duis dolore te feugait nulla facilisi. Nam liber tempor cum soluta nobis eleifend option congue nihil imperdiet doming id quod mazim placerat facer possim assum.

Lorem ipsum dolor sit amet, consectetuer adipiscing elit, sed diam nonummy nibh euismod tincidunt ut laoreet dolore magna aliquam erat volutpat. Ut wisi enim ad minim veniam, quis nostrud exerci tation ullamcorper suscipit lobortis nisl ut aliquip ex ea commodo consequat. Duis autem vel eum iriure dolor in hendrerit in vulputate velit esse molestie consequat, vel illum dolore eu feugiat nulla facilisis at vero eros et accumsan et iusto odio dignissim qui blandit praesent luptatum zzril delenit augue duis dolore te feugait nulla facilisi. Lorem ipsum dolor sit amet, consectetuer adipiscing elit, sed diam nonummy nibh euismod tincidunt ut laoreet dolore magna aliquam erat volutpat.

Ut wisi enim ad minim veniam, quis nostrud exerci tation ullamcorper suscipit lobortis nisl ut aliquip ex ea commodo consequat. Duis autem vel eum iriure dolor in hendrerit in vulputate velit esse molestie consequat, vel illum dolore eu feugiat nulla facilisis at vero eros et accumsan et iusto odio dignissim qui blandit praesent luptatum zzril delenit augue duis dolore te feugait nulla facilisi.

In the example at left, the headline lacks impact because it is submerged in the text.

The example at right presents an easier-to-read impression because of the horizontal band of white space at the top. This white space also makes the headline easier to read.

12 Build white space into the bottom of each page.

Add white space to the bottom of each page. Add white space between the bottom border of the page and the footer text or footer rule, as well as white space between the footer and the bottom of each column of text. Often, simply eliminating two lines of text from each column can make a major difference in the overall appearance of the page, as the bottom example shows.

In addition, unless you are creating a formal document, consider using uneven, or scalloped columns. Scalloped columns end where paragraphs end (unless the paragraph is so long that at least four or five lines continue at the top of the next column). These designs are easier to produce and create more interesting pages because the bottom of each column contains a different amount of white space.

The top example lacks breathing room. Text closely approaches the rule at the bottom of the the page. In addition, note the single line beginning the new paragraph in the center column.

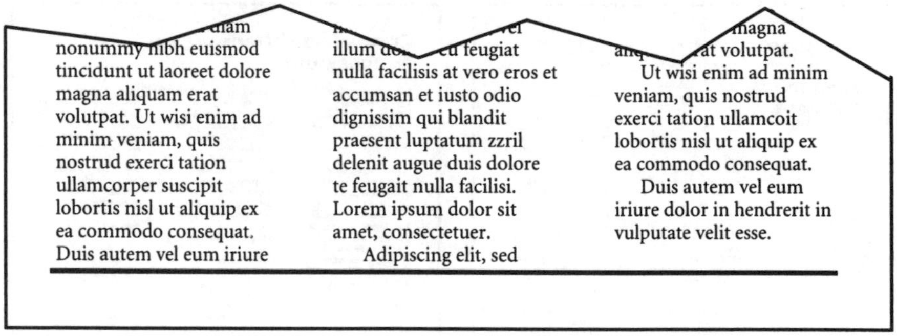

nonummy nibh euismod
tincidunt ut laoreet dolore
magna aliquam erat
volutpat. Ut wisi enim ad
minim veniam, quis
nostrud exerci tation
ullamcorper suscipit
lobortis nisl ut aliquip ex
ea commodo consequat.
Duis autem vel eum iriure

illum dolore eu feugiat
nulla facilisis at vero eros et
accumsan et iusto odio
dignissim qui blandit
praesent luptatum zzril
delenit augue duis dolore
te feugait nulla facilisi.
Lorem ipsum dolor sit
amet, consectetuer.
Adipiscing elit, sed

magna
aliquam erat volutpat.
Ut wisi enim ad minim
veniam, quis nostrud
exerci tation ullamcoit
lobortis nisl ut aliquip ex
ea commodo consequat.
Duis autem vel eum
iriure dolor in hendrerit in
vulputate velit esse.

The white space separating the text from the horizontal rule in the bottom example is emphasized by starting the new paragraph at the top of the last column.

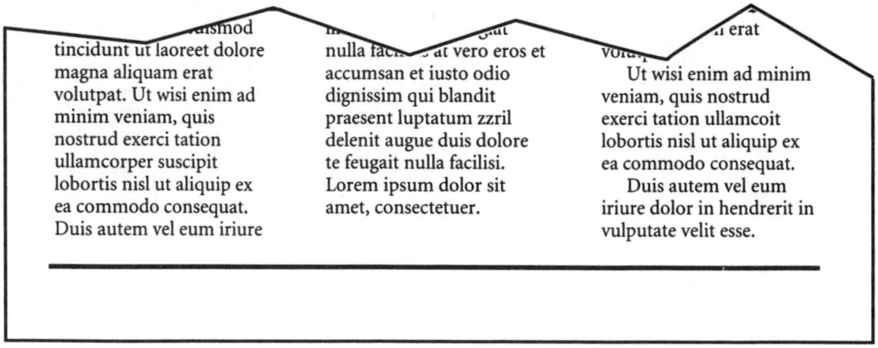

euismod
tincidunt ut laoreet dolore
magna aliquam erat
volutpat. Ut wisi enim ad
minim veniam, quis
nostrud exerci tation
ullamcorper suscipit
lobortis nisl ut aliquip ex
ea commodo consequat.
Duis autem vel eum iriure

nulla facilisis at vero eros et
accumsan et iusto odio
dignissim qui blandit
praesent luptatum zzril
delenit augue duis dolore
te feugait nulla facilisi.
Lorem ipsum dolor sit
amet, consectetuer.

erat
volutpat.
Ut wisi enim ad minim
veniam, quis nostrud
exerci tation ullamcoit
lobortis nisl ut aliquip ex
ea commodo consequat.
Duis autem vel eum
iriure dolor in hendrerit in
vulputate velit esse.

Use five- and seven-column grids to add white space to the sides of your pages.

13

Two- and three-column grids often create unwanted page symmetry. Two- and three-column grids restrict options for placing text and visuals and often result in pages with an undesirable amount of left- and right-hand balance. In addition, two-column grids force you to use a relatively large type size or add extra line spacing.

You can improve the appearance of your pages by using five- and seven-column grids and *combining adjacent pairs of columns.* This builds vertical white space into your pages. Headlines, pull-quotes, and photographs emerge with greater impact when they extend into the narrow columns of white space at the outer edges of each page or two-page spread. The slightly narrower columns also permit a more comfortable relationship between type size and line length.

Notice how "full" the page on the left, based on a two-column grid, appears compared to the same material placed on a five-column grid on the right.

(The seven-column grid, not shown, works in a similar fashion, building in even more flexibility and white space.)

14 Base column spacing on type size.

The default column spacing found in most software programs is too generous for most applications. This is especially true if you are using flush-left/ragged-right type (i.e. columns of text containing lines of different lengths). Get in the habit of replacing your software program's default column spacing with a choice based on the particular layout you're using.

Choose column spacing wide enough to keep readers from reading across the columns, yet narrow enough to avoid creating unconnected columns or vertical bands of white space between the columns.

In general, increase the amount of white space between columns as you increase type size. In addition, use a bit more column spacing when using justified text because flush-left/ragged-right columns contain irregular amounts of white space at the end of each line.

As the top example shows, default column spacing is usually too generous, especially if you choose flush-left/ragged-right alignment.

tincidunt ut laoreet dolore magna aliquam erat volutpat. Ut wisi enim ad minim veniam, quis nostrud exerci tation ullamcorper suscipit lobortis nisl ut aliquip ex ea commodo consequat. Duis autem vel eum iriure dolor in hendrerit in vulputate velit esse molestie consequat, vel illum

luptatum zzril delenit augue duis dolore te feugait nulla facilisi. Lorem ipsum dolor sit amet, consectetuer adipiscing elit, sed diam nonummy nibh euismod tincidunt ut laoreet dolore magna aliquam erat volutpat. Ut wisi enim ad minim veniam, quis nostrud exerci tation ullamcorper

As shown in the bottom example, by reducing column spacing you can eliminate the distracting vertical bands of white space that appear between widely-spaced columns.

tincidunt ut laoreet dolore magna aliquam erat volutpat. Ut wisi enim ad minim veniam, quis nostrud exerci tation ullamcorper suscipit lobortis nisl ut aliquip ex ea commodo consequat. Duis autem vel eum iriure dolor in hendrerit in vulputate velit esse molestie consequat, vel illum dolore eu

delenit augue duis dolore te feugait nulla facilisi. Lorem ipsum dolor sit amet, consectetuer adipiscing elit, sed diam nonummy nibh euismod tincidunt ut laoreet dolore magna aliquam erat volutpat. Ut wisi enim ad minim veniam, quis nostrud exerci tation ullamcorper suscipit lobortis nisl ut aliquip ex ea

Add vertical rules between columns only when necessary.

15

Use vertical downrules between columns only when they are absolutely necessary. All too often, vertical rules are added out of habit rather than necessity, resulting in unnaturally cluttered pages.

Think of vertical downrules as barriers to prevent readers from reading across the columns. As such, they are more often needed with justified text than flush-left/ragged-right text.

When used with flush-left/ragged-right text, vertical downrules often appear to be improperly centered between the columns because the differing amounts of white space at the ends of each left-hand column make the rules appear closer to the right-hand column.

Vertical downrules also slow down production since they have to be resized on pages containing headlines or visuals spanning more than one column.

Lorem ipsum

Lorem ipsum dolor sit amet, consectetuer adipiscing elit, sed diam nonummy nibh euismod tincidunt ut laoreet dolore magna aliquam erat volutpat. Ut wisi enim ad minim veniam, quis nostrud exerci tation ullamcorper suscipit lobortis nisl ut aliquip ex ea commodo consequat. Duis autem vel eum iriure dolor in hendrerit in vulputate velit esse molestie consequat, vel illum dolore eu feugiat nulla facilisis at vero eros et accumsan et iusto odio dignissim qui blandit praesent luptatum zzril delenit augue duis dolore te feugait nulla facilisi. Lorem ipsum dolor sit amet, consectetuer adipiscing elit, sed diam nonummy nibh euismod tincidunt ut laoreet dolore magna aliquam erat volutpat.

Ut wisi enim ad minim veniam, quis nostrud exerci tation ullamcoit lobortis nisl ut aliquip ex ea commodo consequat.

Duis autem vel eum iriure dolor in hendrerit in vulputate velit esse molestie consequat, vel illum dolore eu feugiat facilisis at vero eros et accumsan et iusto odio dignissim qui blandit praesent luptatum zzril delenit augue duis dolore te feugait nulla facilisi. Nam liber tempor cum soluta nobis eleifend option congue nihil imperdiet doming id adipiscing elit, sed diam nonummy nibh euismod tincidunt ut laoreet dolore magna aliquam erat volutpat. Ut wisi enim ad minim veniam, quis nostrud exerci tation ullamcorper suscipit lobortis nisl ut aliquip ex ea commodo consequat.

Ut wisi

Duis autem vel eum iriure dolor in hendrerit in vulputate velit esse molestie consequat, vel illum dolore eu feugiat nulla facilisis at vero eros et accumsan et iusto odio dignissim qui blandit praesent luptatum zzril delenit augue duis dolore te feugait nulla facilisi. Nam liber tempor cum soluta nobis eleifend option congue nihil imperdiet doming id quod mazim placerat facer possim assum.

Lorem ipsum dolor sit amet, consectetuer adipiscing elit, sed diam nonummy nibh euismod tincidunt ut laoreet dolore magna aliquam erat volutpat. Ut wisi enim ad minim veniam, quis nostrud exerci tation ullamcorper suscipit lobortis nisl ut aliquip ex ea commodo consequat. Duis autem vel eum iriure dolor in hendrerit in vulputate velit esse molestie consequat, vel illum dolore eu feugiat nulla facilisis at vero eros et accumsan et iusto odio dignissim qui blandit praesent luptatum zzril delenit augue duis dolore te feugait nulla facilisi. Lorem ipsum dolor sit amet, consectetuer adipiscing elit, sed diam nonummy nibh euismod tincidunt ut laoreet dolore magna aliquam erat volutpat.

Ut wisi enim ad minim veniam, quis nostrud exerci tation ullamcorper suscipit lobortis nisl ut aliquip ex ea commodo consequat. Duis autem vel eum iriure dolor in hendrerit in vulputate velit esse molestie consequat, vel illum dolore eu feugiat nulla facilisis at vero eros et accumsan et iusto odio dignissim qui blandit praesent luptatum zzril delenit augue duis dolore te feugait nulla facilisi. Lorem ipsum dolor sit amet, consectetuer adipiscing elit, sed diam nonummy nibh euismod tincidunt ut laoreet dolore magna aliquam erat volutpat.

Ut wisi enim ad minim veniam, quis nostrud exerci tation ullamcorper

Lorem ipsum

Lorem ipsum dolor sit amet, consectetuer adipiscing elit, sed diam nonummy nibh euismod tincidunt ut laoreet dolore magna aliquam erat volutpat. Ut wisi enim ad minim veniam, quis nostrud exerci tation ullamcorper suscipit lobortis nisl ut aliquip ex ea commodo consequat. Duis autem vel eum iriure dolor in hendrerit in vulputate velit esse molestie consequat, vel illum dolore eu feugiat nulla faci lisis at vero eros et accum san et iusto odio dignissim qui blandit praesent luptatum zzril delenit augue duis dolo re te feugait nulla facilisi. Lorem ipsum dolor sit amet, consectetuer adipiscing elit, sed diam nonummy nibh euismod tincidunt ut laoreet dolore magna aliquam erat volutpat.

Ut wisi enim ad minim veniam, quis nostrud exerci tation ullamcoit lobortis nisl ut aliquip ex ea commodo consequat.

Duis autem vel eum iriure dolor in hendrerit in vulp utate velit esse molestie consequat, vel illum dolore eu feugiat facilisis at vero eros et accumsan et iusto odio dignissim qui blandit praesent luptatum zzril delenit augue duis dolore te feugait nulla facilisi. Nam liber tempor cum soluta nobis eleifend option congue nihil imperdiet doming id adipiscing elit, sed diam nonummy nibh euismod tincidunt ut laoreet dolore magna aliquam erat volutpat. Ut wisi enim ad minim veniam, quis nostrud exerci tation ullamcorper suscipit lobortis nisl ut aliquip ex ea commodo consequat.

Ut wisi

Duis autem vel eum iriure dolor in hendrerit in vulputate velit esse molestie consequat, vel illum dolore eu feugiat nulla facilisis at vero eros et accumsan et iusto odio dignissim qui blandit praesent luptatum zzril delenit augue duis dolore te feugait nulla facilisi. Nam liber tempor cum soluta nobis eleifend option congue nihil imperdiet doming id quod mazim placerat facer possim assum.

Lorem ipsum dolor sit amet, consectetuer adipis cing elit, sed diam nonummy nibh euismod tincidunt ut laoreet dolore magna ali quam erat volutpat. Ut wisi enim ad minim veniam, quis nostrud exerci tation ullam corper suscipit lobortis nisl ut aliquip ex ea commodo consequat. Duis autem vel eum iriure dolor in hendrerit in vulputate velit esse moles tie consequat, vel illum dolo re eu feugiat nulla facilisis at vero eros et accumsan et iust o odio dignissim qui blandit praesent luptatum zzril delenit augue duis dolore te feugait nulla facilisi. Lorem ipsum dolor sit amet, con sectetuer adipiscing elit, sed diam nonummy nibh euis mod tincidunt ut laoreet dolore magna aliquam erat volutpat.

Ut wisi enim ad minim veniam, quis nostrud exerci tation ullamcorper suscipit lobortis nisl ut aliquip ex ea commodo consequat. Duis autem vel eum iriure dolor in hendrerit in vulputate velit esse molestie consequat, vel illum dolore eu feugiat nulla facilisis at vero eros et accumsan et iusto odio dignissim qui blandit praesent luptatum zzril delenit augue duis dolore te feugait nulla facilisi. Lorem ipsum dolor sit amet, consectetuer adipiscing elit, sed diam nonummy nibh euismod tincidunt ut laoreet dolore magna aliquam erat volutpat.

Ut wisi enim ad minim veniam, quis nostrud exerci tation ullamcorper suscipit lobortis nisl ut aliquip ex ea commodo consequat. Duis autem vel eum iriure dolor in hendrerit in vulputate velit esse molestie consequat, vel illum dolore eu feugiat nulla facilisis at vero eros et accumsan et iusto odio dignissim qui blandit praesent luptatum zzril delenit augue duis dolore te feugait nulla facilisi.

Lorem ipsum dolor sit

In the example at left, the vertical rules appear closer to the right-hand column because of the white space characteristically found at the ends of text aligned flush-left/ragged-right.

Eliminating the vertical rules and reducing column spacing creates a more unified page, as shown in the example at right.

16 Use symmetrical page elements to communicate a conservative image.

Symmetrical pages communicate strength and a "classic" or "no surprises" image. Centered elements include headlines, subheads, page numbers, and visuals.

You can emphasize the symmetry of centered page elements by using justified text, i.e. columns containing lines of equal length. The column structure is typically based on one-, two-, or three-column grids. Use visuals of relatively equal size.

The text areas of two-page spreads should appear centered, with equal amounts of white space at the left- and right-hand edges of each page.

Centered headlines, subheads, page numbers, and justified text are hallmarks of symmetrical page layouts.

In this case, the symmetry is reinforced by page numbers centered in the gutter, or space, between the two columns on each page.

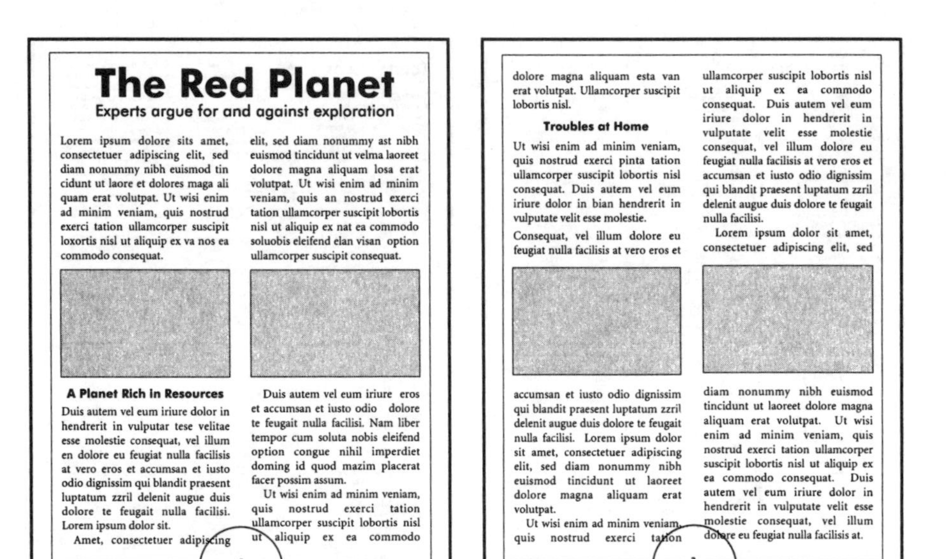

The Red Planet

Experts argue for and against exploration

Lorem ipsum dolore sits amet, consectetuer adipiscing elit, sed diam nonummy nibh euismod tin cidunt ut laore et dolores maga ali quam erat volutpat. Ut wisi enim ad minim veniam, quis nostrud exerci tation ullamcorper suscipit loxortis nisl ut aliquip ex va nos ea commodo consequat.

elit, sed diam nonummy ast nibh euismod tincidunt ut velma laoreet dolore magna aliquam losa erat volutpat. Ut wisi enim ad minim veniam, quis an nostrud exerci tation ullamcorper suscipit lobortis nisl ut aliquip ex nat ea commodo soluobis eleifend elan visan option ullamcorper suscipit consequat.

A Planet Rich in Resources

Duis autem vel eum iriure dolor in hendrerit in vulputar tese velitae esse molestie consequat, vel illum en dolore eu feugiat nulla facilisis at vero eros et accumsan et iusto odio dignissim qui blandit praesent luptatum zzril delenit augue duis dolore te feugait nulla facilisi. Lorem ipsum dolor sit.

Amet, consectetuer adipiscing

Duis autem vel eum iriure eros et accumsan et iusto odio dolore te feugait nulla facilisi. Nam liber tempor cum soluta nobis eleifend option congue nihil imperdiet doming id quod mazim placerat facer possim assum.

Ut wisi enim ad minim veniam, quis nostrud exerci tation ullamcorper suscipit lobortis nisl ut aliquip ex ea commodo

2

dolore magna aliquam esta van erat volutpat. Ullamcorper suscipit lobortis nisl.

Troubles at Home

Ut wisi enim ad minim veniam, quis nostrud exerci pinta tation ullamcorper suscipit lobortis nisl consequat. Duis autem vel eum iriure dolor in bian hendrerit in vulputate velit esse molestie.

Consequat, vel illum dolore eu feugiat nulla facilisis at vero eros et

ullamcorper suscipit lobortis nisl ut aliquip ex ea commodo consequat. Duis autem vel eum iriure dolor in hendrerit in vulputate velit esse molestie consequat, vel illum dolore eu feugiat nulla facilisis at vero eros et accumsan et iusto odio dignissim qui blandit praesent luptatum zzril delenit augue duis dolore te feugait nulla facilisi.

Lorem ipsum dolor sit amet, consectetuer adipiscing elit, sed

accumsan et iusto odio dignissim qui blandit praesent luptatum zzril delenit augue duis dolore te feugait nulla facilisi. Lorem ipsum dolor sit amet, consectetuer adipiscing elit, sed diam nonummy nibh euismod tincidunt ut laoreet dolore magna aliquam erat volutpat.

Ut wisi enim ad minim veniam, quis nostrud exerci tation

diam nonummy nibh euismod tincidunt ut laoreet dolore magna aliquam erat volutpat. Ut wisi enim ad minim veniam, quis nostrud exerci tation ullamcorper suscipit lobortis nisl ut aliquip ex ea commodo consequat. Duis autem vel eum iriure dolor in hendrerit in vulputate velit esse molestie consequat, vel illum dolore eu feugiat nulla facilisis at.

3

Use asymmetrical page elements to project a dynamic image.

17

Use grids with an unequal number of columns, left-aligned (or right or staggered) headlines, and visuals of widely differing sizes to create a disciplined yet "engineered" image. Asymmetrical layouts frequently employ left-aligned headlines and subheads, along with flush-left/ragged-right text. Right-aligned and staggered headlines are also common. Photographs can be of widely differing sizes.

Often, top and bottom borders signal the underlying grid and provide order to apparently unrelated visual elements. Notice, in the example below, the unequal left/right weight on the two page spread, with the reversed headline right-aligned along the right edge of the left-hand page. The result is disciplined, even though the first impression is of apparent randomness.

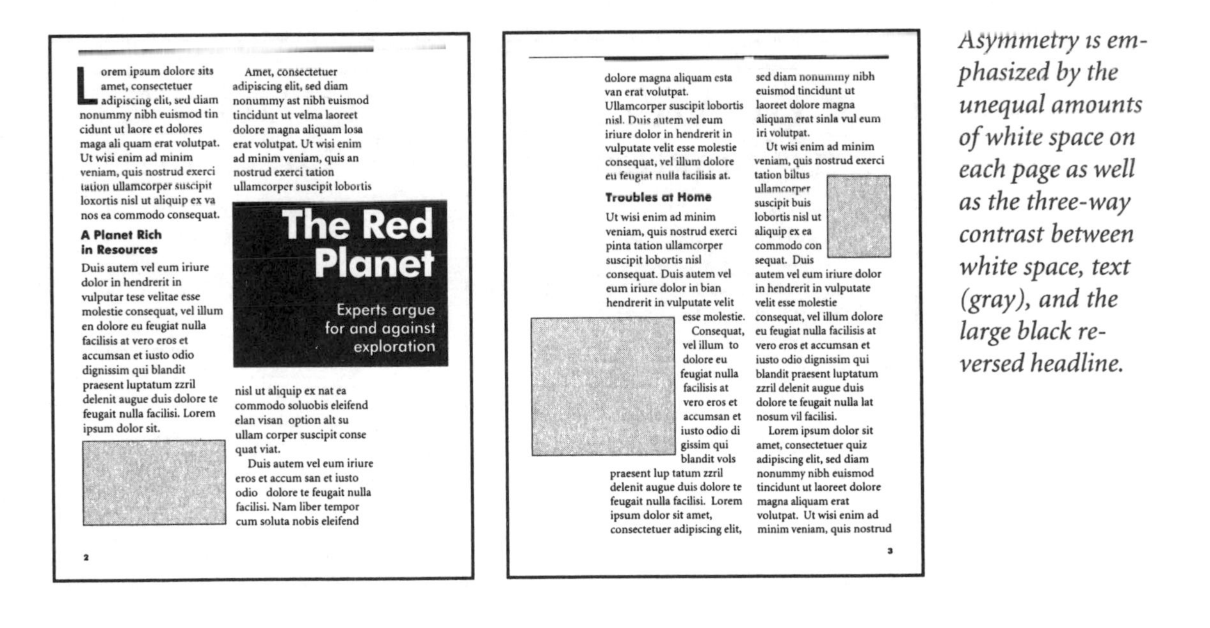

Lorem ipsum dolore sits amet, consectetuer adipiscing elit, sed diam nonummy nibh euismod tin cidunt ut laore et dolores maga ali quam erat volutpat. Ut wisi enim ad minim veniam, quis nostrud exerci tation ullamcorper suscipit loxortis nisl ut aliquip ex va nos ea commodo consequat.

A Planet Rich in Resources

Duis autem vel eum iriure dolor in hendrerit in vulputar tese velitae esse molestie consequat, vel illum en dolore eu feugiat nulla facilisis at vero eros et accumsan et iusto odio dignissim qui blandit praesent luptatum zzril delenit augue duis dolore te feugait nulla facilisi. Lorem ipsum dolor sit.

Amet, consectetuer adipiscing elit, sed diam nonummy ast nibh euismod tincidunt ut velma laoreet dolore magna aliquam losa erat volutpat. Ut wisi enim ad minim veniam, quis an nostrud exerci tation ullamcorper suscipit lobortis

The Red Planet

Experts argue for and against exploration

nisl ut aliquip ex nat ea commodo soluobis eleifend elan visan option alt su ullam corper suscipit conse quat viat.

Duis autem vel eum iriure eros et accum san et iusto odio dolore te feugait nulla facilisi. Nam liber tempor cum soluta nobis eleifend

2

dolore magna aliquam esta van erat volutpat. Ullamcorper suscipit lobortis nisl. Duis autem vel eum iriure dolor in hendrerit in vulputate velit esse molestie consequat, vel illum dolore eu feugiat nulla facilisis at.

Troubles at Home

Ut wisi enim ad minim veniam, quis nostrud exerci pinta tation ullamcorper suscipit lobortis nisl consequat. Duis autem vel eum iriure dolor in bian hendrerit in vulputate velit esse molestie. Consequat, vel illum to dolore eu feugiat nulla facilisis at vero eros et accumsan et iusto odio di gissim qui blandit vols praesent lup tatum zzril delenit augue duis dolore te feugait nulla facilisi. Lorem ipsum dolor sit amet, consectetuer adipiscing elit, sed diam nonummy nibh euismod tincidunt ut laoreet dolore magna aliquam erat sinla vul eum iri volutpat.

Ut wisi enim ad minim veniam, quis nostrud exerci tation biltus ullamcorper suscipit buis lobortis nisl ut aliquip ex ea commodo con sequat. Duis autem vel eum iriure dolor in hendrerit in vulputate velit esse molestie consequat, vel illum dolore eu feugiat nulla facilisis at vero eros et accumsan et iusto odio dignissim qui blandit praesent luptatum zzril delenit augue duis dolore te feugait nulla lat nosum vil facilisi.

Lorem ipsum dolor sit amet, consectetuer quiz adipiscing elit, sed diam nonummy nibh euismod tincidunt ut laoreet dolore magna aliquam erat volutpat. Ut wisi enim ad minim veniam, quis nostrud

3

Asymmetry is emphasized by the unequal amounts of white space on each page as well as the three-way contrast between white space, text (gray), and the large black reversed headline.

18 Use only functional page borders.

Page borders should reflect the desired image. Boxes are often placed around pages out of habit rather than necessity. This often results in unnecessary clutter and conflicts with the desired image.

Use boxes around pages when you want to create a "classic" image. Boxed borders reinforce centered page elements, sometimes at the expense of creating boundries that discourage uninterrupted reading.

Contemporary designs employ horizontal and vertical rules more sparingly, resulting in more "open" pages.

Contemporary designs often use horizontal or vertical rules to provide structure. The varying length and width of these borders emphasize the text and visuals they enclose.

Notice how the page at left looks "wrong" because the centered border conflicts with the asymmetrical placement of the publication name and columns of text.

At right, the heavy horizontal rules reinforce the text area. The narrower rules define the adjacent white space.

QUARTET
Quarterly

Surprise Guest to
Appear at Tanglewood

Season
Opener
Page 4

Inside

Benefit
Concert a
Ringing
Success

QUARTET
Quarterly

Surprise Guest to
Appear at Tanglewood

Season
Opener
Page 4

Inside

Benefit
Concert a
Ringing
Success

Section 3

Display Type

In large part, you can determine the success of your publication by how successfully you handle display type: headlines, titles, subheads, and pull-quotes. Since these are likely to be the most prominent text elements on a page, they play a crucial role in the image you project as well as the readability of your document.

Headlines play a major role in determining the success or failure of your publication. If readers don't read your headlines, they are unlikely to read your body copy. Subheads and pull-quotes provide multiple entry points to long text passages.

19 Choose a contrasting typeface family to add impact to headlines.

The traditional "safe bet" is to combine sans serif headlines with body copy set in a serif typeface. Sans serif headlines are excellent for legibility. The individual letters are clearly defined and easily read from a distance. This differentiation clearly sets your headlines apart from the body copy that follows, making your headlines easier to locate.

Serif typefaces are frequently used for body copy because of their readability – the measure of how easily readers can read extended text blocks. When serif headlines introduce serif text, however, their similarities often weaken their impact unless the headlines are made significantly larger.

Notice how much stronger the sans serif headline introducing the serif text in the right-hand example appears compared to the serif headline introducing serif text in the left-hand example.

Drain cleaner friendly to environment

Lorem ipsum dolor sit amet, consectetuer adipiscing elit, sed diam nonummy nibh euismod tincidunt ut laoreet dolore magna aliquam erat volutpat.

Ut wisi enim ad minim veniam, quis nostrud exerci tation ullamcorper suscipit lobortis nisl ut aliquip ex ea commodo consequat. Duis autem vel eum iriure dolor in hendrerit in vulputate velit esse molestie.

Consequat, vel illum dolore eu feugiat nulla facilisis at vero eros et accumsan et iusto odio dignissim qui blandit praesent luptatum zzril delenit augue duis dolore te feugait nulla facilisi. Lorem ipsum dolor sit amet, consectetuer adipiscing elit, sed diam

Drain cleaner friendly to environment

Lorem ipsum dolor sit amet, consectetuer adipiscing elit, sed diam nonummy nibh euismod tincidunt ut laoreet dolore magna aliquam erat volutpat.

Ut wisi enim ad minim veniam, quis nostrud exerci tation ullamcorper suscipit lobortis nisl ut aliquip ex ea commodo consequat. Duis autem vel eum iriure dolor in hendrerit in vulputate velit esse molestie.

Consequat, vel illum dolore eu feugiat nulla facilisis at vero eros et accumsan et iusto odio dignissim qui blandit praesent luptatum zzril delenit augue duis dolore te feugait nulla facilisi. Lorem ipsum dolor sit amet, consectetuer adipiscing elit, sed diam

Unless there is a significant size difference between a headline and its body text, a headline set in a serif typeface often lacks the impact that a headline set in a sans serif typeface of the same size.

Note the difference between the serif headline/serif text combination in the example at left compared to the sans serif headline/serif text combination in the example at right.

20 Make type size contrasts significant.

Headlines should be significantly larger than the text they introduce. Type is measured in points. There are 72 points to the inch. Most body copy text is set in sizes ranging from 8 to 12 points. With the exception of headlines set in heavy, condensed sans serif typefaces, set headlines in a type size at least three or four times larger than body text.

When headlines are only marginally larger than body text, the headlines are apt to be overlooked or considered "mistakes" rather than deliberate applications of contrast.

The need for significant size contrast is especially true in designs where the same typeface is used for both headlines and body copy. Here, a four- or even five-to-one ratio may be appropriate, especially when designing advertisements.

You may need to edit your headlines in order to create the space needed for large headlines.

The headline in the top example lacks impact because it is not significantly larger than the text it introduces.

Birds flying west

Duis autem vel eum iriure dolor in hendrerit in vulputate velit esse molestie consequat, vel illum dolore vero eros et accumsan et iusto odio dignissim qui blandit praesent luptatum zzril delenit augue duis dolore te feugait nulla facilisi. Lorem ipsum dolor sit amet, consectetuer adipiscing elit, sed diam nonummy nibh euismod tincidunt ut laoreet dolore magna aliquam erat volutpat. Ut wisi enim ad minim veniam, quis nostrud exerci tation ullamcorper suscipit lob... liquip ex ea ...modo conse...

iusto odio dolore te feugait nulla facilisi. Nam liber tempor cum soluta nobis eleifend option congue nihil imperdiet doming id quod mazim placerat facer possim assum.

Lorem ipsum dolor sit amet, consectetuer adipiscing elit, sed diam nonummy nibh euismod tincidunt ut laoreet dolore magna aliquam erat.

Ut wisi enim ad minim veniam, quis nostrud exerci tation ullamcorper suscipit lobortis nisl ut aliquip ex ea commodo consequat. Duis autem vel eum iriure dolor in hendrerit in vulputate velit esse molestie consequat, vel illum dolore e...iat nulla ...eros et accumsan e...

In the bottom example, a significant size difference helps readers quickly locate the headline. In addition, the headline's large size allows readers to appreciate the beauty of the typeface.

Birds flying west

Duis autem vel eum iriure dolor in hendrerit in vulputate velit esse molestie consequat, vel illum dolore vero eros et accumsan et iusto odio dignissim qui blandit praesent luptatum zzril delenit augue duis dolore te feugait nulla facilisi. Lorem ipsum dolor sit amet, consectetuer adipiscing elit, sed diam nonummy nibh euismod tincidunt ut laoreet dolore magna aliquam erat volutpat. Ut wisi enim ad minim veniam, quis...

iusto odio dolore te feugait nulla facilisi. Nam liber tempor cum soluta nobis eleifend option congue nihil imperdiet doming id quod mazim placerat facer possim assum.

Lorem ipsum dolor sit amet, consectetuer adipiscing elit, sed diam nonummy nibh euismod tincidunt ut laoreet dolore magna aliquam erat.

Ut wisi enim ad minim veniam, qui...ostrud ...ullamcorper suscipit...

Use type size to create a visible hierarchy of importance.

21

There should be a close relationship between the size of the headline and the importance of the article it introduces. At a glance, readers should be able to identify the most important article, followed by lesser articles.

When all headlines on a page appear the same size, it is difficult for readers to separate lead – or important – articles from secondary – or supporting – articles.

In addition, visual boredom can easily set in when all headlines are set approximately the same size. The example on the left provides no clue to indicate which article is of greater importance and, hence, no starting point for your eye's travel through the page. In the example on the right, your eye is immediately drawn to the larger, stronger headline.

Board Report on Travel Expenses Budget Cuts

Lorem ipsum dolor sit amet, consectetuer adipiscing elit, sed diam nonummy nibh euismod tincidunt ut laoreet dolore magna al iquam erat volutpat. Ut wisi enim ad minim veniam, quis nostrud exerci tation ullamcorper suscipit lobortis nisl ut aliquip ex ea commodo consequat.

Duis autem vel eum iriure dolor in hendrerit in vulputate velit esse molestie consequat, vel illum dolore eu feugiat nulla facilisis at vero eros et accumsan et iusto odio dignissim qui blandit praesent luptatum zzril delenit augue duis dolore te feugait nulla facilisi. Lorem ipsum dolor sit amet, consectetuer adipiscing elit, sed diam nonummy nibh euismod tincidunt ut laoreet dolore magna aliquam erat volutpat.

Ut wisi enim ad minim veniam, quis nostrud exerci tation ullamcoit lobortis nisl ut aliquip ex ea commodo consequat.

Duis autem vel eum iriure dolor in hendrerit in vulputate velit esse molestie consequat, vel illum dolore eu feugiat facilisis at vero eros et accumsan et iusto odio dignissim qui blandit praesent luptatum zzril delenit augue duis dolore te feugait nulla facilisi. Nam liber tempor cum soluta nobis eleifend option congue nihil imperdiet doming id adipiscing elit, sed diam nonummy nibh euismod tincidunt ut laoreet.

Ice Cream Vendor Lowers Prices

Dolore magna aliquam erat volutpat. Ut wisi enim ad minim veniam, quis nostrud exerci tation ullamcorper suscipit lobortis nisl ut aliquip ex ea commodo consequat.

Duis autem vel eum iriure dolor in hendrerit in vulputate velit esse molestie consequat, vel illum dolore eu feugiat nulla facilisis at vero eros et accumsan et iusto odio dignissim qui blandit praesent luptatum zzril delenit augue duis dolore te feugait nulla facilisi. Nam liber tempor cum soluta nobis eleifend option congue nihil imperdiet doming id quod mazim placerat facer possim assum.

Lorem ipsum dolor sit amet, consectetuer adipiscing elit, sed diam nonummy nibh euismod tincidunt ut laoreet dolore magna aliquam erat volutpat. Ut wisi enim ad minim veniam, quis nostrud exerci tation ullamcorper suscipit lobortis nisl ut aliquip ex ea commodo consequat. Duis autem vel eum iriure dolor in hendrerit.

New Bases Ordered

In vulputate velit esse molestie consequat, vel illum dolore eu feugiat nulla facilisis at vero eros et accumsan et iusto odio dignissim qui blandit praesent luptatum zzril delenit augue duis dolore te feugait nulla facilisi. Lorem ipsum dolor sit amet, consectetuer adipiscing elit, sed diam nonummy nibh euismod tincidunt ut laoreet dolore magna aliquam erat volutpat.

Ut wisi enim ad minim veniam, quis nostrud exerci tation ullamcorper suscipit lobortis nisl ut aliquip ex ea commodo consequat. Duis autem vel eum iriure dolor in hendrerit in vulputate velit.

3

Board Report on Travel Expenses Budget Cuts

Lorem ipsum dolor sit amet, consectetuer adipiscing elit, sed diam nonummy nibh euismod tincidunt ut laoreet dolore magna al iquam erat volutpat. Ut wisi enim ad minim veniam, quis nostrud exerci tation ullamcorper suscipit lobortis nisl ut aliquip ex ea commodo consequat.

Duis autem vel eum iriure dolor in hendrerit in vulputate velit esse molestie consequat, vel illum dolore eu feugiat nulla facilisis at vero eros et accumsan et iusto odio dignissim qui blandit praesent luptatum zzril delenit augue duis dolore te feugait nulla facilisi. Lorem ipsum dolor sit amet, consectetuer adipiscing elit, sed diam nonummy nibh euismod tincidunt ut laoreet dolore magna aliquam erat volutpat.

Ut wisi enim ad minim veniam, quis nostrud exerci tation ullamcoit lobortis nisl ut aliquip ex ea commodo consequat.

Duis autem vel eum iriure dolor in hendrerit in vulputate velit esse molestie consequat, vel illum dolore eu feugiat facilisis at vero eros et accumsan et iusto odio dignissim qui blandit praesent luptatum zzril delenit augue duis dolore te feugait nulla facilisi. Nam liber tempor cum soluta nobis eleifend option congue nihil imperdiet doming id adipiscing elit, sed diam nonummy nibh euismod tincidunt ut laoreet.

New Bases Ordered

In vulputate velit esse molestie consequat, vel illum dolore eu feugiat nulla facilisis at vero eros et accumsan et iusto odio dignissim qui blandit praesent luptatum zzril delenit augue duis dolore te feugait nulla facilisi. Lorem ipsum dolor sit amet, consectetuer adipiscing elit, sed diam nonummy nibh euismod tincidunt ut laoreet dolore magna aliquam erat volutpat.

Ut wisi enim ad minim veniam, quis nostrud exerci tation ullamcorper suscipit lobortis nisl ut aliquip ex ea commodo consequat. Duis autem vel eum iriure dolor in hendrerit in vulputate velit.

Ice Cream Vendor Lowers Prices

Dolore magna aliquam erat volutpat. Ut wisi enim ad minim veniam, quis nostrud exerci tation ullamcorper suscipit lobortis nisl ut aliquip ex ea commodo consequat.

Duis autem vel eum iriure dolor in hendrerit in vulputate velit esse molestie consequat, vel illum dolore eu feugiat nulla facilisis at vero eros et accumsan et iusto odio dignissim qui blandit praesent luptatum zzril delenit augue duis dolore te feugait nulla facilisi. Nam liber tempor cum soluta nobis eleifend option congue nihil imperdiet doming id quod mazim placerat facer possim assum.

Lorem ipsum dolor sit amet, consectetuer adipiscing elit, sed diam nonummy nibh euismod tincidunt ut laoreet dolore magna aliquam erat volutpat. Ut wisi enim ad minim veniam, quis nostrud exerci tation ullamcorper suscipit lobortis nisl ut aliquip ex ea commodo consequat. Duis autem vel eum iriure dolor in hendrerit.

3

The headlines in the example at left compete with each other, virtually canceling each other out.

In the example at right, size indicates that one headline is clearly more important than the others.

22 Use white space to add impact to headlines.

One of the easiest ways you can add impact to your headlines is to surround them with a significant amount of white space. White space acts as a magnet, drawing the reader's attention to the text it surrounds.

Be sure to place most of the white space above and to the right of your headline, so that your reader's eyes can make a smooth transition into the body copy your headline introduces.

Notice that flush-left headlines appear to have more white space around them than centered headlines. This is because the white space is concentrated in one place (i.e. to the right of the headline) rather than divided equally between the left and right sides of the headline.

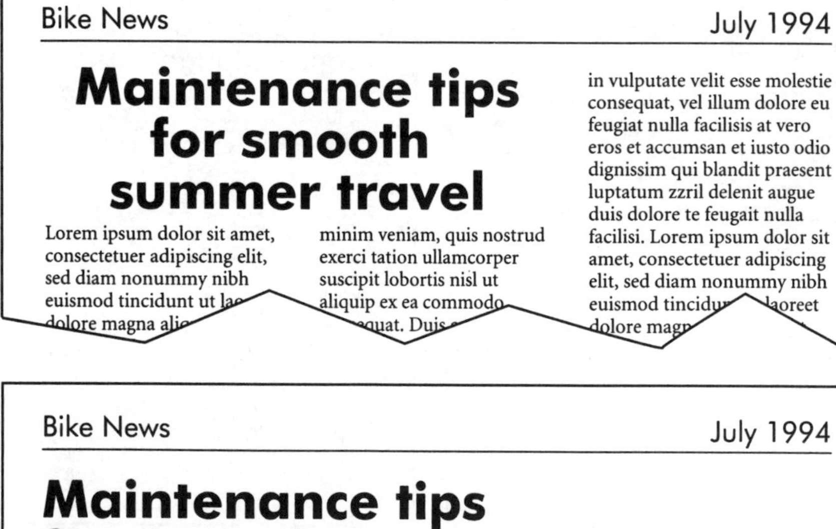

The top headline lacks impact because white space is divided between its left and right sides. In addition, the headline is dwarfed by the text in the third column.

The lower headline concentrates white space to the right.

Replace white space inside headlines with white space around headlines.

23

Reduce headline letterspacing and line spacing as headline size increases. There are three ways you can eliminate unwanted white space within headlines:

Tracking. Tracking, or uniformly reducing letterspacing throughout a headline, helps words emerge as distinct visual elements.

Kerning. Kerning, or reducing unwanted spacing between selected pairs of letters, is especially important with combinations of upper- and lowercase letters, such as Wa, Wi, Ta, To, Ya, and Yo.

Tracking and kerning create horizontal white space to the left and right of the headline.

Leading. Software programs' default leading, or line spacing, is usually too generous. Reducing line spacing creates vertical white space to frame the headline and helps the headline emerge as a distinct visual unit instead of unconnected lines.

Mysterious red and green lights hover over city

Mysterious red and green lights hover over city

Mysterious red and green lights hover over city

Often a three-line headline becomes an easier-to-read two-line headline when you remove unnecessary white space.

The top example shows default letterspacing and default line spacing.

The center example shows reduced letterspacing.

The bottom example shows how reduced line spacing helps even more.

24 Use condensed, heavy sans serif typefaces for headlines.

Set headlines in typeface designs characterized by thick strokes and reduced character width. Heavy, condensed typeface designs offer increased contrast with body text and occupy less horizontal space, adding to the surrounding white space.

The first example below, set in Frutiger Bold, lacks impact.

The second example, set in Frutiger Black, has more impact, but occupies too much horizontal space.

The third example, set in Condensed Frutiger Black, combines the impact of Frutiger Black yet occupies less space than Frutiger Bold.

Hint: Most sans serif typefaces come in a variety of weights and widths.

The Frutiger Bold headline in the top example lacks impact.

The Frutiger Black used in the middle example emerges stronger, yet occupies too much space.

Frutiger Condensed Black has the impact of Frutiger Black but saves space.

Board accepts major reorganization plan

Board accepts major reorganizationplan

Board accepts major reorganization plan

Edit your headlines.

25

Restrict headlines to a three-line maximum. Two-line headlines are even better. Replace long words with short words and eliminate unnecessary words.

Remember that each time you eliminate words in a headline, you gain the space needed to set the remaining words in a larger type size, use a heavier typeface, or add white space around the headline.

Avoid telling too much of the story in your headlines. Headlines should simply tease, or attract readers into the story. If you include too many details you risk discouraging readership by giving so much information that readers don't need to read the associated story, or they may reject the story that follows because of its content or outlook.

New lease on life promised by steroid-based cardiac breakthrough developed at St. Joseph's Hospital

The four-line headline in the top example lacks visual impact and tells so much information you don't need to read the story.

St. Joseph's Hospital announces cardiac care breakthrough

The three-line version occupies the same amount of space, yet has more impact because it contains fewer words set in a larger type size.

26 Break long headlines into shorter elements.

Use fewer words in the headline itself and elaborate on the headline in kickers, decks, and blurbs – terms used for words, phrases, or sentences placed above and below the headline.

Kickers, or *eyebrows,* are short phrases or department heads that categorize or provide a frame of reference for headlines. They cue the reader to whether the headline relates to people, products, or things.

Decks are short, often italicized, introductory phrases that precede a headline.

Blurbs are amplifications of the headline appearing between the headline and the adjacent story. They amplify the headline, helping relate the story topic to the reader's frame of reference. Blurbs are often set in the same typeface as the headline, but in a smaller type size.

Compare the "gray" appearance and tone of the top headline with the example at bottom.

New health insurance plan helps self-employed graphic designers save thousands of dollars a year

Notice how the bottom example offers more visual interest and provides a logical, gentle transition into the detailed text that follows.

Attention Designers

New health insurance plan announced

Now you can save thousands of dollars a year on insurance premiums and broaden coverage for your entire household.

27

Break headlines at logical pauses.

Think of headlines as sentences that you're reading aloud to your readers. Read your headlines out loud to yourself. Notice how you automatically pause between certain phrases.

Long headlines set on single lines spanning several columns are often harder to read than short headlines set in the same type size on two or three lines.

Break your headlines where you would pause when reading them aloud.

Notice the difference in the examples below. The stacked flush-left headlines in the second example open up the page with the extra white space added on the right.

Note: When breaking headlines, avoid inadvertently adding paragraph spacing between the lines. Many software programs include a special line-break command that can prematurely break the headline, but preserve normal line spacing.

Vertmont judge convicts elderly Hollis grandmother of reckless driving

The top example is awkward to read because the adjective is separated from the noun.

**Vermont judge convicts
elderly Hollis grandmother
of reckless driving**

In the bottom example, the headline is broken at a natural point. In addition, the three-line setting creates a pool of white space to the right of the headline, adding visual impact.

28 Avoid underlining headlines and subheads.

Use typographic contrast instead of underlining to add impact to headlines and subheads. Underlining is an unfortunate holdover from the days of typewriters when one of the few ways you could add emphasis was by underlining. Instead of attracting attention, underlining makes words harder to read.

Underlined headlines set in uppercase type are especially difficult to read because the underlining distracts readers from paying full attention to the shapes of the letters.

Underlining interferes with lowercase type by obscuring the descenders, or portions of letters like g, y, and p that extend below the baseline. These play an essential role in word recognition.

Hardest to read of all are subheads set in small, underlined italics.

As the top example shows, underlining adds clutter to the rectangular shape created by the uppercase letters. In addition, the descenders of the italicized subhead are obscured by underlining.

RECYCLING CENTER OPENS

They'll take it all, from appliances to batteries . . .

Duis autem vel eum iriure dolor in hendrerit in vulputate velit esse molestie consequat, vel illum dolore vero eros et accumsan et iusto odio dignissim qui blandit praesent luptatum zzril delenit augue duis dolore te feugait nulla facilisi. Lorem ipsum dolor sit amet, consectetuer adipiscing elit, sed diam nonummy nibh euismod ti... ut laoreet dolore magna aliquam erat ...

Duis autem vel eum iriure eros et accumsan et iusto odio dolore te feugait nulla facilisi. Nam liber tempor cum soluta nobis eleifend option congue nihil imperdiet doming id quod mazim placerat facer possim assum.

Lorem ipsum dolor sit amet, consectetuer adipiscing elit, sed diam nonummy ni... laoreet dolore magna ...

In the bottom example, the headline set in a heavy sans serif type is easier to read, as is the subhead set in a heavier sans serif type.

RECYCLING CENTER OPENS

They'll take it all, from appliances to batteries . . .

Duis autem vel eum iriure dolor in hendrerit in vulputate velit esse molestie consequat, vel illum dolore vero eros et accumsan et iusto odio dignissim qui blandit praesent luptatum zzril delenit augue duis dolore te feugait nulla facilisi. Lorem ipsum dolor sit amet, consectetuer adipiscing elit, sed diam nonummy nibh euismod ti... ut laoreet dolore magna aliquam erat ...

Duis autem vel eum iriure eros et accumsan et iusto odio dolore te feugait nulla facilisi. Nam liber tempor cum soluta nobis eleifend option congue nihil imperdiet doming id quod mazim placerat facer possim assum.

Lorem ipsum dolor sit amet, consectetuer adipiscing elit, sed diam nonummy ni... laoreet dolore magna ...

Use uppercase letters with discretion.

29

Avoid the temptation to capitalize the first letter of every word in a headline. This is often done out of habit rather than necessity. The result is unnecessary confusion. When you capitalize only the first letter of the headline and proper nouns, it's immediately obvious whether words are modifiers or nouns.

In the top example, it's difficult to know whether "Small" refers to the size of the landfill or to its name. Likewise, is "Major Progress" a World War II hero coming to town, or does it refer to what's going on at the landfill? These ambiguities are eliminated in the bottom example where only proper nouns are set in uppercase letters.

Notice how the overuse of uppercase letters creates longer headlines, reducing the amount of white space surrounding the headlines and also legibility (*see next page*).

Major Progress Scheduled for Small East End Landfill

MAJOR PROGRESS SCHEDULED FOR SMALL EAST END LANDFILL

Major progress scheduled for small East End landfill

Using uppercase letters to introduce each word creates ambiguity. Is "Progress" a process or a person? Is "Small" the landfill's name?

The middle example set entirely in uppercase type requires three lines instead of the two required in the other examples.

In the bottom example, it's obvious that "East End" is the name of the landfill.

30 Restrict the use of all-caps text to short headlines.

Headlines set in all uppercase type are harder to read and occupy more space. Readers depend on word shapes to decode your message. Thus, headlines set in all-caps are harder to read than headlines set in a combination of upper- and lowercase letters because words set in uppercase type lack distinctive shapes. Compare the two settings of the word "photography." Which is easier to read?

Words set in uppercase text also occupy more space. Compare the lengths of the two examples. Notice how the top "photography" is much longer than the lowercase example, which reduces available white space.

The best all-cap headlines consist of a few key words set very large, amplified by a strong subhead.

In the example at left, the headline lacks impact and is difficult to read because there are so many words of equal visual weight lacking distinctive shapes.

The headline in the example at right works better because of the visual contrast between a few key words set large and amplified by the "interpretive" subhead.

APPLIANCE WAREHOUSE ANNOUNCES LOWEST PRICES ON WASHERS, DRYERS, TVs AND STEREOS

Lorem ipsum dolor sit amet, consectetuer adipiscing elit, sed diam nonummy nibh euismod tincidunt ut laoreet dolore magna aliquam erat volutpat. Ut wisi enim ad minim veniam, quis nostrud exerci tation ullamcorper suscipit lobortis nisl ut aliquip ex ea commodo consequat. Duis autem vel eum i in vulputate velit esse molestie consequat, vel illum dolore eu feugiat nulla facilisis at vero eros et accumsan et iusto odio dignissim qui blandit praesent luptatum zzril delenit augue duis dolore te feugait nulla facilisi. Lorem ipsum dolor sit amet, consectetuer adipiscing elit, sed diam nonummy nibh euismod tincidunt ut laoreet dolore magna aliquam erat volutpat. Ut wisi enim ad minim veniam, quis nostrud exerci tation ullamcorper suscipit lobortis nisl ut aliquip ex ea commodo consequat.

Duis autem vel eum iriure eros et accumsan et iusto odio dolore te feugait nulla facilisi. Nam liber tempor cum soluta nobis eleifend option congue nihil imperdiet doming id quod mazim placerat facer possim assum.

Ut wisi enim ad minim veniam, quis nostrud exerci tation ullamcorper suscipit lobortis nisl ut aliquip ex ea commodo consequat. Lorem ipsum dolor sit amet, consectetuer adipiscing elit, sed diam nonummy nibh euismod tincidunt ut laoreet dolore magna aliquam erat volutpat. Duis autem vel eum iriure dolor in hendrerit in vulputate velit esse molestie consequat, vel illum dolore eu feugiat nulla facilisis at vero eros et accumsan et iusto odio dignissim qui blandit praesent luptatum zzril delenit augue duis dolore te feugait nulla facilisi. Lorem ipsum dolor sit amet, consectetuer adipiscing

PRICE WAR!

All major appliances 50% off

Lorem ipsum dolor sit amet, consectetuer adipiscing elit, sed diam nonummy nibh euismod tincidunt ut laoreet dolore magna aliquam erat volutpat. Ut wisi enim ad minim veniam, quis nostrud exerci tation ullamcorper suscipit lobortis nisl ut aliquip ex ea commodo consequat. Duis autem vel eum i in vulputate velit esse molestie consequat, vel illum dolore eu feugiat nulla facilisis at vero eros et accumsan et iusto odio dignissim qui blandit praesent luptatum zzril delenit augue duis dolore te feugait nulla facilisi. Lorem ipsum dolor sit amet, consectetuer adipiscing elit, sed diam nonummy nibh euismod tincidunt ut laoreet dolore magna aliquam erat volutpat. Ut wisi enim ad minim veniam, quis nostrud exerci tation ullamcorper suscipit lobortis nisl ut aliquip ex ea commodo consequat.

Duis autem vel eum iriure eros et accumsan et iusto odio dolore te feugait nulla facilisi. Nam liber tempor cum soluta nobis eleifend option congue nihil imperdiet doming id quod mazim placerat facer possim assum.

Ut wisi enim ad minim veniam, quis nostrud exerci tation ullamcorper suscipit lobortis nisl ut aliquip ex ea commodo consequat. Lorem ipsum dolor sit amet, consectetuer adipiscing elit, sed diam nonummy nibh euismod tincidunt ut laoreet dolore magna aliquam erat volutpat. Duis autem vel eum iriure dolor in hendrerit in vulputate velit esse molestie consequat, vel illum dolore eu feugiat nulla facilisis at vero eros et accumsan et iusto odio dignissim qui blandit praesent luptatum zzril delenit augue duis dolore te feugait nulla facilisi. Lorem ipsum dolor sit amet, consectetuer adipiscing

PHOTOGRAPHY

photography

Add extra letterspacing and reduce line spacing when setting headlines in uppercase type. 31

Add extra letterspacing when setting headlines in uppercase type. Extra spacing provides the breathing room readers need to decipher the shapes of the individual letters.

Remember that uppercase letters are typically designed to be used in combination with lowercase letters. When uppercase letters appear next to each other, the white space that normally appears to their right is missing. The result is reduced legibility.

You can improve the appearance of headlines set in uppercase type by reducing line spacing. Line spacing can be reduced since uppercase words lack descenders, or portions of letters which extend below the line the words rest on.

WILMINGTON MILLIONAIRE WINS WASHINGTON AWARD

Duis autem vel eum iriure dolor in hendrerit in vulputate velit esse molestie consequat, vel illum dolore vero eros et accumsan et iusto odio dignissim qui blandit praesent luptatum zzril delenit augue duis dolore te feugait nulla facilisi. Lorem ipsum dolor sit amet, consectetuer adipiscing elit, sed diam nonummy nibh euismod tincidunt ut laoreet dolore magna aliquam erat ... im ad

Duis autem vel eum iriure eros et accumsan et iusto odio dolore te feugait nulla facilisi. Nam liber tempor cum soluta nobis eleifend option congue nihil imperdiet doming id quod mazim placerat facer possim assum.

Lorem ipsum dolor sit amet, consectetuer adipiscing elit, sed diam nonummy nibh euismod ... laoreet dolore magna ... inim ve

The headline in the top example is difficult to read because the default letterspacing causes the letters to run together.

W I L M I N G T O N M I L L I O N A I R E W I N S W A S H I N G T O N A W A R D

Duis autem vel eum iriure dolor in hendrerit in vulputate velit esse molestie consequat, vel illum dolore vero eros et accumsan et iusto odio dignissim qui blandit praesent luptatum zzril delenit augue duis dolore te feugait nulla facilisi. Lorem ipsum dolor sit amet, consectetuer adipiscing elit, sed diam nonummy nibh euismod tincidunt ut laoreet dolore magna aliquam erat ... im ad

Duis autem vel eum iriure eros et accumsan et iusto odio dolore te feugait nulla facilisi. Nam liber tempor cum soluta nobis eleifend option congue nihil imperdiet doming id quod mazim placerat facer possim assum.

Lorem ipsum dolor sit amet, consectetuer adipiscing elit, sed diam nonummy nibh euismod ... laoreet dolore magna ... inim ve

In the bottom example, the headline benefits from additional letterspacing which helps the individual letters to emerge with enhanced clarity.

32 Optically align the first letters of headlines set in a large type size.

Move the first line of flush-left headlines beginning with letters like T and Y to the left so the letter's "center of gravity" aligns with the left-hand margin of the text that follows. In the top example, notice how the overhanging horizontal stroke at the top of the T forces the T's vertical stem to the right. As a result, the T looks like it has been inadvertently indented, even though – to the computer – it is perfectly lined up.

As shown in the bottom example, moving the T and Y to the left aligns their stems with the left margin and elimates the appearance of unintentional indents.

The larger your headlines, the more important it is to fine-tune the optical alignment of the first letters, especially letters wider at the top or bottom.

In the bottom example, notice how the headline appears lined up, even though the Y has been moved to the left.

Ysleta Election Results

Duis autem vel eum iriure dolor in hendrerit in vulputate velit esse molestie consequat, vel illum dolore vero eros et accumsan et iusto odio dignissim qui blandit praesent luptatum zzril delenit augue duis dolore te feugait nulla facilisi. Lorem ipsum dolor sit amet, consectetuer adipiscing elit, sed diam nonummy nibh euismod tincidunt ut laoreet dolore magna aliquam erat volutpat.

Ut wisi enim ad minim quis nostrud exerci tation ullamc isl ut aliquip ex ea minim veniam, quis nostrud exerci tation ullamcorper suscipit lobortis nisl ut aliquip exea commodo consequat.

Duis autem vel eum iriure eros et accumsan et iusto odio dolore te feugait nulla facilisi. Nam liber tempor cum soluta nobis eleifend option congue nihil imperdiet doming id quod mazim placerat facer possim assum.

Lorem ipsum dolor sit amet, conse sed diam nonumm

In the bottom example, notice how each line of the headline appears lined up, even though the T and the Y have been moved to the left.

Ysleta Election Results

Duis autem vel eum iriure dolor in hendrerit in vulputate velit esse molestie consequat, vel illum dolore vero eros et accumsan et iusto odio dignissim qui blandit praesent luptatum zzril delenit augue duis dolore te feugait nulla facilisi. Lorem ipsum dolor sit amet, consectetuer adipiscing elit, sed diam nonummy nibh euismod tincidunt ut laoreet dolore magna aliquam erat volutpat.

Ut wisi enim ad minim quis nostrud exerci tation ullamc isl ut aliquip ex ea minim veniam, quis nostrud exerci tation ullamcorper suscipit lobortis nisl ut aliquip exea commodo consequat.

Duis autem vel eum iriure eros et accumsan et iusto odio dolore te feugait nulla facilisi. Nam liber tempor cum soluta nobis eleifend option congue nihil imperdiet doming id quod mazim placerat facer possim assum.

Lorem ipsum dolor sit amet, conse sed diam nonumm

Avoid parallel headlines.

33

Avoid side-by-side headline placement. Parallel, or "tombstone" headlines create unwanted parallelism between columns, and you lose the visual variety and page-to-page "surprises" that occur when headlines appear at different locations on a page.

In addition, tombstone headlines encourage readers to read across rather than down. Unless you have provided sufficient visual barriers in the form of white space between columns or vertical downrules, readers might "jump the column" and read the second headline as part of the first line, inadvertently reading two headlines as one long headline.

The only exception to avoiding parallel headlines is when you are using consistent headline placement as an intentional design tool, as in the bottom example.

Senate To Take Action On Bill

Duis autem vel eum iriure dolor in hendrerit in vulputate velit esse molestie consequat, vel illum dolore vero eros et accumsan et iusto odio dignissim qui blandit praesent luptatum zzril delenit augue duis dolore te feugait nulla facilisi. Lorem ipsum dolor sit amet, consectetuer adipiscing elit, sed diam nonummy nibh euismod tincidunt

Your Money – How It Works

Lorem ipsum dolor duis autem vel eum iriure eros et accumsan et iusto odio dolore te feugait nulla facilisi. Nam liber tempor cum soluta nobis eleifend option congue nihil imperdiet doming id quod mazim placerat facer possim assum.

Lorem ipsum dolor sit amet, consectetuer adipiscing elit, sed diam nonummy

As the top example shows, parallel headline placement can encourage readers to read across columns, rather than reading each headline as a distinct unit.

Senate to take action on banking bill

Duis autem vel eum iriure dolor in hendrerit in vulputate velit esse molestie consequat,

Take charge of your paycheck

Amet, consectetuer adipiscing elit, sed diam nonummy nibh euismod

Interest rates predicted to soar

Amet, consectetuer adipiscing elit, sed diam nonummy nibh euismod tincidunt ut

Protect your credit cards and your rating

Dolor duis autem vel eum iriure eros et accumsan et iusto odio dolore te feugait nulla facilisi.

How to take that second mortgage

Consectetuer adipiscing elit, sed diam nonummy nibh euismod

As the bottom example shows, parallel headlines can work, if small, condensed typefaces are used and there is plenty of white space to the right of each headline.

34 Avoid redundant emphasis.

Use the minimum number of contrast tools necessary to add emphasis to headlines and subheads. The use of multiple contrast tools often results in clutter rather than emphasis.

Two strong contrast tools, such as a Condensed Black sans serif typeface that contrasts with a serif body copy typeface, applied consistently and in conjunction with white space, often adds more emphasis and projects a more professional appearance than a seemingly random assortment of less effective typographic and graphic tools.

Compare the professional image projected by the Condensed Heavy sans serif headline and subheads in the bottom example with the underlined, italicized, centered, and shadowed serif headline at top. The bottom example projects strength, the other projects indecision and simply showcases the tools at the user's command.

Clutter overwhelms emphasis in the top example.

Lorem ipsum dolor sit amet

Duis autem vel eum iriure dolor in hendrerit in vulputate velit esse molestie consequat, vel illum dolore vero eros et accumsan et iusto odio dignissim qui blandit praesent luptatum zzril delenit augue duis dolore te feugait nulla facilisi.

Consectetuer adipiscing

Elit, sed diam nonummy nibh euismod tincidunt ut laoreet dolore magna al... tpat. Ut wisi

iusto odio dolore te feugait nulla facilisi. Nam liber tempor cum soluta nobis eleifend option congue nihil imperdiet doming id quod mazim placerat facer possim assum.

Odio dignissim

Lorem ipsum dolor sit amet, consectetuer adipiscing elit, sed diam nonummy nibh euismod tincidunt ut lao... magna aliquam erat.

The lower example, based on a left-aligned, large, heavy sans serif typeface projects a more professional appearance.

Lorem ipsum dolor sit amet

Duis autem vel eum iriure dolor in hendrerit in vulputate velit esse molestie consequat, vel illum dolore vero eros et accumsan et iusto odio dignissim qui blandit praesent luptatum zzril delenit augue duis dolore te feugait nulla facilisi.

Consectetuer adipiscing

Elit, sed diam nonummy nib... smod tincidunt ut laoreet dolore magn... at. Ut wisi

iusto odio dolore te feugait nulla facilisi. Nam liber tempor cum soluta nobis eleifend option congue nihil imperdiet doming id quod mazim placerat facer possim assum.

Odio dignissim

Lorem ipsum dolor sit amet, consectetuer adipiscing elit, sed diam nonummy nibh euismod ti...idunt ut la... agna aliquam erat,

Use slab serif typefaces to communicate strength.

35

Because of headlines' large sizes, your headline typeface decisions have a lot of impact upon the impression your documents create. Slab serif typefaces, such as Rockwell, Glypha, and Memphis, are characterized by heavy, thick horizontal serifs.

Because of their precise, no-nonsense serifs, and relatively uniform stroke widths, slab serif typefaces project a high-impact "architectural" or "engineering" image, making them suitable for headlines projecting accuracy and preciseness. Slab serif typefaces are definitely the choice when you want to project a no-nonsense, frivolity-free image.

Compare the "blandness" of the Helvetica Bold sample in the middle with the impact of the same headline set in Rockwell on the bottom.

An added benefit: Slab serif typefaces also look good when reproduced by low-resolution output devices like fax machines.

Federal Bureau of Petroleum Exploration and Land Reclamation

The Times Roman used in the top example is at odds with the image of an "outdoors" firm.

Federal Bureau of Petroleum Exploration and Land Reclamation

The Helvetica in the middle example lacks strength.

Federal Bureau of Petroleum Exploration and Land Reclamation

But the sturdy serifs of Rockwell project an appropriate "heavy equipment" image in the bottom example.

36 Use rounded typefaces to create an informal, friendly atmosphere.

Use rounded typefaces when you want to project a warm and friendly, "hometown," personalized image. The smooth edges of these typefaces present a nonthreatening image.

Souvenir is an excellent example of a rounded typeface. Notice its freedom from pretension or rigidity. Souvenir is available in a large range of weights, from light to heavy. Notice the subtle amount of stress, or difference in thickness between thick and thin strokes.

Compare the lack of image presented by the headline in the top example, set in Helvetica, with the warmth of the same headline set in Souvenir in the middle example and VAG Rounded in the bottom example.

The top logo, set in Helvetica, lacks character. If it presents any image at all, it's one of no-nonsense "function" rather than "informal family."

Souvenir's rounded shapes and smooth serifs present a friendlier image in the center example, as does the playful VAG Rounded sample in the bottom example.

TRAVELER'S FRIEND
FAMILY DINING AND RV CAMPGROUND

TRAVELER'S FRIEND
FAMILY DINING AND RV CAMPGROUND

TRAVELER'S FRIEND
FAMILY DINING AND RV CAMPGROUND

Use Modern typefaces at large sizes to create an elegant image.

37

Modern typefaces' sharply defined serifs and significant stress – or differences between thick and thin strokes – become design statements when used at large sizes. Although the serifs and extreme stress characteristic of Modern typefaces can become detriments when used in body copy – creating body copy so "busy" that it draws attention to itself – typefaces such as Monotype's Ellington or any of the numerous versions of Bodoni can be positively beautiful when set at large size and surrounded by sufficient white space.

Again, compare the relatively "characterless" restaurant names in the top two examples with the same words set in Fairfield in the bottom example.

Where would you rather go for a fancy meal to celebrate a promotion or engagement?

Newfield Street
Bistro and Fine Dining — By Reservation Only

The neutrality that makes Times Roman a strong text font works against using it to establish an image.

Newfield Street
Bistro and Fine Dining — By Reservation Only

Although Helvetica might work well if you were aiming for a contemporary clientele, the center example lacks character.

Newfield Street
Bistro and Fine Dining — By Reservation Only

Fairfield, used in the bottom example, does a better job of establishing an upscale presence.

38 Use Geometric sans serif typefaces with restraint.

Although Geometric typefaces can communicate a contemporary image, they are best used for short headlines set in a large type size. Geometric typefaces are typically assembled from lines and circles – or portions of circles. They lack stress: their stroke thickness typically remains the same throughout the letter. The most common examples are Avant Garde and Futura. Both are available in a variety of weights and widths.

Although their "constructed" precision permits geometric typefaces to make strong design statements in logos and titles, they are often harder to read than the same headlines set in sans serif typefaces that more closely resemble handwritten letters.

Notice how much easier your eyes can read the examples in the right-hand column below, than the examples in the left-hand columm.

Note how it is easier to read the right-hand headlines and text, set in Gill Sans (top) and Frutiger (bottom), than the same words in the left-hand examples.

The geometric shapes and uniform stroke weight of Avant Garde (top left) and Futura (bottom left) make it harder to decipher individual letters.

Millions attend military honors ceremony

Lorem ipsum dolor sit amet, consectetuer adipiscing elit, sed diam nonummy nibh euismod tincidunt ut laoreet dolore magna aliquam erat volutpat.

Millions attend military honors ceremony

Lorem ipsum dolor sit amet, consectetuer adipiscing elit, sed diam nonummy nibh euismod tincidunt ut laoreet dolore magna aliquam erat volutpat.

Millions attend military honors ceremony

Lorem ipsum dolor sit amet, consectetuer adipiscing elit, sed diam nonummy nibh euismod tincidunt ut laoreet dolore magna aliquam erat volutpat.

Millions attend military honors ceremony

Lorem ipsum dolor sit amet, consectetuer adipiscing elit, sed diam nonummy nibh euismod tincidunt ut laoreet dolore magna aliquam erat volutpat.

Use shaded or open typefaces to reduce the mass of large headlines.

39

Avoid large, heavy headlines that dwarf the text that follows them. You can maintain the size of a large headline and yet reduce its weight by reproducing the headline in a shade of gray.

Or, consider using typeface alternatives like Caslon Open Face; or choose one of the options available with the URW TypeWorks collection – these contain a variety of outline and relief typeface options for every typeface.

Open, outline, and relief designs reduce the visual weight of the headlines and avoid dominating the page.

You can also use drawing or font manipulation programs to achieve the same effects with your current typefaces.

The use of Caslon Open Face provides a delicate touch that would be lost if the letters of the headline were totally filled in.

40 Fine-tune letterspacing.

As headline size increases, fine-tuning becomes more and more necessary. Kerning, or optically adjusting spacing between letters, is especially important when "overhanging" uppercase letters like Ws, Ts, and Ps are placed next to lowercase vowels (a, e, i, o, u). Certain pairs of lowercase letters as well as combinations of uppercase letters and punctuation also require optical fine-tuning.

Letterspacing should be adjusted until the letters appear evenly spaced, even if they have been brought significantly closer together.

Under some circumstances, you should *add* letterspacing. In some typefaces, r's and n's can optically combine to create m's.

Here are the top 20 kerning pairs likely to require attention, as identified by Frank Romano, founder of ***TypeWorld,*** *and contained in his* TypeEncyclopedia *(R.R. Bowker, 1984). (Reprinted with permission.)*

Yo	Wo	P.	T.
We	Tu	Ty	Y.
To	Tw	Wa	TA
Tr	Ya	Yo	PA
Ta	Te	we	wa

Subheads

Subheads help convert "skimmers" into "readers." Subheads provide additional points for you to advertise the content of your article and give readers additional opportunities to become involved. To succeed, however, subheads have to stand out clearly from the surrounding text.

Use subheads to break up long text passages.

41

Use subheads to organize your material and provide visual breaks. Long, uninterrupted columns of body copy discourage readers. You can increase the readability of your publication by adding a subhead each time a new idea is introduced. Each subhead provides a valuable opportunity to attract readers' attention and invite them to read the text.

The hierarchy of your subheads should reflect the complexity of your documents. Although a single level of subheads may be sufficient for newsletters, technical documentation may require a multilevel hierarchy.

Subhead appearance should reflect subhead importance. Level one subheads should be more noticeable than level two or level three subheads. You can use subhead length to reinforce their hierarchy by using sentences for level one subheads but only key phrases for level two and level three subheads.

Lorem ipsum dolor sit amet, consectetuer adipiscing elit, sed diam nonummy nibh euismod tincidunt ut laoreet dolore magna aliquam erat volutpat. Ut wisi enim ad minim veniam, quis nostrud exerci tation ullamcorper suscipit lobortis nisl ut aliquip ex ea commodo consequat. Duis autem vel eum iriure dolor in hendrerit in vulputate velit esse molestie consequat, vel illum dolore eu feugiat nulla facilisis at vero eros et accumsan et iusto odio dignissim qui blandit praesent luptatum zzril delenit augue duis dolore te feugait nulla facilisi. Lorem ipsum dolor sit amet, consectetuer adipiscing elit, sed diam nonummy nibh euismod tincidunt ut laoreet dolore magna aliquam erat volutpat. Ut wisi enim ad minim veniam, quis nostrud exerci tation ullamcorper suscipit lobortis nisl ut aliquip ex ea commodo consequat.

Duis autem vel eum iriure eros et accumsan et iusto odio dolore te feugait nulla facilisi. Nam liber tempor cum soluta nobis eleifend option congue nihil imperdiet doming id quod mazim placerat facer possim assum.

Ut wisi enim ad minim veniam, quis nostrud exerci tation ullamcorper suscipit lobortis nisl ut aliquip ex ea commodo consequat. Lorem ipsum dolor sit amet, consectetuer adipiscing elit, sed diam nonummy nibh euismod tincidunt ut laoreet dolore magna aliquam erat volutpat. Duis autem vel eum iriure dolor in hendrerit in vulputate velit esse molestie consequat, vel illum dolore eu feugiat nulla facilisis at vero eros et accumsan et iusto odio dignissim qui blandit praesent luptatum zzril delenit augue duis dolore te feugait nulla facilisi. Lorem ipsum dolor sit amet, consectetuer adipiscing elit, sed diam nonummy nibh euismod tincidunt ut laoreet dolore magna aliquam erat volutpat.

Ut wisi enim ad minim veniam, quis nostrud exerci tation ullamcorper suscipit lobortis nisl ut aliquip ex ea commodo consequat. Duis autem vel eum iriure dolor in hendrerit in vulputate velit esse molestie. Consequat, vel illum dolore eu feugiat nulla facilisis at vero eros et accumsan et iusto odio dignissim qui blandit praesent luptatum zzril

2

Lorem ipsum dolor sit amet, consect etuer adipiscing elit, sed diam nonummy nibh euismod tincidunt ut laoreet dolore magna aliquam erat volutpat.

Organic Gardening Tips

Lorem ipsum dolor sit amet, consectetuer adipiscing elit, sed diam nonummy nibh euismod tincidunt ut laoreet dolore magna aliquam erat volutpat. Ut wisi enim ad minim veniam, quis nostrud exerci tation ullamcorper suscipit lobortis nisl ut aliquip ex ea commodo consequat.

Pest Control

Duis autem vel eum iriure dolor in hendrerit in vulputate velit esse molestie consequat, vel illum dolore eu feugiat nulla facilisis at vero eros et accumsan et iusto odio dignissim qui blandit praesent luptatum zzril delenit augue duis dolore te feugait nulla facilisi.

Fertilizing

Lorem ipsum dolor sit amet, consectetuer adipiscing elit, sed diam nonummy nibh euismod tincidunt ut laoreet dolore magna aliquam erat volutpat. Ut wisi enim ad minim veniam, quis nostrud exerci tation ullam corper suscipit lobortis nisl ut aliquip ex ea commodo consen quat. Duis autem vel eum iriure eros et accumsan et iusto odio dolore te feugait nulla facilisi. Nam liber tempor cum soluta nobis eleifend option congue nihil imperdiet doming id quod mazim placerat facer possim branve assum.

Preserving Your Crops

Ut wisi enim ad minim veniam, quis nostrud exerci tation ullam corper suscipit lobortis nisl ut aliquip ex ea commodo consequat.

Canning

Lorem ipsum dolor sit amet, consectetuer adipiscing elit, sed diam nonummy nibh euismod tincidunt ut laoreet dolore mag na aliquam erat volutpat. Duis autem vel eum iriure dolor in hendrerit in vulputate.

Freezing

Velit esse molestie consequat, vel illum dolore eu feugiat nulla facilisis at vero eros et accumsan et iusto odio dignissim qui bland it praesent luptatum zzril delenit augue duis dolore te feugait nul la facilisi. Lorem ipsum dolor sit

2

The example at left discourages readership. There are no clues to attract your interest at a glance.

The subheads in the example at right, however, allow you to preview the contents of the page without reading the text.

42 Use white space to separate and connect.

Use white space to signal the relationship between subheads and adjacent text. In general, you should leave more space above subheads than below them.

In the example on the left, the subhead "floats" between the paragraphs, leaving readers wondering which paragraph the subhead relates to. This ambiguity is reinforced by the fact that the subhead is centered.

In the example on the right, there is more space between the subhead and the text that precedes it than there is between the subhead and the text it introduces. This eliminates ambiguity, making the subhead's relationship obvious.

The subhead's flush-left alignment also makes it easier for the reader's eyes to make a smooth transition to the first paragraph.

Use your software program's "space before" and "space after" settings to insert the appropriate amounts of space before and after subheads.

Once you have determined optimum spacing, save the settings as part of your document's styles.

The quick brown fox jumped over the lazy dog. This is the previous paragraph.

Subhead introduces new material

This is the long-awaited new material. The quick brown fox was terribly upset that he was not associated with the winning team. When in the course of human events.

The quick brown fox jumped over the lazy dog. This is the previous paragraph.

Subhead introduces new material

This is the long-awaited new material. The quick brown fox was terribly upset that he was not associated with the winning team. When in the course of human events.

Use horizontal rules to separate subheads from preceding text.

43

You can emphasize your subheads and visually reinforce their relationship to adjacent text with rules, or horizontal lines. Remember that rules often signal "stop!"

In the example on the left, although the horizontal rule adds impact to the subhead, its position under the subhead inadvertently creates a barrier between the subhead and the text it introduces.

The example on the right is more logical. Placing the rule over the subhead visually reinforces the intended relationship between the subhead and adjacent text.

The rule definitely emphasizes the ending of one text block and "locks" the subhead to the text that follows.

The quick brown fox jumped over the lazy dog. This is the previous paragraph.

Subhead introduces new material

This is the long-awaited new material. The quick brown fox was terribly upset that he was not associated with the winning team. When in the course of human events.

The quick brown fox jumped over the lazy dog. This is the previous paragraph.

Subhead introduces new material

This is the long-awaited new material. The quick brown fox was terribly upset that he was not associated with the winning team. When in the course of human events.

You can save time and ensure consistent spacing between rules and text by incorporating the rules into the subhead styles you establish for your publication.

You can also emphasize different subhead levels by the presence or absence of rules, as well as by their thickness.

44 Use hanging indents to emphasize subheads.

Add emphasis to subheads by beginning them to the left of the text they introduce. Beginning a subhead to the left of the text columns surrounds the subhead's first words with white space which makes the subheads easier to find.

Use the depth of the hanging indent in conjunction with type size to signal the desired subhead hierarchy. For example, level one subheads should begin farther to the left than level two subheads, and so forth. This visually reinforces the subhead's hierarchy of importance.

Hanging indents reinforce other forms of typographic contrast. Notice how much added impact the subheads in the right-hand example have than the subheads in the left-hand example, even though both are the same size.

In the example to the left, the subheads are harder to locate because they are submerged in the text columns.

In the example to the right, the subheads are hung to the left, enhancing the reader's ability to quickly locate them.

enim ad minim veniam, quis nostrud exerci tation ullam corper suscipit lobortis nisl ut aliquip ex ea commodo consequat diat lud van wig.

Automatic Reactor Safety

Low water related

Lorem ipsum dolor sit amet, consectetuer adipiscing elit, sed diam nonummy nibh euismod tincidunt ut laoreet dolore magna aliquam erat volutpat. Ut wisi enim ad minim veniam, quis nostrud exerci tation ullamcorper suscipit lobortis nisl ut aliquip ex ea commodo consequat. Duis autem vel eum iriure dolor in hendrerit in vulputate velit esse molestie consequat, vel illum dolore eu feugiat nulla facilisis at vero eros et accum san et iusto odio dignissim qui blandit praesent luptatum zzril delenit augue duis dolore te feugait nulla facilisi.

Lorem ipsum dolor sit amet, consectetuer adipiscing elit, sed diam nonummy nibh euismod tincidunt ut laoreet dolore magna aliquam erat volutpat. Ut wisi enim ad minim veniam, quis nostrud exerci tation ullamcorper suscipit lobortis nisl ut aliquip ex ea commodo consequat.

Duis autem vel eum iriure eros et accumsan et iusto odio dolore te feugait nulla facilisi. Nam liber tempor cum soluta nobis eleifend option congue nihil imperdiet doming id quod mazim placerat facer possim assum.

Employee vacation related

Lorem ipsum dolor sit amet, consectetuer adipiscing elit, sed diam nonum3my nibh euismod tincidunt ut laoreet dolore magna aliquam erat volutpat. Ut wisi enim ad minim veniam, quis nostrud exerci tation ullamcorper suscipit lobortis nisl ut aliquip ex ea commodo consequat.

enim ad minim veniam, quis nostrud exerci tation ullam corper suscipit lobortis nisl ut aliquip ex ea commodo consequat diat lud van wig.

Automatic Reactor Safety

Low water related

Lorem ipsum dolor sit amet, consectetuer adipiscing elit, sed diam nonummy nibh euismod tincidunt ut laoreet dolore magna aliquam erat volutpat. Ut wisi enim ad minim veniam, quis nostrud exerci tation ullamcorper suscipit lobortis nisl ut aliquip ex ea commodo consequat. Duis autem vel eum iriure dolor in hendrerit in vulputate velit esse molestie consequat, vel illum dolore eu feugiat nulla facilisis at vero eros et accum san et iusto odio dignissim qui blandit praesent luptatum zzril delenit augue duis dolore te feugait nulla facilisi.

Lorem ipsum dolor sit amet, consectetuer adipiscing elit, sed diam nonummy nibh euismod tincidunt ut laoreet dolore magna aliquam erat volutpat. Ut wisi enim ad minim veniam, quis nostrud exerci tation ullamcorper suscipit lobortis nisl ut aliquip ex ea commodo consequat.

Duis autem vel eum iriure eros et accumsan et iusto odio dolore te feugait nulla facilisi. Nam liber tempor cum soluta nobis eleifend option congue nihil imperdiet doming id quod mazim placerat facer possim assum.

Employee vacation related

Lorem ipsum dolor sit amet, consectetuer adipiscing elit, sed diam nonummy nibh euismod tincidunt ut laoreet dolore magna aliquam erat volutpat. Ut wisi enim ad minim veniam, quis nostrud exerci tation ullamcorper suscipit lobortis nisl ut aliquip ex ea commodo consequat.

45

Replace subheads with side heads.

Use side heads to conserve vertical space and avoid text interruptions instead of using subheads in the text columns. Side heads are subheads placed in columns alongside the body copy they introduce.

Subheads often interfere with reading speed, as they interrupt the flow of the text. They also take up valuable vertical space, which is especially bothersome with short documents (like résumés).

In addition, subheads within the body copy column often lack sufficient contrasting white space.

Side heads, however, do not take up vertical space and are completely surrounded by white space. You can set side heads either flush left or flush right. When set flush right in the column to the left of the text they introduce, the side heads become visually "locked" to that text, which makes their connection obvious.

enim ad minim veniam, quis nostrud exerci tation ullam corper suscipit lobortis nisl ut aliquip ex ea commodo consequat diat lud van wig.

Automatic Reactor Safety

Low water related

Lorem ipsum dolor sit amet, consectetuer adipiscing elit, sed diam nonummy nibh euismod tincidunt ut laoreet dolore magna aliquam erat volutpat. Ut wisi enim ad minim veniam, quis nostrud exerci tation ullamcorper suscipit lobortis nisl ut aliquip ex ea commodo consequat. Duis autem vel eum iriure dolor in hendrerit in vulputate velit esse molestie consequat, vel illum dolore eu feugiat nulla facilisis at vero eros et accum san et iusto odio dignissim qui blandit praesent luptatum zzril delenit augue duis dolore te feugait nulla facilisi.

Lorem ipsum dolor sit amet, consectetuer adipiscing elit, sed diam nonummy nibh euismod tincidunt ut laoreet dolore magna aliquam erat volutpat. Ut wisi enim ad minim veniam, quis nostrud exerci tation ullamcorper suscipit lobortis nisl ut aliquip ex ea commodo consequat.

Duis autem vel eum iriure eros et accumsan et iusto odio dolore te feugait nulla facilisi. Nam liber tempor cum soluta nobis eleifend option congue nihil imperdiet doming id quod mazim placerat facer possim assum.

Employee vacation related

Lorem ipsum dolor sit amet, consectetuer adipiscing elit, sed diam nonummy nibh euismod tincidunt ut laoreet dolore magna aliquam erat volutpat. Ut wisi enim ad minim veniam, quis nostrud exerci tation ullamcorper suscipit lobortis nisl ut aliquip ex ea commodo consequat.

enim ad minim veniam, quis nostrud exerci tation ullam corper suscipit lobortis nisl ut aliquip ex ea commodo consequat diat lud van wig.

Automatic Reactor Safety

Water related Lorem ipsum dolor sit amet, consectetuer adipiscing elit, sed diam nonummy nibh euismod tincidunt ut laoreet dolore magna aliquam erat volutpat. Ut wisi enim ad minim veniam, quis nostrud exerci tation ullamcorper suscipit lobortis nisl ut aliquip ex ea commodo consequat. Duis autem vel eum iriure dolor in hendrerit in vulputate velit esse molestie consequat, vel illum dolore eu feugiat nulla facilisis at vero eros et accumsan et iusto odio dignissim qui blandit praesent luptatum zzril delenit augue duis dolore te feugait nulla facilisi.

Lorem ipsum dolor sit amet, consectetuer adipiscing elit, sed diam nonummy nibh euismod tincidunt ut laoreet dolore magna aliquam erat volutpat. Ut wisi enim ad minim veniam, quis nostrud exerci tation ullamcorper suscipit lobortis nisl ut aliquip ex ea commodo consequat.

Duis autem vel eum iriure eros et accumsan et iusto odio dolore te feugait nulla facilisi. Nam liber tempor cum soluta nobis eleifend option congue nihil imperdiet doming id quod mazim placerat facer possim assum.

Employee related Lorem ipsum dolor sit amet, consectetuer adipiscing elit, sed diam nonummy nibh euismod tincidunt ut laoreet dolore magna aliquam erat volutpat. Ut wisi enim ad minim veniam, quis nostrud exerci tation ullamcorper suscipit lobortis nisl ut aliquip ex ea commodo consequat.
Duis autem vel eum iriure dolor in hendrerit in vulputate velit esse molestie consequat, vel illum dolore eu feugiat nulla

You can use side heads in conjunction with subheads hung to the left to indicate information hierarchy.

You can also use side heads to introduce fields of information, like "to," "from," and "date" information in memos and fax covering sheets.

46 Match the x-height of sans serif run-ins with the x-height of adjacent serif text.

To avoid dominating adjacent text, match the x-height of run-ins with the adjacent body text. Run-ins are often used for level two or level three subheads. Run-ins consist of a word or phrase set in a contrasting typeface.

Often, sans serif run-ins introduce serif text. When this happens, the x-height of the run-in is significantly larger than the x-height of the adjacent serif text, even if both are set the same size. This destroys the desired even texture of the passage.

You can achieve a smoother, more even texture by reducing the type size of the sans serif typeface until its x-height matches that of the adjacent serif text.

Often, a two-, three-, or four-point difference is needed to properly match x-heights. Experiment with half-point differences.

In the top example, the sans serif run-in dominates the adjacent text, even though both are set the same size.

Read Before Using: Lorem ipsum dolor sit amet, consec tetuer adipiscing elit, sed diam nonummy nibh euismod tincidunt ut laoreet dolore magna aliquam erat volutpat. Ut wisi enim ad minim veniam, quis nostrud exerci tation ullamcorper suscipit lobortis nisl ut aliquip ex ea commodo consequat.

In the lower example, there is a much smoother transition.

Read Before Using: Lorem ipsum dolor sit amet, consec tetuer adipiscing elit, sed diam nonummy nibh euismod tincidunt ut laoreet dolore magna aliquam erat volutpat. Ut wisi enim ad minim veniam, quis nostrud exerci tation ullamcorper suscipit lobortis nisl ut aliquip ex ea commodo consequat.

A comparison of Minion and Frutiger x-heights shows how much they differ when set the same size.

Use matching typography for headlines, subheads, and pull-quotes.

47

Use different weights, widths, styles, and alignments of a single typeface for all display type. The major sans serif typefaces are available in weights and widths ranging from light to heavy, condensed to expanded. By choosing variations of a single typeface, you can make each category of type stand apart without visually cluttering your page.

In the right-hand example, Helvetica Extra Black is used for the headline, Helvetica Condensed Black for level one subheads, Helvetica Bold for level two subheads, and Helvetica Light for pull-quotes. The result is a unified page, yet each element of page architecture stands apart from the body copy.

Although your readers may not be aware of the consistency on a perceptual level, subconsciously they will respond favorably to your professionalism and attention to detail.

Yesterday's railroad tracks become today's bicycle paths

Lorem ipsum dolor sit amet, consectetuer adipiscing elit, sed diam nonummy nibh euismod tincidunt ut laoreet dolore magna aliquam erat volutpat. Ut wisi enim ad minim veniam, quis nostrud exerci tation ullamcorper suscipit lobortis nisl ut aliquip ex ea commodo consequat.

Duis autem vel eum iriure dolor in hendrerit in vulputate velit esse molestie consequat, vel illum dolore eu feugiat nulla facilisis at vero eros et accumsan et iusto odio dignissim qui blandit praesent luptatum zzril delenit augue duis dolore te feugait nulla facilisi. Lorem ipsum dolor sit amet, consectetuer adipiscing elit, sed diam nonummy nibh euismod tincidunt ut laoreet dolore magna aliquam erat volutpat.

Cycling for Recreation

Ut wisi enim ad minim veniam, quis nostrud exerci tation ullamcoit lobortis nisl ut aliquip ex ea commodo consequat.

Duis autem vel eum iriure dolor in hendrerit in vulputate velit esse molestie consequat, vel illum dolore eu feugiat facilisis at vero eros et accumsan et iusto odio dignissim qui blandit praesent luptatum zzril delenit augue duis dolore te feugait nulla facilisi. Nam liber tempor cum soluta nobis eleifend option congue nihil imperdiet doming id adipiscing elit, sed diam nonummy nibh euismod tincidunt ut laoreet dolore magna aliquam erat volutpat.

Scenic Trails

Ut wisi enim ad minim veniam, quis nostrud exerci tation ullamcorper suscipit lobortis nisl ut aliquip ex ea commodo consequat.

Duis autem vel eum iriure dolor in hendrerit in vulputate velit esse molestie consequat, vel illum dolore eu feugiat nulla facilisis at vero eros et accumsan et iusto odio dignissim qui blandit praesent luptatum zzril delenit augue duis dolore te feugait nulla facilisi. Nam liber tempor cum soluta nobis eleifend option congue nihil imperdiet doming id quod mazim placerat facer possim assum.

Lorem ipsum dolor sit amet, consectetuer adipiscing elit, sed diam nonummy nibh euismod tincidunt ut laoreet dolore magna aliquam erat volutpat. Ut wisi enim ad minim veniam, quis nostrud exerci tation ullamcorper suscipit lobortis nisl ut aliquip ex ea commodo consequat. Duis autem vel eum iriure dolor in hendrerit in vulputate velit esse molestie consequa.

Vel illum dolore eu feugiat nulla facilisis at vero eros et accumsan et iusto odio dignissim qui blandit praesent luptatum zzril delenit augue duis dolore te feugait nulla facilisi. Lorem ipsum dolor sit amet, consectetuer adipiscing elit, sed diam nonummy nibh euismod tincidunt ut laoreet dolore magna aliquam erat volutpat.

Ut wisi enim ad minim veniam, quis nostrud exerci tation ullamcorper suscipit lobortis nisl ut aliquip ex ea

The big rage is mountain biking on smoothly paved bicycle paths

commodo consequat. Duis autem vel eum iriure dolor in hendrerit in vulputate velit esse molestie consequat, vel illum dolore eu feugiat nulla facilisis at vero eros et accumsan et iusto odio dignissim qui blandit

3

Yesterday's railroad tracks become today's bicycle paths

Lorem ipsum dolor sit amet, consectetuer adipiscing elit, sed diam nonummy nibh euismod tincidunt ut laoreet dolore magna aliquam erat volutpat. Ut wisi enim ad minim veniam, quis nostrud exerci tation ullamcorper suscipit lobortis nisl ut aliquip ex ea commodo consequat.

Duis autem vel eum iriure dolor in hendrerit in vulputate velit esse molestie consequat, vel illum dolore eu feugiat nulla facilisis at vero eros et accumsan et iusto odio dignissim qui blandit praesent luptatum zzril delenit augue duis dolore te feugait nulla facilisi. Lorem ipsum dolor sit amet, consectetuer adipiscing elit, sed diam nonummy nibh euismod tincidunt ut laoreet dolore magna aliquam erat volutpat.

Cycling for Recreation

Ut wisi enim ad minim veniam, quis nostrud exerci tation ullamcoit lobortis nisl ut aliquip ex ea commodo consequat.

Duis autem vel eum iriure dolor in hendrerit in vulputate velit esse molestie consequat, vel illum dolore eu feugiat facilisis at vero eros et accumsan et iusto odio dignissim qui blandit praesent luptatum zzril delenit augue duis dolore te feugait nulla facilisi. Nam liber tempor cum soluta nobis eleifend option congue nihil imperdiet doming id adipiscing elit, sed diam nonummy nibh euismod tincidunt ut laoreet dolore magna aliquam erat volutpat.

Scenic Trails

Ut wisi enim ad minim veniam, quis nostrud exerci tation ullamcorper suscipit lobortis nisl ut aliquip ex ea commodo consequat.

Duis autem vel eum iriure dolor in hendrerit in vulputate velit esse molestie consequat, vel illum dolore eu feugiat nulla facilisis at vero eros et accumsan et iusto odio dignissim qui blandit praesent luptatum zzril delenit augue duis dolore te feugait nulla facilisi. Nam liber tempor cum soluta nobis eleifend option congue nihil imperdiet doming id quod mazim placerat facer possim assum.

Lorem ipsum dolor sit amet, consectetuer adipiscing elit, sed diam nonummy nibh euismod tincidunt ut laoreet dolore magna aliquam erat volutpat. Ut wisi enim ad minim veniam, quis nostrud exerci tation ullamcorper suscipit lobortis nisl ut aliquip ex ea commodo consequat. Duis autem vel eum iriure dolor in hendrerit in vulputate velit esse molestie consequa.

Vel illum dolore eu feugiat nulla facilisis at vero eros et accumsan et iusto odio dignissim qui blandit praesent luptatum zzril delenit augue duis dolore te feugait nulla facilisi. Lorem ipsum dolor sit amet, consectetuer adipiscing elit, sed diam nonummy nibh euismod tincidunt ut laoreet dolore magna aliquam erat volutpat.

Ut wisi enim ad minim veniam, quis nostrud exerci

The big rage is mountain biking on smoothly paved bicycle paths

tation ullamcorper suscipit lobortis nisl ut aliquip ex ea commodo consequat. Duis autem vel eum iriure dolor in hendrerit in vulputate velit esse molestie consequat, vel illum dolore eu feugiat nulla facilisis at vero eros et accumsan et iusto odio

3

The example at left lacks unity, because different typefaces are employed for headlines, subheads, and pull-quotes.

The example at right presents a more unified appearance, because the same typeface is used for headlines, subheads, and pull-quotes.

48 Avoid isolated subheads.

Always precede and follow subheads with at least three lines of text. When a subhead appears by itself at the top of a column or page, it attracts unwanted attention and readers may mistake it for a headline.

Likewise, subheads that introduce less than three lines of text at the bottom of a column or page look awkward and are apt to be overlooked as the reader's eyes move to the top of the next column.

Note: Most software programs permit you to create styles that automatically lock subheads and a specified number of lines together.

In the left-hand example, the first subhead could be confused with a headline introducing a new topic and the last subhead could be easily overlooked.

At right, it is obvious that the text continues from a previous page and continues on to the next page.

Atmospheric conditions

Lorem ipsum dolor sit amet, consectetuer adipiscing elit, sed diam nonummy nibh euismod tincidunt ut laoreet dolore magna . Ut wisi enim ad minim veniam, quis nostrud exerci tation ullamcorper suscipit lobortis nisl ut aliquip ex ea commodo consequat.

Duis autem vel eum iriure dolor in hendrerit in vulputate velit esse molestie consequat, vel illum dolore eu feugiat nulla facilisis at vero eros et accumsan et iusto odio dignissim qui blandit praesent luptatum zzril delenit augue duis dolore te feugait nulla facilisi.

Economic constraints

Lorem ipsum dolor sit amet, consectetuer adipiscing elit, sed diam nonummy nibh euismod tincidunt ut ullamcorper suscipitlaoreet dolore magna aliquam erat volutpat.

Ut wisi enim ad minim veniam, quis nostrud exerci tation ullamcorper suscipit lobortis nisl ut aliquip ex ea commodo con equat molestie consequat, vel ill.

Duis autem vel eum iriure eros et accumsan et iusto odio dolore te feugait nulla facilisi. Nam liber tempor cum utem illum dolore eu feugiat nullavel eum iriure dolor in hendreritsoluta nobis eleifend option congue nihil imperdiet doming id quod mazim placerat facer possim assum.

Local politics

Lorem ipsum dolor sit amet, consectetuer adipiscing elit, sed diam nonummy nibh euismod tincidunt ut laoreet dolore magna aliquam erat volutpat.

Ut wisi enim ad minim veniam, quis nostrud exerci tation ullamcorper suscipit lobortis nisl ut aliquip ex ea commodo consequat. Duis autem vel eum iriure dolor in hendrerit in vulputate velit esse molestie consequat, vel illum dolore eu feugiat nulla facilisis at vero eros et accumsan et iusto odio dignissim delenit augue duis dolore te feugait nulla facilisi. Lorem ipsum dolor sit amet, consectetuer adipiscing elit, sed dolore magna aliquam erat volutpat.

National politics

tincidunt ut ullamcorper suscipitlaoreet dolore magna aliquam erat volutpat nihi aliquip .

Atmospheric conditions

Lorem ipsum dolor sit amet, consectetuer adipiscing elit, sed diam nonummy nibh euismod tincidunt ut laoreet dolore magna . Ut wisi enim ad minim veniam, quis nostrud exerci tation ullamcorper suscipit lobortis nisl ut aliquip ex ea commodo consequat.

Duis autem vel eum iriure dolor in hendrerit in vulputate velit esse molestie consequat, vel illum dolore eu feugiat nulla facilisis at vero eros et accumsan et iusto odio dignissim qui blandit praesent luptatum zzril delenit augue duis dolore te feugait nulla facilisi.

Economic constraints

Lorem ipsum dolor sit amet, consectetuer adipiscing elit, sed diam nonummy nibh euismod tincidunt ut ullamcorper suscipitlaoreet dolore magna aliquam erat volutpat.

Ut wisi enim ad minim veniam, quis nostrud exerci tation ullamcorper suscipit lobortis nisl ut aliquip ex ea comodo consequat.

Duis autem vel eum iriure eros et accumsan et iusto odio dolore te feugait nulla facilisi. Nam liber tempor cum utem vel eum iriure dolor in hendreritsoluta nobis eleifend option congue nihil imperdiet doming id quod mazim placerat facer possim assum.

Local politics

Lorem ipsum dolor sit amet, consectetuer adipiscing elit, sed diam nonummy nibh euismod tincidunt ut laoreet dolore magna aliquam erat volutpat.

Ut wisi enim ad minim veniam, quis nostrud exerci tation ullamcorper suscipit lobortis nisl ut aliquip ex ea commodo consequat. Duis autem vel eum iriure dolor in hendrerit in vulputate velit esse molestie consequat, vel illum dolore eu f.

National politics

Ut wisiem et enim ad sed minim veniam, sed quis nostrud exerci tation ullamcorper suscipit lobortis nisl ut aliquip ex ea commodo consequat. Duis autem vel eum iriure dolor in hendrerit in

Pull-Quotes

Use pull-quotes—short phrases or sentences extracted from body copy—to add visual interest to a page and provide readers with an additional text-entry point. Pull-quotes attract reader by providing "skimmers" with a brief, tantalizing summary of the information covered in the adjacent text.

Place pull-quotes within paragraphs rather than between paragraphs.

49

Readers should not be able to confuse pull-quotes with headlines or subheads. Pull-quotes must appear *within* paragraphs rather than *between* paragraphs. If pull-quotes appear between paragraphs, they can easily be mistaken for headlines or subheads.

Extract pull-quotes from the page they appear on, but they should not repeat information from the same paragraph in which they appear. When the pull-quote appears within the originating paragraph, readers are apt to become confused, thinking that they've just read the same sentence twice.

Lorem ipsum dolor sit amet, consectetuevel illum dolore eu feugiat nulla facilisis at vero eros et accumsan et iusto odio dignissim qui blandit praesent luptatum zzril delenit augue duis dolore te feugait nulla facilisi.

Many times the illusion of wealth is as satisfying as its attainment.

Lorem ipsum dolor sit amet, consectetuer adipiscing elit, sed diam nonummy nibh euismod tincidunt ut laoreet dolore magna aliquam erat volutpat. Ut wisi enim ad minim veniam, quis nostrud exerci tation ullamcorper suscipit lobortis nisl ut aliquip ex ea commodo consequat.

Duis autem vel eum iriure eros et accumsan et iusto odio dolore te feugait nulla facilisienim ad minim veniam. Nam liber tempor cum soluta nobis eleifend option congue nihil imperdiet doming id quod mazim placerat facer possim assum.

Lorem ipsum dolor sit amet, consectetuer adipiscing elit, sed diam nonummy nibh euismod tincidunt ut laoreet dolore magna aliquam erat volutpat. Ut wisi elit, sed diam nonummy nibh euismod tincidunt ut laoreet dolore magna aliquam erat volutpat.

Ut wisi enim ad minim veniam, quis nostrud exerci tation ullamcorper suscipit lobortis nisl ut aliquip ex ea commodo consequat. Duis autem vel eum iriure dolor in hendrerit in vulputate velit esse molestie consequat, vel illum dolore eu feugiat nulla facilisis at vero eros et accumsan et iusto odio dignissim qui blandit praesent luptatum zzril delenit augue duis dolore te feugait nulla facilisi.

Often, the very wealthy masquerade their wealth to avoid jealousy.

Lorem ipsum dolor sit amet, consectetuer adipiscing elit, sed diam nonummy nibh euismod tincidunt ut laoreet dolore magna

Lorem ipsum dolor sit amet, consectetuevel illum dolore eu feugiat nulla facilisis at vero eros et accumsan et iusto odio dignissim qui blandit praesent luptatum zzril delenit augue duis dolore te feugait nulla facilisi.

Lorem ipsum dolor sit amet, consectetuer adipiscing elit, sed diam nonummy nibh euismod tincidunt ut laoreet dolore magna aliquam erat volutpat dolore mag

Many times the illusion of wealth is as satisfying as its attainment.

tut wisi enim ad minim veniam, quis nostrud exerci tation ullamcorper suscipit lobortis nisl ut aliquip ex ea commodo consequat.

Duis autem vel eum iriure eros et accumsan et iusto odio dolore te feugait nulla facilisienim ad minim veniam. Nam liber tempor cum soluta nobis eleifend option congue nihil imperdiet doming id quod mazim placerat facer possim assum.

Lorem ipsum dolor sit amet, consectetuer adipiscing elit, sed diam nonummy nibh euismod aliquam erat volutpat. Ut wisi elit, sed diam nonummy nibh euismod tincidunt ut laoreet dolore magna aliquam erat volutpat.

Ut wisi enim ad minim veniam, quis nostrud exerci tation ullamcorper suscipit lobortis nisl ut aliquip ex ea commodo consequat.

Duis autem vel eum iriure dolor in hendrerit in vulputate velit esse molestie consequat, vel facilisis at dolore eu feugiatvero eros et accumsan et iusto odio

Often, the very wealthy masquerade their wealth to avoid jealousy.

dignissim qui blandit praesent luptatum zzril delenit augue duis dolore te feugait nulla facilisi.

Lorem ipsum dolor sit amet, consectetuer adipiscing elit, sed diam nonummy nibh euismod

In the example at left, the pull-quote could be confused with a headline or subhead.

In the example at right, the pull-quote's placement within the paragraph eliminates this ambiguity.

50 Avoid pull-quotes at the tops of columns, near headlines, or next to each other.

Pull-quotes at the tops of columns can be easily mistaken for headlines or subheads. Pull-quotes look best when you place them within the middle three-fifths of a page. In other words, a pull-quote should begin at least one-fifth of the page's length down from the top of the page. Others should end at least one-fifth of a page length up from the bottom of the page.

Avoid parallel placement of pull-quotes. Visual distraction and a "cancellation effect" is likely to occur when you align pull-quotes in adjacent columns. Parallel placement could also cause readers to read across the columns.

Pull-quotes should be far enough away from headlines to avoid competing with them.

When pull-quotes are placed at the tops of columns or next to each other, as in the example at left, they can appear to be headlines or section dividers.

Pull-quotes work better when they appear within columns, apart from each other or adjacent headlines, as shown in the example at right.

Ut wisi enim ad min veniam, quis nos execitation.

Duisa nibh amla nostro ma dolor sit vero.

Lorem ipsum

Lorem ipsum dolor sit amet, consectetuer adipiscing elit, sed diam nonummy nibh euismod tincidunt ut laoreet dolore magna aliquam erat volutpat.

Ut wisi enim ad minim veniam, quis nostrud exerci tation ullamcorper suscipit lobortis nisl ut aliquip ex ea commodo consequat. Duis autem vel eum iriure dolor in hendrerit in vulputate velit esse molestie consequat, vel illum dolore eu feugiat nulla facilisis at vero eros et accumsan et iusto odio dignissim qui blandit praesent luptatum zzril delenit augue duis dolore te feugait nulla facilisi. Lorem ipsum dolor sit amet, consectetuer adipiscing elit, sed diam nonummy nibh euismod tincidunt ut laoreet dolore magna aliquam erat volutpat.

Ut wisi enim ad minim veniam, quis nostrud exerci tation ullamcoit lobortis nisl ut aliquip ex ea commodo consequat.

Duis autem vel eum iriure dolor in hendrerit in vulputate velit esse molestie consequat, vel illum dolore eu feugiat facilisis at vero eros et accumsan et iusto odio dignissim qui blandit praesent luptatum zzril delenit augue duis dolore te feugait nulla facilisi. Nam liber tempor cum soluta nobis eleifend option congue nihil imperdiet doming id adipiscing elit, sed diam nonummy nibh euismod tincidunt ut laoreet dolore magna aliquam erat volutpat. Ut wisi enim ad minim veniam, quis nostrud exerci tation ullamcorper suscipit lobortis nisl ut aliquip ex ea commodo consequat.

Ut wisi

Duis autem vel eum iriure dolor in hendrerit in vulputate velit esse molestie consequat, vel illum dolore eu feugiat nulla facilisis at vero eros et accumsan et iusto odio dignissim qui blandit.

Praesent luptatum zzril delenit augue duis dolore te feugait nulla facilisi. Nam liber tempor cum soluta nobis eleifend option congue nihil imperdiet doming id quod mazim placerat facer possim assum.

Lorem ipsum dolor sit amet, consectetuer adipiscing elit, sed diam nonummy nibh euismod tincidunt ut laoreet dolore magna aliquam erat volutpat.

Ut wisi enim ad minim veniam, quis nostrud exerci tation ullamcorper suscipit lobortis nisl ut aliquip ex ea commodo consequat. Duis autem vel eum iriure dolor in hendrerit in vulputate velit esse molestie consequat, vel illum dolore eu feugiat nulla facilisis at vero eros et accumsan et iusto odio dignissim qui blandit praesent luptatum zzril.

Delenit augue duis dolore te feugait nulla facilisi. Lorem ipsum dolor sit amet, consectetuer adipiscing elit, sed diam nonummy nibh euismod tincidunt ut laoreet dolore magna aliquam erat volutpat.

Ut wisi enim ad minim veniam, quis nostrud exerci tation ullamcorper suscipit lobortis nisl ut aliquip ex ea commodo consequat. Duis autem vel eum iriure dolor in hendrerit in vulputate velit esse molestie consequat, vel illum dolore eu feugiat nulla facilisis at vero eros et accumsan et iusto odio dignissim qui blandit praesent luptatum zzril delenit augue duis dolore te feugait nulla facilisi. Lorem ipsum dolor sit amet, consectetuer adipiscing elit,

Facili augue iust ulla blandit zzril delen qui.

Lorem ipsum

Lorem ipsum dolor sit amet, consectetuer adipiscing elit, sed diam nonummy nibh euismod tincidunt ut laoreet dolore magna aliquam erat volutpat.

Ut wisi enim ad minim veniam, quis nostrud exerci

Ut wisi enim ad min veniam, quis nos execitation.

tation ullamcorper suscipit lobortis nisl ut aliquip ex ea commodo consequat. Duis autem vel eum iriure dolor in hendrerit in vulputate velit esse molestie consequat, vel illum dolore eu feugiat nulla facilisis at vero eros et accumsan et iusto odio dignissim qui blandit praesent luptatum zzril delenit augue duis dolore te feugait nulla facilisi. Lorem ipsum dolor sit amet, consectetuer adipiscing elit, sed diam nonummy nibh euismod tincidunt ut laoreet dolore magna aliquam erat volutpat.

Ut wisi enim ad minim veniam, quis nostrud exerci tation ullamcoit lobortis nisl ut aliquip ex ea commodo consequat.

Duis autem vel eum iriure dolor in hendrerit in vulputate velit esse molestie consequat, vel illum dolore eu feugiat facilisis at vero eros et accumsan et iusto odio dignissim qui blandit praesent luptatum zzril delenit augue duis dolore te feugait nulla facilisi. Nam liber tempor cum soluta nobis eleifend option congue nihil imperdiet doming id adipiscing elit, sed diam nonummy nibh euismod tincidunt ut laoreet dolore magna aliquam erat volutpat. Ut wisi enim ad minim veniam, quis nostrud exerci tation ullamcorper suscipit lobortis nisl ut aliquip ex ea commodo consequat.

Ut wisi

Duis autem vel eum iriure dolor in hendrerit in vulputate velit esse molestie consequat, vel illum dolore

Duisa nibh amla nostro ma dolor sit vero.

eu feugiat nulla facilisis at vero eros et accumsan et iusto odio dignissim qui blandit.

Praesent luptatum zzril delenit augue duis dolore te feugait nulla facilisi. Nam liber tempor cum soluta nobis eleifend option congue nihil imperdiet doming id quod mazim placerat facer possim assum.

Lorem ipsum dolor sit amet, consectetuer adipiscing elit, sed diam nonummy nibh euismod tincidunt ut laoreet dolore magna aliquam erat volutpat.

Ut wisi enim ad minim veniam, quis nostrud exerci tation ullamcorper suscipit lobortis nisl ut aliquip ex ea commodo consequat. Duis autem vel eum iriure dolor in hendrerit in vulputate velit esse molestie consequat, vel illum dolore eu feugiat nulla facilisis at vero eros et accumsan et iusto odio dignissim qui blandit praesent luptatum zzril.

Delenit augue duis dolore te feugait nulla facilisi. Lorem ipsum dolor

Facili augue iust ulla blandit zzril delen qui.

sit amet, consectetuer adipiscing elit, sed diam nonummy nibh euismod tincidunt ut laoreet dolore magna aliquam erat volutpat.

Ut wisi enim ad minim veniam, quis nostrud exerci tation ullamcorper suscipit lobortis nisl ut aliquip ex ea commodo consequat. Duis autem vel eum iriure dolor in hendrerit in vulputate velit esse molestie consequat, vel illum dolore eu feugiat nulla facilisis at vero eros et accumsan et iusto odio dignissim qui blandit praesent luptatum zzril delenit augue duis dolore te feugait nulla facilisi. Lorem

Choose short pull-quotes set in a large type size.

51

Limit pull-quotes to a maximum of four lines; three lines is even better. Short pull-quotes work best. Readership declines as pull-quotes increase in length. Edit pull-quotes to the minimum number of words sufficient to summarize related material. Long pull-quotes are difficult to read and contribute to "gray pages."

Tease your readers with pull-quotes rather than tell a complete story. Pull-quotes should tell enough of the story to attract readers into the adjacent text, yet not tell so much that readers don't have to read the adjacent text.

Like headlines, pull-quotes reflect a trade-off between type size and number of words. Long pull-quotes require more lines and/or a smaller type size. Both alternatives reduce pull-quotes' effectiveness.

Lorem ipsum

Duisa nibh amla nostro ma dolor sit vero. Delenit wisi autem dolor vel feugiat ban de facilis.

Ut wisi enim ad min veniam, quis nos excitation. A voce lat duis sin ex volup tat ut laoreet qui blandit delenit ague.

Ut wisi

Facili augue iust ulla blandit zzril delen qui. Volun elit sed diamne con eu ullam copter va lom.

Lorem ipsum

Ut wisi enim ad min veniam, quis nos excitation.

Ut wisi

Duisa nibh amla nostro ma dolor sit vero.

Facili augue iust ulla blandit zzril delen qui.

The extended pull-quotes in the example at left appear to be sidebars, or mini-articles. Their length detracts from their ability to attract the reader's attention.

The shorter pull-quotes in the example at right present a far less challenging reading experience.

52 Use contrast to make pull-quotes stand out.

Use contrasting typography so pull-quotes contrast with adjacent text. A typical solution is to use a contrasting typeface design, like sans serif pull-quotes with serif body copy. Different style and weight variations often work well. Try pull-quotes set in the Condensed Light Italics, for example.

There should be a significant amount of type size contrast. Make pull-quotes at least twice the size of adjacent body copy; a three-to-one relation often works even better.

You can further emphasize pull-quotes by adding graphic accents. For example, place your pull-quotes below heavy rules, against screened or graduated tints, or against colored backgrounds.

You can also use oversize quotation marks to call attention to quotations used as pull-quotes.

The pull-quotes in the example at left, set in a size only slightly larger than the body copy text, do not clearly emerge from the adjacent text.

In the example at right, the pull-quotes are significantly larger, set in a contrasting typeface, and emphasized by horizontal rules.

Lorem ipsum

Duisa nibh amla nostro ma dolor sit vero.

Facili augue iust ulla blandit zzril delen qui.

Ut wisi

Ut wisi enim ad min veniam, quis nos excitation.

Lorem ipsum

Ut wisi enim ad min veniam, quis nos excitation.

Facili augue iust ulla blandit zzril delen qui.

Ut wisi

Duisa nibh amla nostro ma dolor sit vero.

Align pull-quotes with columns. 53

Avoid unnecessary text wraps, often caused by placing pull-quotes between columns or extending into adjacent columns. Text wraps interfere with reading by forcing readers to readjust their rhythm. Text wraps also create narrow columns, which can result in unwanted extra hyphenation and unnatural word spacing in columns of justified text.

Text wraps around flush-left/ragged-right columns are equally unattractive because of the unwanted difference between the ragged right-hand edge of the left-hand column compared to the razor sharp straight edge on the right-hand column.

Lorem ipsum

Lorem ipsum dolor sit amet, consectetuer adipiscing elit, sed diam nonummy nibh euismod tincidunt ut laoreet dolore magna aliqu am erat vusa volutpat.
Ut wisi enim ad minim veniam, quis nostrud exerci tation ullamcorper suscipit lobortis nisl ut aliquip ex ea commodo consequat. Duis autem vel eum iriure dolor in hendrerit in vulputate velit esse mole stie consequat, vel illum dolore eu feugiat nulla facilisis at vero eros et accumsan et iusto odio dignissim qui blandit praesent luptatum zzril delenit augue duis dolore te feugait nulla facilisi. Lorem ipsum dolor sit amet, consec tetuer dilmin adipiscing elit, sed diam quod nonummy sin nibh euismod tincidunt ut laoreet dolore magna aliquam erat volutpat.
Ut wisi enim ad minim veniam, quis nostrud exerci tation ullamcoit lob ortis nisl ut aliquip ex ea commodo consequat.
Duis autem vel eum iriure dolor in hendrerit in vulputate velit esse

Ut wisi enim ad min veniam, quis nos execitation.

Duisa nibh amla nostro ma dolor sit vero.

praesent luptatum zzril delenit augue duis dolore te feugait nulla facilisi. Nam liber tempor cum soluta nobis eleifend option congue nihil imperdiet doming id adipiscing elit, sed diam nonummy nibh euismod tincidunt ut laoreet dolore magna aliquam erat volut pat. Ut wisi enim ad minim veniam, quis nostrud exe rci tation ullamcorper suscipit lob ortis nisl ut aliquip ex ea commodo consequat.

Ut wisi

Duis autem vel eum iriure dolor in hendrerit in vulputate velit esse molestie consequat, vel illum dolore eu feugiat nulla facilisis at vero eros et accumsan et iusto odio dignissim qui blandit.
Praesent luptatum zzril delenit aug ue duis dolore te feugait nulla facilisi. Nam liber tempor cum soluta nobis eleifend option congue nihil imperdiet doming id quod mazim placerat facer possim assum.
Lorem ipsum dolor sit amet, consectetuer vostu

Facili augue lust ulla blandit zzril delen qui.

veniam, quis nostrud vina exerci tation ullamcorper suscipit lobortis nisl ut va aliquip ex ea commodo consequat. Duis autem vel eum iriure dolor in hendre rit in vulputate velit esse molestie consequat, vel illum dolore eu feugiat nulla facilisis at vero eros et accumsan et iusto odio dignissim qui blandit que praesent luptatum zzril.
Delenit augue duis dolore te feugait nulla facilisi. Lorem ipsum dolor sit amet, consectetuer adip iscing elit, sed diam no nummy nibh euismod tin cidunt ut laoreet dolore magna aliquam ert voltpat.
Ut wisi enim ad minim dus veniam, tu quis nos trud exerci tation ullam corper suscipit lobortis nisl ut aliquip ex ea commodo consequat. Duis autem vel eum iriure dolor in hen drerit in vulputate velit esse molestie consequat, vel illum dolore eu feugiat nulla facilisis at vero eros et accumsan et iusto odio dignissim qui blandit praesent luptatum zzril delenit augue duis dolore te feugait nulla facilisi. Lorem ipsum dolor sit amet, consectetuer adipiscing elit, sed diam nonummy nibh euismod tincidunt ut laoreet dolore

Lorem ipsum

Lorem ipsum dolor sit amet, consectetuer adipiscing elit, sed diam nonummy nibh euismod tincidunt ut laoreet dolore magna aliquam erat volutpat.
Ut wisi enim ad minim veniam, quis nostrud exerci tation ullamcorper suscipit lobortis nisl ut

Ut wisi enim ad min veniam, quis nos execitation.

aliquip ex ea commodo consequat. Duis autem vel eum iriure dolor in hendrerit in vulputate velit esse molestie consequat, vel illum dolore eu feugiat nulla facilisis at vero eros et accumsan et iusto odio dignissim qui blandit praesent luptatum zzril delenit augue duis dolore te feugait nulla facilisi. Lorem ipsum dolor sit amet, consectetuer adipiscing elit, sed diam nonummy nibh euismod tincidunt ut laoreet dolore magna aliquam erat volutpat.
Ut wisi enim ad minim veniam, quis nostrud exerci tation ullamcoit lobortis nisl ut aliquip ex ea commodo consequat.
Duis autem vel eum iriure dolor in hendrerit in

praesent luptatum zzril delenit augue duis dolore te feugait nulla facilisi. Nam liber tempor cum soluta nobis eleifend option congue nihil imperdiet doming id adipiscing elit, sed diam nonummy nibh euismod tincidunt ut laoreet dolore magna aliquam erat volutpat. Ut wisi enim ad minim veniam, quis nostrud exerci tation ullamcorper suscipit lobortis nisl ut aliquip ex ea commodo consequat.

Ut wisi

Duis autem vel eum iriure dolor in hendrerit in vulputate velit esse molestie consequat, vel illum dolore eu feugiat nulla facilisis at vero eros et accumsan et iusto odio dignissim qui blandit.
Praesent luptatum zzril delenit augue duis dolore te feugait nulla facilisi.

Duisa nibh amla nostro ma dolor sit vero.

Nam liber tempor cum soluta nobis eleifend option congue nihil imperdiet doming id quod mazim placerat facer possim assum.
Lorem ipsum dolor sit amet, consectetuer vostu

veniam, quis nostrud exerci tation ullamcorper suscipit lobortis nisl ut aliquip ex ea commodo consequat. Duis autem vel eum iriure dolor in hendrerit in vulputate velit esse molestie consequat, vel illum dolore eu feugiat nulla facilisis at vero eros et

Facili augue lust ulla blandit zzril delen qui.

accumsan et iusto odio dignissim qui blandit praesent luptatum zzril.
Delenit augue duis dolore te feugait nulla facilisi. Lorem ipsum dolor sit amet, consectetuer adipiscing elit, sed diam nonummy nibh euismod tincidunt ut laoreet dolore magna aliquam erat volutpat.
Ut wisi enim ad minim veniam, quis nostrud exerci tation ullamcorper suscipit lobortis nisl ut aliquip ex ea commodo consequat. Duis autem vel eum iriure dolor in hendrerit in vulputate velit esse molestie consequat, vel illum dolore eu feugiat nulla facilisis at vero eros et accumsan et iusto odio dignissim qui blandit praesent luptatum zzril delenit augue duis dolore te feugait nulla facilisi. Lorem ipsum dolor sit

Pull-quotes set between columns, as in the example at left, create narrow columns which disturb the reader's rhythm and create extra hyphenation.

Pull-quotes within columns, as in the example at right, do not interfere with easy, uninterrupted reading of the adjacent columns.

Section 4

Body Copy

The bulk of this book is based on body copy typography because most of your message is likely to be contained in type set in columns at small sizes. Indeed, 80 percent of the typical document's contents appear in body text type.

Your first body copy decision involves choosing the right typeface and type size. These decisions form the basis of later decisions involving line, letter, word, and paragraph spacing.

Choose a "familiar" or "transparent" typeface.

54

Choose a serif typeface with moderate stress for extended text. Serif typefaces are usually easier to recognize than sans serif typefaces. Serifs play an important role in character recognition because they help readers identify each letter. Serifs also help "pull" the reader's eyes from letter to letter.

Stress refers to the difference in stroke thickness. Stress adds visual interest and aids letter identification. Typefaces composed of strokes of equal thickness are less recognizable than typefaces with varying thick and thin strokes. Typefaces with exaggerated stress, however, are often too "busy" to be used for comfortable reading of extended text passages.

Notice how the top paragraph, set in Didot, is more distracting (and perhaps, too "formal") than the same paragraph set in Palatino in the bottom example.

It was destined to be an eventful day. On this day, Bill Jackson was going to have his Armed Forces physical. He was apprehensive but excited. He had always wanted to travel. But, he had an aversion to authority. He had even been thrown out of summer camp for subverting his den mother's authority!

It was destined to be an eventful day. On this day, Bill Jackson was going to have his Armed Forces physical. He was apprehensive but excited. He had always wanted to travel. But, he had an aversion to authority. He had even been thrown out of summer camp for subverting his den mother's authority!

The following are a few "safe" alternatives to the Times Roman likely to be included with your laser printer: Berling, Janson, Joanna, Melior.

Refer to the typeface specimen catalogs offered by the major typeface foundries for more information.

55 Avoid using stylized typefaces.

Choose a typeface that contains enough distinguishing features both to establish an image and allow the shapes of the individual letters to emerge clearly without interfering with ease of reading. Reading depends on familiarity. Readability is enhanced by the use of familiar typefaces.

Stylized serifs typefaces with exaggerated stress may be acceptable at large sizes when used for brochure titles or newsletter headlines, but are often too "busy" to look good when set at small sizes.

Notice how Monotype's Ellington looks great when used as a headline, but creates a "busy" and hard-to-read appearance when used as a body copy typeface at small size.

Roaring Twenties gallery features our new vintage railroad collection

Lorem ipsum dolor sit amet, consectetuer adipiscing elit, sed diam nonummy nibh euismod tincidunt ut laoreet dolore magna aliquam erat volutpat.

Ut wisi enim ad minim veniam, quis nostrud exerci tation suscipit lobortis nisl ut aliquip ex ea commodo consequat. Duis autem vel eum iriure dolor in hendrerit in vulputate velit esse molestie consequat, vel illum dolore eu feugiat nulla facilisis at vero eros et accumsan et iusto odio dignissim qui blandit praesent luptatum zzril delenit augue duis dolore te feugait nulla facilisi. Lorem ipsum dolor sit amet, consectetuer adipiscing elit, sed diam nonummy nibh euismod tincidunt ut laoreet dolore magna aliquam erat volutpat. Ut wisi enim ad minim veniam, quis nostrud exerci tation ullamcorper suscipit lobortis nisl ut aliquip ex ea commodo consequat.

Duis autem vel eum iriure dolor in hendrerit in vulputate velit esse molestie consequat, vel illum dolore eu feugiat nulla facilisis at vero eros et accumsan et iusto odio dignissim qui blandit praesent luptatum zzril delenit augue duis dolore te feugait nulla facilisi. Nam liber tempor cum soluta nobis eleifend option congue nihil imperdiet doming id quod mazim placerat facer possim assum.

Create templates for comparing typefaces, type sizes, and software commands. 56

Templates permit you to make easy side-by-side comparisons of typefaces and the effects of subtle changes in size and spacing. Base your templates on a three-column grid.

Use your software program's Copy and Paste commands to place the same text in each column. Fill the columns with nonsense words – such as the Latin phrase beginning "Lorem ipsum" – so you can concentrate on the appearance of the type rather than its meaning.

Describe the typeface specifications or software command used at the top of each column.

You'll be surprised at how subtle manipulation of letter, line, or word spacing quickly changes the appearance of the columns of type.

Hint: Be sure you experiment with only one variable each time– i.e. don't change both typeface and type size in the same template.

14 point
16-point leading

Lorem ipsum dolor sit amet, consectetuer adipiscing elit, sed diam nonummy nibh euismod tincidunt ut laoreet dolore magna aliquam erat volutpat. Ut wisi enim ad minim veniam, quis nostrud exerci tation ullamcorper suscipit lobortis nisl ut aliquip ex ea commodo consequat. Duis autem vel eum iriure dolor in hendrerit in vulputate velit esse molestie consequat, vel illum dolore eu feugiat nulla facilisis at vero eros et accumsan et iusto odio dignissim qui blandit praesent luptatum zzril delenit augue duis dolore te feugait nulla facilisi. Lorem ipsum dolor sit amet, consectetuer adipiscing elit, sed diam nonummy nibh euismod tincidunt ut laoreet dolore magna aliquam erat volutpat. Ut wisi enim ad minim veniam, quis nostrud exerci tation ullamcorper suscipit lobortis nisl ut aliquip ex ea commodo consequat.
Duis autem vel eum iriure dolor in hendrerit in vulputate velit esse molestie consequat, vel illum dolore eu feugiat nulla facilisis at vero eros et accumsan et iusto odio dignissim qui blandit praesent luptatum zzril

14 point
15.5-point leading

Lorem ipsum dolor sit amet, consectetuer adipiscing elit, sed diam nonummy nibh euismod tincidunt ut laoreet dolore magna aliquam erat volutpat. Ut wisi enim ad minim veniam, quis nostrud exerci tation ullamcorper suscipit lobortis nisl ut aliquip ex ea commodo consequat. Duis autem vel eum iriure dolor in hendrerit in vulputate velit esse molestie consequat, vel illum dolore eu feugiat nulla facilisis at vero eros et accumsan et iusto odio dignissim qui blandit praesent luptatum zzril delenit augue duis dolore te feugait nulla facilisi. Lorem ipsum dolor sit amet, consectetuer adipiscing elit, sed diam nonummy nibh euismod tincidunt ut laoreet dolore magna aliquam erat volutpat. Ut wisi enim ad minim veniam, quis nostrud exerci tation ullamcorper suscipit lobortis nisl ut aliquip ex ea commodo consequat.
Duis autem vel eum iriure dolor in hendrerit in vulputate velit esse molestie consequat, vel illum dolore eu feugiat nulla facilisis at vero eros et accumsan et iusto odio dignissim qui blandit praesent luptatum zzril

14 point
15-point leading

Lorem ipsum dolor sit amet, consectetuer adipiscing elit, sed diam nonummy nibh euismod tincidunt ut laoreet dolore magna aliquam erat volutpat. Ut wisi enim ad minim veniam, quis nostrud exerci tation ullamcorper suscipit lobortis nisl ut aliquip ex ea commodo consequat. Duis autem vel eum iriure dolor in hendrerit in vulputate velit esse molestie consequat, vel illum dolore eu feugiat nulla facilisis at vero eros et accumsan et iusto odio dignissim qui blandit praesent luptatum zzril delenit augue duis dolore te feugait nulla facilisi. Lorem ipsum dolor sit amet, consectetuer adipiscing elit, sed diam nonummy nibh euismod tincidunt ut laoreet dolore magna aliquam erat volutpat. Ut wisi enim ad minim veniam, quis nostrud exerci tation ullamcorper suscipit lobortis nisl ut aliquip ex ea commodo consequat.
Duis autem vel eum iriure dolor in hendrerit in vulputate velit esse molestie consequat, vel illum dolore eu feugiat nulla facilisis at vero eros et accumsan et iusto odio dignissim qui blandit praesent luptatum zzril

Notice how half-point differences in line spacing affect the "color" of each column as well as the length of each column (indicated by the circles).

These subtle differences cannot be appreciated until you can observe the differences printed out side by side.

Be sure you save your printouts in a 3-ring binder for later reference.

57 Avoid mixing similar typefaces and type sizes.

Use the same typeface and type size for all body copy. Differences should appear deliberate rather than accidental. Two serif or two sans serif typefaces look more alike than different, confusing readers because they notice that "something's wrong – but what?" This is why the use of serif headline, in the left example to introduce body copy with a different serif type is not as satisfactory as the sans serif headline with serif body copy on the right.

Likewise, avoid type size changes that appear "accidental" rather than "planned." Avoid changing type size to "squeeze in" more text. Slight changes in type size are very noticeable and may confuse the reader by implying that the smaller type indicates a message of lesser importance.

The subtleness of the differences between Granjon and Linoletter Roman make the headline/body copy contrast look accidental rather than planned. Notice the differences in the uppercase Js and lowercase a's.

There is nothing "accidental" about the right-hand example, however, which contrasts Frutiger with Minion (used for the body copy of this book).

Bill Jackson Joins the Army

It was destined to be an eventful day. On this day, Bill Jackson was going to have his Armed Forces physical. He was nervous but excited. He had always wanted to travel. But he had an aversion to authority. He had even been thrown out of summer camp for subverting his cabin counselor's authority!

Bill Jackson Joins the Army

It was destined to be an eventful day. On this day, Bill Jackson was going to have his Armed Forces physical. He was nervous but excited. He had always wanted to travel. But he had an aversion to authority. He had even been thrown out of summer camp for subverting his cabin counselor's authority!

Choose a typeface with an appropriate x-height.

58

Pay as much attention to x-height as you do to type size. X-height is a more accurate indicator of how large type will appear on a page, than type size alone. X-height refers to height of lowercase letters without ascenders.

Type is measured by the distance between the top of the ascenders and the bottom of the descenders. Within this distance, there can be great variations in x-height, as the examples below show.

Low x-height letters appear smaller than high x-height letters. As a result, two typefaces of equal size may present totally different appearances.

In addition, x-height also influences word density, or the number of words that can fit on a column inch, as the example below shows. This will also influence the number of pages needed to communicate your message.

Taxjey Taxjey

Antique Olive (top left) looks much larger than Granjon (top right), although both are set the same size (56 points).

abcdefghijklmnopqrstuvw

abcdefghijklmnopqrstuvwxy01234

Note that the lowercase 24-point Granjon sample contains seven more letters than the same size Antique Olive.

59 Avoid long lines of small type or short lines of large type.

Base type size decisions on the design of the typeface you're using, as well as the width of the column – or the length of the line. Increase type size as column width increases. Decrease type size as column width decreases.

Aim for lines containing approximately 1½ alphabets, between 40 and 60 characters.

Large type set in narrow columns forces too many vertical eye movements and is frequently characterized by irregular word spacing and excessive hyphenation.

When type is too small for line length, readers inadvertently reread lines, returning to the beginning of the current line instead of advancing to the next line.

Experiment with half-point type size differences. Sometimes 11-point type is too small, 12-point type too large, but 11.5-points is just right!

Note that the left example, set in 20-point Minion, is much harder to read than text set at 11 points placed in a column of the same width.

Notice that the wide column below, set in 9-point Minion, is visually gray and is very difficult to read.

Monday was destined to be an eventful day. On this day, Bill Jackson was going to have his Armed Forces physical. He was very apprehensive but extremely excited. He

Monday was destined to be an eventful day. On this day, Bill Jackson was going to have his Armed Forces physical. He was very apprehensive but extremely excited. He had always wanted to travel. But, he had an aversion to authority. He had even been thrown out of summer camp for subverting his den mother's authority!

Monday was destined to be an eventful day. On this day, Bill Jackson was going to have his Armed Forces physical. He was very apprehensive but extremely excited. He had always wanted to travel. But, he had an aversion to authority. He had even been thrown out of summer camp for subverting his den mother's authority!

Reduce letterspacing and word spacing.

60

You can create better-looking, easy-to-read body copy type by slightly reducing letterspacing and word spacing. Default letterspacing is typically too generous. Reduce letterspacing to increase word density (permitting you to add more white space to each page) and improve readability by making it easier for readers to identify word shapes.

Most word processing and page layout software programs have commands to reduce letterspacing uniformly. The correct term for controlling letterspacing is *tracking,* which normally must be turned "on" because the default is "off."

Even slight reductions in letterspacing pay big dividends in improving the appearance of your pages by increasing word density, which allows you to add more white space to the page.

It was destined to be an eventful day. On this day, Bill Jackson was going to have his Armed Forces physical. He was apprehensive but excited. He had always wanted to travel. But, he had an aversion to authority. He had even been thrown out of summer camp for subverting his den mother's authority!

It was destined to be an eventful day. On this day, Bill Jackson was going to have his Armed Forces physical. He was apprehensive but excited. He had always wanted to travel. But, he had an aversion to authority. He had even been thrown out of summer camp for subverting his den mother's authority!

It was destined to be an eventful day. On this day, Bill Jackson was going to have his Armed Forces physical. He was apprehensive but excited. He had always wanted to travel. But, he had an aversion to authority. He had even been thrown out of summer camp for subverting his den mother's authority!

Default letter-spacing results in very "open" sentences (top).

A slight reduction in letter-spacing saves space and makes your text easier to read (middle). Note the different line endings emphasized by the circles.

But know when to stop! Readability suffers when letter-spacing is reduced too much.

61 Let the resolution of your output device influence your choice of typeface.

Avoid low x-height typefaces with rounded edges and thin serifs when using 300 dots-per-inch (dpi) laser printers. Rounded edges become jaggy – creating stair-stepping – thin serifs get lost, and open spaces inside the letters close in. In addition, horizontal and vertical strokes often reproduce thicker than the typeface designer intended.

There are three ways to avoid these type appearance problems. If you are preparing final artwork on a 300 dpi laser printer, one alternative is to choose typefaces like Bitstream Charter or Adobe Stone that were designed for optimum reproduction at 300 dpi.

Another alternative is to upgrade your printer to one that prints at 600, 800, 1000, or 1,200 dots-per-inch.

A third alternative is to send your files to an outside service bureau for imaging at 1,250 or 2,450 dpi.

Thin serifs and curved letters are particularly susceptible to the limitations of low-resolution output.

Low stress, high x-height typefaces like Charter, Stone Serif, and Lucida work well on 300 dots-per-inch laser printers.

Reserve Modern typefaces like Bodoni, Didot, and Monotype Scotch Roman for projects to be imaged on high-resolution output devices.

S

Charter
Stone Serif
Lucida

Bodoni
Didot
Scotch Roman

Paper surface and color should also influence your choice of typeface.

62

Do not print typefaces containing thin strokes and delicate serifs on very porous paper or a white, coated paper. On a porous or textured paper, the serifs get lost and the white spaces inside the letters fill in at small sizes.

A different problem occurs when printing your projects on a shiny, coated stock: The serifs and details of the letters become too noticeable, adding "shimmer" or "sparkle," especially when read in a bright environment. (You may have encountered the problem of trying to read the captions and text of an expensive photography book in a room brilliantly illuminated by fluorescent ceiling fixtures.)

Eliminating unnecessary glare is the reason many design books are printed on an ivory or off-white paper. This reduces the harsh contrast of black type against a white background.

Fairfield Light

Lorem ipsum dolor sit amet, consectetuer adipiscing elit, sed diam nonummy nibh euismod tincidunt ut laoreet dolore magna aliquam erat volutpat. Ut wisi enim ad minim veniam, quis nostrud exerci tation ullamcorper suscipit lobortis nisl ut aliquip ex ea commodo consequat. Duis autem vel eum iriure dolor in.

Didot

Lorem ipsum dolor sit amet, consectetuer adipiscing elit, sed diam nonummy nibh euismod tincidunt ut laoreet dolore magna aliquam erat volutpat. Ut wisi enim ad minim veniam, quis nostrud exerci tation ullamcorper suscipit lobortis nisl ut aliquip ex ea commodo consequat.

Monotype Bodoni

Lorem ipsum dolor sit amet, consectetuer adipiscing elit, sed diam nonummy nibh euismod tincidunt ut laoreet dolore magna aliquam erat volutpat. Ut wisi enim ad minim veniam, quis nostrud exerci tation ullamcorper suscipit lobortis nisl ut aliquip ex ea commodo consequat. Duis autem vel eum iriure dolor.

Scotch Roman

Lorem ipsum dolor sit amet, consectetuer adipiscing elit, sed diam nonummy nibh euismod tincidunt ut laoreet dolore magna aliquam erat volutpat. Ut wisi enim ad minim veniam, quis nostrud exerci tation ullamcorper suscipit lobortis nisl ut aliquip ex ea commodo consequat. Duis

Typefaces that present problems when printed on porous or textured paper, or on bright, shiny paper.

63 Replace underlined text with words set in bold, italic, or small caps.

Avoid using your software program's underscore command. Underlining obscures word shapes by interfering with the reader's ability to recognize descenders (portions of letters that extend below the baseline, or invisible line, the text rests on). Descenders help readers identify the unique shapes of words containing them.

Underlining darkens a page and is especially objectionable when used with italicized type – especially italicized text set in all caps.

Underlining is a holdover from typewriter days, when the only way to add emphasis to words was either to set them in uppercase type or underline them. Today's computers and the availability of typeface options like bold, italic, bold-italic, and small caps eliminate the need to underline type.

If you *do* decide to underline key words, use your software program's ability to control the horizontal placement of the line to avoid interference with text descenders.

Underlining makes words harder to read because it interferes with word shapes.

Lisa strongly disagreed with the ideas conveyed in the popular book <u>The Happy Bliss Of Ignorance</u>, and so wrote her own book, <u>Both Eyes Open</u>, which catapulted her to fame.

Bold type adds emphasis without seriously compromising readability.

Lisa strongly disagreed with the ideas conveyed in the popular book **The Happy Bliss of Ignorance,** and so wrote her own book, **Both Eyes Open,** which catapulted her to fame.

Words set in italics add emphasis without calling too much attention to themselves.

Lisa strongly disagreed with the ideas conveyed in the popular book *The Happy Bliss of Ignorance,* and so wrote her own book, *Both Eyes Open,* which catapulted her to fame.

Small caps allow words to stand out without undue emphasis.

Lisa strongly disagreed with the ideas conveyed in the popular book THE HAPPY BLISS OF IGNORANCE, and so wrote her own book, BOTH EYES OPEN, which catapulted her to fame.

Avoid overusing bold and italicized text.

64

Exercise restraint when using bold or italicized type. Bold type is ideal for emphasizing second- or third-level subheads, but bold words, names, or short passages within paragraphs can be very distracting. Bold "shouts" at the reader. In addition, bold text is harder to read because the strokes are thicker and there is less white space within the letters to help readers identify the letters.

Paragraphs containing numerous proper nouns set in bold create a blotchy "Morse code" effect. Bold text also occupies more space than roman or medium text.

It is difficult to read long passages of italicized text because readers have to reorient themselves to reading letters at an angle to their normal orientation. Also, italicized letters are closer together. Italicized text communicates a conversational, often ironic, tone of voice.

Jeanne Schultz from the **Confetti Department** ipsum dolor sit amet, consectetuer adipiscing elit, sed diam non. **Fred Larson,** the new **Assistant Manager** for the **Round Things Department,** magna aliquam erat volutpat. Ut aliquip, **Susan Howard,** retiring **Head of Security,** commodo consequat vit. As it stands now, **Larry Jones,** of **Secretarial Services** at our new **Portsmouth** offices, vel illum dolore eu feugiat nulla facilisis.

Jeanne Schultz from the Confetti Department ipsum dolor sit amet, consectetuer adipiscing elit, sed diam non. *Fred Larson, the new Assistant Manager for the Round Things Department, magna aliquam erat volutpat. Ut aliquip, Susan Howard, retiring Head of Security, commodo consequat vit.* As it stands now, Larry Jones, of Secretarial Services at our new Portsmouth offices, vel illum dolore eu feugiat nulla facilisis.

Note the staccato texture of the left-hand example and how tiring it is to read the long passage set in italics at right.

In the letters at the bottom, notice how bold text reduces the amount of white space within letters. This reduces legibility.

Notice, also, that Times Roman italic was redrawn, but Helvetica italic was just angled.

agex**agex***agex*

agex**agex***agex*

65 Invest in alternative text weights to add selective emphasis.

Semi-bold and extra bold typeface designs permit you to add just the right amount of emphasis. Many serif typefaces are available in these versions. Semi-bold (often called demi-bold) and extra bold typeface variations permit you to "voice" your documents without the visual distractions that a totally different typeface would create.

Semi-bold and extra bold options appear as separate listings in your font menu.

Semi-bold serif typefaces permit you to add emphasis within a paragraph without "shouting." Extra bold permits you to add extra emphasis to subheads.

Notice how there is no visible hierarchy in the example on the left because the title within the text is the same weight as the subhead. As a result, they simply compete with each other.

In the example on the right, however, the extra bold subhead definitely carries more emphasis than the semi-bold title within the text.

Lorem ipsum dolor sit amet, consectetuer adipiscing elit, sed diam nonummy nibh.

Conclusion

Ut wisi enim ad minim veni am, quis nostrud exer citation ullamcorper **Bay State Reporter** ut aliquip ex ea commodo consequat. Duis autem vel eum iriure dolor in hendrerit in vul putate velit esse molestie con sequat, vel illum dolore eu feugiat nulla facilisis at vero eros et accumsan et iusto odio dignissim qui

Lorem ipsum dolor sit amet, consectetuer adipiscing elit, sed diam nonummy nibh.

Conclusion

Ut wisi enim ad minim veni am, quis nostrud exer citation ullamcorper **Bay State Reporter** ut aliquip ex ea commodo consequat. Duis autem vel eum iriure dolor in hendrerit in vul putate velit esse molestie con sequat, vel illum dolore eu feugiat nulla facilisis at vero eros et accumsan et iusto odio dignissim qui

Use small caps for abbreviations, titles, and acronyms.

Use small capitals to add selective emphasis without disturbing the texture of the body copy or changing the tone of your words. Small caps offer an ideal replacement for bold or italicized text within body copy paragraphs. Small caps allow you to add emphasis to book titles, honorary titles, and acronyms (like time of day) without the visual distraction or tone of voice changes caused by using bold, italic, or uppercase letters.

Notice how your "internal voice" changes as you read the same paragraph with the same titles set (from left) in bold, italic, and small caps. The bottom example allows you to add emphasis without distraction or interpretation.

Note: Since small caps lack descenders, you can also use them for tightly spaced headlines, which allows you to clearly indicate proper nouns.

Jane Lewis earned her PH.D. in history while working at IBM and DEC, where she would often arrive at 6:00 A.M. in time to read **Leisure World** and **USA Yesterday.**

Jane Lewis earned her PH.D. in history while working at IBM and DEC, where she would often arrive at 6:00 A.M. in time to read LEISURE WORLD and USA YESTERDAY.

In the top example, acronyms, titles, and abbreviations set in uppercase letters attract unnecessary emphasis.

In the bottom example, acronyms, titles, and abbreviations stand out without unnecessarily disturbing the smooth, even texture of the body copy.

Line Spacing

Line spacing is next in order of importance, closely following your choice of typeface and type size. Vertical distance between lines plays a major role in determining the appearance of your pages as well as how quickly and easily readers can comprehend your message.

Never use default or "automatic" line spacing. 67

Leading, or line spacing, is second only to type size in terms of its importance in determining the "look" and readability of your publications. Leading is a term that originated in days when type was set in metal because thin strips of lead were inserted between lines of type to achieve desired spacing.

Appropriate line spacing is based on the correct relationship between typeface design, type size, and column width (or line length).

Default line spacing is an approximation based on a "typical" combination of typeface, type size, and column width that may bear no relation to your particular layout.

The best way to determine the appropriate leading is to try out various settings using the three-column template described in Point 56. Experiment with half-point changes in line spacing.

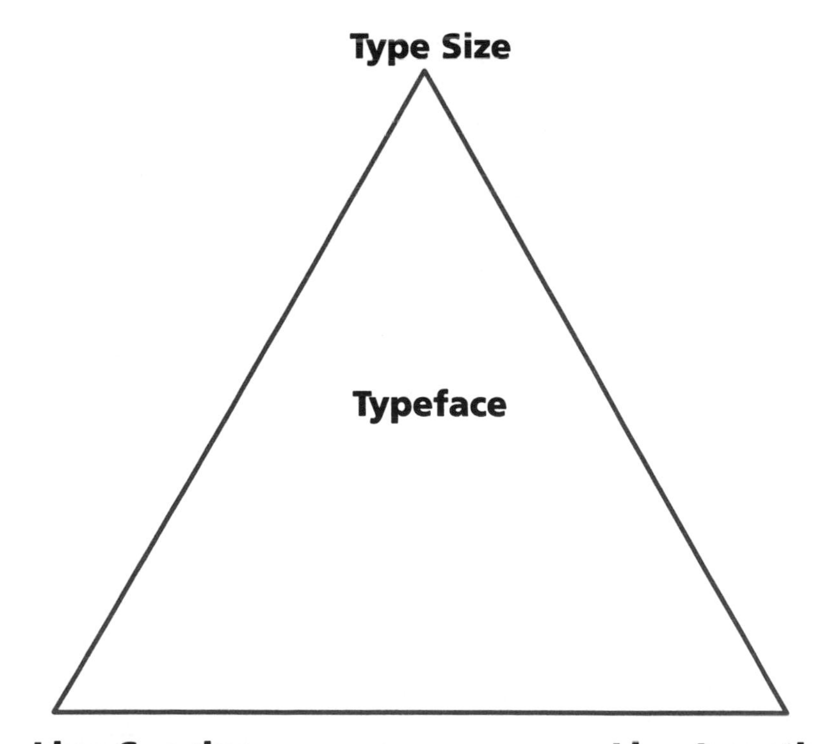

Never consider type size without considering line spacing and line length.

The correct relationship is different for every typeface.

The right choice usually becomes immediately obvious when you arrive at the right combination of typeface, type size, line spacing, and line length.

68 Add leading when setting type in long lines.

Add extra leading to type set in long lines (or wide columns). Extra leading prevents readers from doubling, or inadvertently returning to the starting point of the line they just finished reading.

In the examples below, notice how a combination of typeface, type size and line length that works for a narrow column (in the top example) does not work in the middle example, where the line length is doubled. (Notice, also, how the type in the middle example seems smaller.)

Adding four points of extra leading, as shown in the bottom example, restores harmony.

The exact amount of leading needed is determined by the particular combination of typeface, type size, and line length your design specifies.

The top example uses 12-point type with 14 points leading.

Lorem ipsum ea commodo consequat. Duis autem vel eum iriure dolor in hendrerit in vulputate velit esse molestie consequat, vel illum dolore eu feugiat nulla facilisis at vero eros et accumsan et iusto odio dignissim qui blandit praesent luptatum zzril delenit.

The same type becomes difficult to read when line length is doubled without changing leading.

Lorem ipsum ea commodo consequat. Duis autem vel eum iriure dolor in hendrerit in vulputate velit esse molestie consequat, vel illum dolore eu feugiat nulla facilisis at vero eros et accumsan et iusto odio dignissim qui blandit praesent luptatum zzril delenit augue duis dolore te feugait nulla facilisi. Lorem ipsum dolor sit amet, consectetuer adipiscing elit.

But, adding four additional points of leading makes the same combination of type and line length more readable.

Lorem ipsum ea commodo consequat. Duis autem vel eum iriure dolor in hendrerit in vulputate velit esse molestie consequat, vel illum dolore eu feugiat nulla facilisis at vero eros et accumsan et iusto odio dignissim qui blandit praesent luptatum zzril delenit augue duis dolore te feugait nulla facilisi. Lorem ipsum dolor sit amet, consectetuer adipiscing elit.

Add extra leading when using sans serif typefaces.

You can enhance the readability of sans serif typefaces by adding extra line spacing. Body copy set in sans serif typefaces typically looks better when extra line spacing is added. This is partly because sans serif typefaces typically have higher x-heights than serif typefaces.

Extra leading also provides additional white space that is needed to compensate for their lack of serifs, which aid recognizability.

Notice how much easier the sans serif example below becomes after adding additional leading.

Lorem ipsum ea commodo consequat. Duis autem vel eum iriure dolor in hendrerit in vulputate velit esse molestie consequat, vel illum dolore eu feugiat nulla facilisis at vero eros et accumsan et iusto odio dignissim qui blandit praesent luptatum zzril delenit augue duis dolore te feugait nulla facilisi. Lorem ipsum dolor sit amet, consectetuer adipiscing elit.

Lorem ipsum ea commodo consequat. Duis autem vel eum iriure dolor in hendrerit in vulputate velit esse molestie consequat, vel illum dolore eu feugiat nulla facilisis at vero eros et accumsan et iusto odio dignissim qui blandit praesent luptatum zzril delenit augue duis dolore te feugait nulla facilisi. Lorem ipsum dolor sit amet, consectetuer adipiscing elit.

Compare how much easier it is to read the top example, set in 12-point Times Roman on 15-point leading, than the middle example, set in Helvetica in the same size, with the same leading. The middle example looks cramped and hard to read.

Lorem ipsum ea commodo consequat. Duis autem vel eum iriure dolor in hendrerit in vulputate velit esse molestie consequat, vel illum dolore eu feugiat nulla facilisis at vero eros et accumsan et iusto odio dignissim qui blandit praesent luptatum zzril delenit augue duis dolore te feugait nulla facilisi. Lorem ipsum dolor sit amet, consectetuer adipiscing elit.

Adding three points of additional leading to the Helvetica sample makes the bottom example far easier to read.

70 Add leading when using serif typefaces with high x-heights.

Add extra leading to high x-height typefaces to compensate for their less pronounced ascenders and descenders. High x-height typefaces require extra line spacing because the reduced space between ascenders and x-height, and descenders and the baseline reduces the word shapes readers depend on for word recognition.

By increasing leading, you can compensate for the shorter ascenders and descenders of high x-height typefaces like Adobe Utopia. Adding leading increases the white space around the ascenders and descenders and makes the word shapes easier to recognize.

Since there are no "absolutes," the best way to determine the proper amount of leading is to prepare a sample paragraph, set in the typeface and line length your design calls for, and experiment with half-point changes in line spacing.

Compare the top example, set in Adobe Garamond, with the middle example, set in Adobe Utopia, a typeface with a high x-height.

Although both are set in 13-point type on 15-point leading, the middle example appears harder to read.

But adding three points of extra leading makes the bottom example far easier to read.

Lorem ipsum ea commodo consequat. Duis autem vel eum iriure dolor in hendrerit in vulputate velit esse molestie consequat, vel illum dolore eu feugiat nulla facilisis at vero eros et accumsan et iusto odio dignissim qui blandit praesent luptatum zzril delenit augue duis dolore te feugait nulla facilisi. Lorem ipsum dolor sit amet.

Lorem ipsum ea commodo consequat. Duis autem vel eum iriure dolor in hendrerit in vulputate velit esse molestie consequat, vel illum dolore eu feugiat nulla facilisis at vero eros et accumsan et iusto odio dignissim qui blandit praesent luptatum zzril delenit augue duis dolore te feugait nulla facilisi. Lorem ipsum dolor sit amet.

Lorem ipsum ea commodo consequat. Duis autem vel eum iriure dolor in hendrerit in vulputate velit esse molestie consequat, vel illum dolore eu feugiat nulla facilisis at vero eros et accumsan et iusto odio dignissim qui blandit praesent luptatum zzril delenit augue duis dolore te feugait nulla facilisi. Lorem ipsum dolor sit amet.

Reduce leading when using low x-height serif typefaces.

71

Typefaces with low x-heights present a different set of challenges. Because their ascenders (portions of letters that extend above the x-height) and descenders (portions of letters that extend below the baseline) are more pronounced, white space is automatically built-in. As a result, default line spacing is often too generous, creating horizontal bands of white between lines.

By reducing line spacing, you can achieve a smoother, more even appearance.

Lorem ipsum ea commodo consequat. Duis autem vel eum iriure dolor in hendrerit in vulputate velit esse molestie consequat, vel illum dolore eu feugiat nulla facilisis at vero eros et accumsan et iusto odio dignissim qui blandit praesent luptatum zzril delenit augue duis dolore te feugait nulla facilisi. Lorem ipsum dolor sit

Lorem ipsum ea commodo consequat. Duis autem vel eum iriure dolor in hendrerit in vulputate velit esse molestie consequat, vel illum dolore eu feugiat nulla facilisis at vero eros et accumsan et iusto odio dignissim qui blandit praesent luptatum zzril delenit augue duis dolore te feugait nulla facilisi. Lorem ipsum dolor sit amet, consectetuer adipiscing elit.

Lorem ipsum ea commodo consequat. Duis autem vel eum iriure dolor in hendrerit in vulputate velit esse molestie consequat, vel illum dolore eu feugiat nulla facilisis at vero eros et accumsan et iusto odio dignissim qui blandit praesent luptatum zzril delenit augue duis dolore te feugait nulla facilisi. Lorem ipsum dolor sit amet, consectetuer adipiscing elit.

The top example is set in Times Roman, 13-point type on 15-point leading.

When the same specifications are used for Granjon, the low x-height typeface shown in the middle, the lines appear unnaturally far apart.

The appearance of the low x-height typeface can be improved by reducing line spacing 1½ points, removing some of the unnecessary white space between lines.

72 Base text interruptions, like subheads, on multiples of the line spacing chosen.

Maintain consistent baseline alignment when working with multicolumn documents. Baseline relates to the invisible line that the typeface rests on. In a well-designed multicolumn page, the baselines of text in the first column should line up with the baselines of the text in the second and (if present) third columns. Pages appear disorganized when baselines are not aligned.

The easiest way to maintain baseline alignment is to base interruptions on multiples of the leading used. The total amount of space devoted to subheads, pull-quotes, or illustrations should be a multiple of the text leading. Thus, if you are using 12-point leading, the total amount of space devoted to subheads, pull-quotes, or illustrations (including type size, space above, and space below) should be 24, 36, 48 or some other multiple of 12.

Notice how distracting the non-aligned baseline below the subhead appears in the top example.

Duis autem vel eum iriure dolor in hendrerit in vulputate velit esse mol estie consequat, vel illum dolore ve ro eros et accumsan etiusto odio dig nissim qui blandit praesent lup tatum zzril delenit augue duis dol ore te feugait nulla facilisi. Lorem ipsum dolor sit amet, consectetuer adipiscing elit ... ummy

tincidunt ut laoreet dolore magna aliquam erat volutpat.

Subhead

Ut wisi enim ad minim veniam, quis nostrud exerci tation ullam corper suscipit lobortis nisl ut ali quip ex ea commodo con...

This example presents a more professional appearance because the baseline of the text in the second column remains aligned with the baseline of the text in the first column.

Duis autem vel eum iriure dolor in hendrerit in vulputate velit esse mol estie consequat, vel illum dolore ve ro eros et accumsan et iusto odio dig nissim qui blandit praesent lup tatum zzril delenit augue duis dol ore te feugait nulla facilisi. Lorem ipsum dolor sit amet, consectetuer adipiscing eli... ummy

tincidunt ut laoreet dolore magna aliquam erat volutpat.

Subhead

Ut wisi enim ad minim veniam, quis nostrud exerci tation ullam corper suscipit lobortis nisl ut ali quip ex ea commodo consequat. ... vel eum iri...

Paragraphs

Pay particular attention to the way you indicate new paragraphs. Paragraphs are the fundamental text-organizing tool. Without paragraphs, your publications would consist of a seemingly endless stream of sentences which would discourage even the most determined reader.

Choose one, and only one, way to indicate new paragraphs.

73

Avoid duplicate paragraph introductions. You can either indent the first line of each new paragraph or add extra space between paragraphs. Either choice is acceptable, but used together they signal typographic inexperience.

Indented paragraphs work best with justified text because the left-hand indents strongly contrast with the straight, aligned right-hand edges of each column.

Blocked paragraphs work best with flush-left/ragged-right text because the added space between lines emerges stronger than the left-hand first-line indent, which is often balanced on the right by differing line lengths.

When you want to create a square or rectangular text block, use the paragraph symbol or one of the special ornamental characters included with many typeface designs.

Lorem ipsum dolor sit amet, consectetuer adipiscing elit, sed diam nonummy nibh euismod tincidunt ut laoreet dolore magna aliquam erat volutpat.

Ut wisi enim ad minim veniam, quis nostrud exerci tation ullamcorper suscipit lobortis nisl ut aliquip ex ea commodo consequat.

Duis autem vel eum iriure dolor in hendrerit in vulputate velit esse molestie consequat, vel illum dolore eu feugiat nulla facilisis at vero eros et accumsan et iusto odio dignissim qui blandit praesent luptatum zzril delenit augue duis dolore te feugait nulla facilisi. Lorem ipsum dolor sit amet, consectetuer adipiscing elit, sed diam nonummy nibh euismod tincidunt ut laoreet dolore magna aliquam erat volutpat.

Ut wisi enim ad minim veniam, quis nostrud exerci tation ullamcorper suscipit lobortis nisl ut aliquip ex ea commodo consequat.

Duis autem vel eum iriure dolor in hendrerit in vulputate velit esse molestie consequat, vel illum dolore eu feugiat nulla facilisis at vero eros et

Lorem ipsum dolor sit amet, con sectetuer adipiscing elit, sed diam nonummy nibh euismod tincidunt ut laoreet dolore magna aliquam erat volutpat.

Ut wisi enim ad minim veniam, quis nostrud exerci tation ullam cor per suscipit lobortis nisl ut aliquip ex ea commodo consequat.

Duis autem vel eum iriure dolor in hendrerit in vulputate velit esse mo lestie consequat, vel illum dolore eu feugiat nulla facilisis at vero eros et accumsan et iusto odio dignissim qui blandit praesent luptatum zzril dele nit augue duis dolore te feugait nulla facilisi. Lorem ipsum dolor sit amet, consectetuer adipiscing elit, sed diam nonummy nibh euismod tincidunt ut laoreet dolore magna aliquam erat volutpat.

Ut wisi enim ad minim veniam, quis nostrud exerci tation ullam cor per suscipit lobortis nisl ut aliquip ex ea commodo consequat.

Duis autem vel eum iriure dolor in hendrerit in vulputate velit esse mol estie consequat, vel illum sodolore eu feugiat nulla facilisis at vero eros et accumsan et iusto odio dignissim qui blandit praesent luptatum zzril dele nit augue duis dolore te feugait nulla facilisi. Nam liber tempor cum soluta nobis eleifend option congue nihil imperdiet ava doming id quod mazim

Lorem ipsum dolor sit amet, consectetuer adipiscing elit, sed diam nonummy nibh euismod tincidunt ut laoreet dolore magna aliquam erat volutpat. ❧ Ut wisi enim ad minim veniam, quis nostrud exerci tation ullamcorper suscipit lobortis nisl ut aliq commodo consequat. ❧ Duis autem vel eum iriure dolor in hendrerit in vulputate velit esse molestie consequat, vel illum dolore eu feugiat nulla facilisis at vero eros et accumsan et iusto odio dignissim qui blandit praesent luptatum zzril delenit augue duis dolore te feugait nulla facilisi. ❧ Lorem ipsum dolor sit amet, consectetuer adipiscing elit, sed diam nonummy nibh euismod tincidunt ut laoreet dolore magna aliquam erat volutpat. Ut wisi enim ad minim veniam, quis nostrud exerci tation ullamcorper suscipit lobortis nisl ut aliquip.

In the first column, extra space between lines creates a clean visual separation between flush-left/ragged-right paragraphs.

In the middle column, an indented first line indicates the start of new paragraphs of justified text.

In the third column, ornaments separate paragraphs and maintain the desired rectangular text shape.

74 Use a measured amount of white space to separate paragraphs.

Avoid pressing the Enter or Return key twice after each paragraph. When adding extra space between paragraphs, let your software program add a carefully chosen amount of space.

Two hard returns between paragraphs creates horizontal bands of white space which destroys the vertical unity of your page and waste space which could better be used to surround your text.

Try out different amounts of paragraph spacing. Spacing must be sufficient to indicate a new paragraph, yet not be so prominent that it interferes with your reader's smooth and even eye movement. You often obtain the best results by separating paragraphs with space equivalent to one-half line of text.

As the example at left illustrates, wide horizontal gaps characterize paragraphs separated by two hard returns.

The right-hand example presents a smoother texture.

In addition, notice how much shorter the right-hand column is, even though it contains the same number of words set at the same size.

Lorem ipsum dolor sit amet, consetuer adipiscing elit, sed diam nonummy nibh euismod tlincidunt ut laoreet dolore magna aliquam erat volutpat.

Ut wisi enim ad minim veniam, quis nostrud exerci tation ull amcorper suscipit lobortis nisl ut aliquip ex ea commodo consequat, duis autem vel eum iriure dolor in hendrerit in vulputate velit esse molestie consequat, vel illum dolore.

Teu feugiat nulla facilisis at vero eros et accumsan et iusto odio dignissim qui blandit praesent luptatum zzril delenit augue duis ve dolore te feugait nulla facilisi.

Lorem ipsum dolor sit amet, consetuer adipiscing elit, sed diam nonummy nibh euismod tlincidunt ut laoreet dolore magna aliquam erat volutpat.

Ut wisi enim ad minim veniam, quis nostrud exerci tation ull amcorper suscipit lobortis nisl ut aliquip ex ea commodo consequat, duis autem vel eum iriure dolor in hendrerit in vulputate velit esse molestie consequat, vel illum dolore.

Teu feugiat nulla facilisis at vero eros et accumsan et iusto odio dignissim qui blandit praesent luptatum zzril delenit augue duis ve dolore te feugait nulla facilisi.

Use paragraph indents appropriate to type size and length.

75

Replace your software program's default tabs and indents with settings determined by the typeface, type size, and line length you're using. Although your software program's default tab and indent settings may be appropriate for type set in a single column extending the width of the page, these settings are usually too generous for text set in two- or three-column layouts.

When working with layouts of three or more columns, the appropriate indent is usually one or two em spaces. An em space is equal to the square of the typeface (or the size of an uppercase M).

Em spaces are deep enough to be noticed, yet not so deep that they attract unnecessary attention.

Lorem ipsum dolor sit amet, con sectetuer adipiscing elit, sed dia nonummy nibh euismod tincidunt ut laoreet dolore magna aliquam erat volutpat. Ut wisi enim ad minim veniam, quis nostrud exerci tation ullamcorper suscipit lobortis nisl ut aliquip ex ea commodo consequat.

Duis autem vel eum iriure dolor in hendrerit in vulputate velit esse molestie consequat, vel illum dolore eu feugiat nulla facilisis at vero eros et accumsan et iusto odio dignissim qui blandit praesent luptatum zzril delenit augue duis dolore te feugait nulla facilisi.

Lorem ipsum dolor sit amet, consectetuer adipiscing elit, sed diam nonummy nibh euismod tincidunt ut laoreet dolore magna aliquam erat volutpat.

Lorem ipsum dolor sit amet, con sectetuer adipiscing elit, sed dia nonummy nibh euismod tincidunt ut laoreet dolore magna aliquam erat volutpat. Ut wisi enim ad minim veniam, quis nostrud exerci tation ullamcorper suscipit lobortis nisl ut aliquip ex ea commodo consequat.

Duis autem vel eum iriure dolor in hendrerit in vulputate velit esse molestie consequat, vel illum dolore eu feugiat nulla facilisis at vero eros et accumsan et iusto odio dignissim qui blandit praesent luptatum zzril delenit augue duis dolore te feugait nulla facilisi.

Lorem ipsum dolor sit amet, consectetuer adipiscing elit, sed diam nonummy nibh euismod tincidunt ut laoreet dolore magna aliquam erat volutpat.

The typical half-inch default paragraph indent, shown at left, is especially bothersome when used with a low x-height typeface like Granjon at a relatively small size.

The more modest paragraph indent in the right-hand example is deep enough to unmistakably indicate a new paragraph, yet doesn't create an unwanted visual distraction.

76 Avoid unnecessary paragraph indents.

Do not indent the first paragraph after a headline or subhead. First-line indents are needed for new paragraphs within text passages. But, text following a headline or subhead is obviously a new paragraph. Thus, there is no need to set it apart or to indent it for emphasis.

Consider creating a separate "first-paragraph" style which eliminates the normal paragraph indent. This style can be automatically activated as a "Next Style" option that follows your headline or subhead styles.

You can then create an "inside paragraph" style to automatically follow the "first paragraph" style. Your "inside paragraph" style would contain an indent and be used for all subsequent paragraphs in the section.

Note the unnecessary eye-travel and trapped white space created by the unnecessary first-line indent in the paragraph in the left-hand example.

The right-hand example presents a smoother transition between the subhead and the text of the first paragraph.

Nonfat Ice Creams

Lorem ipsum dolor sit amet, con sectetuer adipiscing elit, sed dia nonummy nibh euismod tincidunt ut laoreet dolore magna aliquam erat volutpat. Ut wisi enim ad minim veniam, quis nostrud exerci tation ullamcorper suscipit lobortis nisl ut aliquip ex ea commodo consequat.

Duis autem vel eum iriure dolor in hendrerit in vulputate velit esse molestie consequat, vel illum dolore eu feugiat nulla facilisis at vero eros et accumsan et iusto odio dignissim qui blandit praesent luptatum zzril delenit augue duis dolore te feugait nulla facilisi.

Lorem ipsum dolor sit amet, consectetuer adipiscing elit, sed diam nonummy nibh euismod tincidunt ut laoreet dolore magna.

Nonfat Ice Creams

Lorem ipsum dolor sit amet, con sectetuer adipiscing elit, sed dia nonummy nibh euismod tincidunt ut laoreet dolore magna aliquam erat volutpat. Ut wisi enim ad minim veniam, quis nostrud exerci tation ullamcorper suscipit lobortis nisl ut aliquip ex ea commodo consequat.

Duis autem vel eum iriure dolor in hendrerit in vulputate velit esse molestie consequat, vel illum dolore eu feugiat nulla facilisis at vero eros et accumsan et iusto odio dignissim qui blandit praesent luptatum zzril delenit augue duis dolore te feugait nulla facilisi.

Lorem ipsum dolor sit amet, consectetuer adipiscing elit, sed diam nonummy nibh euismod tincidunt ut laoreet dolore magna.

Avoid isolated letters and words.

77

Eliminate letters and lines isolated at the tops and bottoms of your pages. In general, do not begin a column or page with a few words or a single line of text continued from the bottom of the preceding column or page. These "orphans" are distracting and confusing to the reader. (Readers are unlikely to remember the preceding words.)

Likewise, avoid widows – less than a third of a line – isolated at the bottom of a column or page.

In addition, when beginning a new paragraph at the bottom of a column or page, try to include at least three lines. An exception is books with "filled columns" where the design goal is to completely fill each column with text.

You can avoid widows and orphans by transposing words earlier in the paragraph, using discretionary hyphens to control where words break, or subtly adjusting letterspacing.

dolore.

Lorem ipsum dolor sit amet, consectetuer adipiscing elit, sed diam nonummy nibh euismod tincidunt ut laoreet dolore magna aliquam erat volutpat. Ut wisi enim ad minim veniam, quis nostrud exerci tation ullamcorper suscipit lobortis nisl ut aliquip ex ea commodo consequat. Duis autem vel eum iriure dolor in hendrerit in vulputate velit esse molestie consequat, vel illum dolore eu feugiat nulla facilisis at vero eros et et iusto odio.

Northeast States Rebound

Dignissim qui blandit praesent luptatum zzril delenit augue duis dolore te feugait nulla facilisi. Lorem ipsum dolor sit amet, consectetuer adipiscing elit, sed diam nonummy nibh euismod tincidunt ut laoreet dolore magna aliquam erat volutpat.

Ut wisi enim ad minim veniam, quis nostrud exerci tation ullamcorper suscipit lobortis nisl ut aliquip ex ea commodo consequat.

Duis autem vel eum iriure eros et accumsan et iusto odio. Lorem ipsum dolor sit amet, consectetuer adipiscing dolore te feugait nulla facilisi. Nam liber tempor cum soluta nobis eleifend option congue nihil imperdiet doming id quod mazim placerat facer possim.

Ut wisi enim ad minim veniam, quis nostrud exerci tation ullamcorper suscipit lobortis nisl ut aliquip ex ea commodo sit consequat. Lorem ipsum dolor sit amet, consectetuer adipiscing elit, sed diam nonummy nibh euismod tincidunt ut laoreet dolore magna aliquam erat volutpat. Duis autem vel eum iriure dolor in hendrerit in vulputate velit esse molestie feu giat nulla facilisis at vero eros et accumsan et iusto odio dignissim zzril delenit augue duis dolore te feugait nulla facilisi. Ut wisi enim ad minim veniam, quis nostrud exerci tation ullamcorper suscipit lobortis consequat. Duis autem vel eum vulputate velit esse nonummy molestie.

South Holds Firm

Consequat, vel illum dolore eu feugiat nulla facilisis at vero eros et accumsan et iusto odio dignissim qui blandit praesent luptatum zzril delenit augue duis dolore te feugai-nulla.

Lorem ipsum dolor sit amet, consectetuer adipiscing elit, sed diam nonummy nibh euismod tincidunt ut laoreet dolore magna aliquam erat volutpat. Ut wisi enim ad minim veniam, quis nostrud exerci tation ullamcorper suscipit lobortis nisl ut aliquip ex ea commodo consequat. Duis autem vel eum iriure dolor in hendrerit in vulputate velit esse molestie consequat, vel illum dolore eu feugiat nulla facilisis at vero eros et et iusto odio.

Northeast States Rebound

Dignissim qui blandit praesent luptatum zzril delenit augue duis dolore te feugait nulla facilisi. Lorem ipsum dolor sit amet, consectetuer adipiscing elit, sed diam nonummy nibh euismod tincidunt ut laoreet dolore magna aliquam erat volutpat.

Ut wisi enim ad minim veniam, quis nostrud exerci tation ullamcorper suscipit lobortis nisl ut aliquip ex ea commodo consequat.

Duis autem vel eum iriure eros et accumsan et iusto odio. Lorem ipsum dolor sit amet, consectetuer adipiscing dolore te feugait nulla facilisi. Nam liber tempor cum soluta nobis eleifend option congue nihil imperdiet doming id quod mazim placerat facer possim.

Ut wisi enim ad minim veniam, quis nostrud exerci tation ullamcorper suscipit lobortis nisl ut aliquip ex ea commodo sit consequat. Lorem ipsum dolor sit amet, consectetuer adipiscing elit, sed diam nonummy nibh euismod tincidunt ut laoreet dolore magna aliquam erat volutpat. Duis autem vel eum iriure dolor in hendrerit in vulputate velit esse molestie feu giat nulla facilisis at vero eros et accumsan et iusto odio dignissim zzril delenit augue duis dolore te feugait nulla facilisi. Ut wisi enim ad minim veniam, quis nostrud exerci tation ullamcorper suscipit lobortis consequat. Duis autem vel eum vulputate velit esse nonummy molestie.

South Holds Firm

Consequat, vel illum dolore eu feugiat nulla facilisis at vero eros et accumsan et iusto odio dignissim qui blandit praesent luptatum zzril delenit augue duis dolore te feugait nulla sit amet, consectetuer adipiscing elit, sed diam nonummy

The short line at the top of the first column in the left-hand example looks incomplete, as does the last line of the second column.

In the example at right, the page presents a more professional image.

Initial Caps

Initial caps provide a transition between headlines and body text. Initial caps act like magnets, attracting your reader's eyes to the first words of a paragraph following a headline. In addition, you can use initial caps in extended text passages to provide visual relief and a slight pause. You can also use initial caps in place of subheads to signal the introduction of a new topic within an extended text block.

Make initial caps significantly larger than the text they introduce.

78

Avoid "accidental" initial caps: they should be equal in height to at least three lines of text. Use initial caps to help readers quickly locate the beginning of text following a headline and to visually signal the introduction of new topics within extended text passages.

Initial caps work best when they are significantly larger than the text they introduce. Small initial caps often add clutter without directing the reader's eyes to the beginning of a new paragraph.

There are three types of initial caps: raised, dropped and adjacent.

Raised caps are easiest to create and force white space between the new topic and the preceding paragraphs, helping break up long text passages.

Dropped caps are cut into the text columns. These work best following headlines.

Adjacent caps are placed next to text columns.

Yet John often wondered what would have happened if she had married him, even though her family was against him, and her father, the sheriff, had threatened to have him arrested and beheaded if they should continue their plans to elope to Prague and learn PageMaker in time for the races.

Yet John often wondered what would have happened if she had married him, even though her family was against him, and her father, the sheriff, had threatened to have him arrested and beheaded if they should continue their plans to elope to Prague and learn PageMaker in time for the races.

The initial cap at left looks accidental rather than purposeful.

The initial cap in the right-hand example is more effective in attracting the reader's eyes. The significant size contrast also adds visual interest to the page.

79 Use contrast to add impact to initial caps.

Use the tools of contrast to make your initial caps stand out as much as possible from the text they introduce. Although size is often enough to make initial caps emerge clearly from the text they introduce, there are several other ways you can style them:

Typeface contrast. Combine sans serif initial caps with serif body copy (or vice versa).

Weight contrast. Use a lighter or heavier weight of the same typeface as the body copy.

Style contrast. Set initial caps in bold, italic, or bold italic.

Case contrast. Try oversized lowercase initial caps!

Design contrast. Use the special ornamental or "Swash" characters available with several typefaces.

Foreground/background contrast. Reverse the initial caps out of a black or shaded background.

Feel free to combine more than one technique, but use that combination consistently.

Remember that the particular technique you use is not as important as how consistently you use it.

One good rule of thumb is to use initial caps which relate to the headline typeface used.

Typeface Contrast

Yet John often wondered what would have happened if she had married him, even though her family was very much against him and her father had threatened to have him arrested.

Weight Contrast

Yet John often wondered what would have happened if she had married him, even though her family was very much against him and her father had threatened to have him arrested.

Case Contrast

yet John often wondered what would have happened if she had married him, even though her family was very much against him and her father had threatened to have him arrested.

Design Contrast

Yet John often wondered what would have happened if she had married him, even though her family was very much against him and her father had threatened to have him arrested.

Background Contrast

Yet John often wondered what would have happened if she had married him, even though her family was very much against him and her father had threatened to have him arrested.

Style Contrast

Yet John often wondered what would have happened if she had married him, even though her family was very much against him and her father had threatened to have him arrested.

Maintain baseline alignment between initial caps and the paragraphs they introduce.

Always align the baseline of initial caps with one of the baselines of the text they introduce. The baseline of an initial cap should line up with the baseline of the first, or another, line of text within the first paragraph.

If you do not align the baselines, your initial caps appear to "float," lacking a coherent relationship to the text they are supposed to introduce.

Yet John often wondered what would have happened if she had married him, even though her family was very much against him, and her father, the sheriff, had threatened to have him arrested and beheaded if they continued their plans to elope to Prague and learn PageMaker in time for the races.

Yet John often wondered what would have happened if she had married him, even though her family was very much against him, and her father, the sheriff, had threatened to have him arrested and beheaded if they continued their plans to elope to Prague and learn PageMaker in time for the races.

The initial cap in the left-hand example "floats" because its baseline is not aligned with the baseline of the text it introduces.

Precise baseline alignment is a starting point for smooth transitions between initial caps and the text they introduce.

81 Provide a smooth transition between initial caps and the text that follows.

Always wrap body copy as close to the initial cap as possible. Unless the text is clearly associated with the initial cap, the initial cap will be read as an individual letter and fail to introduce the text that follows. Text wraps may be difficult when using initial caps of irregular widths, such as uppercase Ts, Ls, and Ys.

Another way to provide a smooth transition between the initial cap and the text passage is to set the first few words – or even the first line – of the text in a larger type size, bold text, or small caps.

Note: You may need to rewrite your text when the initial cap is a one-letter word or part of a two- or three-letter word. Readers may read "The" as "T he" or "In" as "I n." Other common problem words include "As" and "To."

Although "correct" as far as the page layout program is concerned, the top of the initial cap at left doesn't appear aligned with the text that follows.

Precise alignment and a smooth transition into the text is achieved at right by setting the first line of the paragraph in small caps. The initial cap now becomes both top and bottom aligned.

Yet he often wondered how things might be if she had married him, even though her family was very much against him, and her father, the sheriff, had threatened to have him arrested and beheaded if they should continue their plans to elope to Prague and learn PageMaker in time for the races.

YET HE OFTEN WONDERED how things might be if she had married him, even though her family was very much against him, and her father, the sheriff, had threatened to have him arrested and beheaded if they should continue their plans to elope to Prague and learn PageMaker in time for the races.

Omit quotation marks before initial caps. 82

Avoid punctuation that competes with initial caps. When a quotation appears as the first sentence in a paragraph introduced with an initial cap, consider omitting the opening quotation mark. The tone of the words and the closing quotation mark will make it clear to readers that the paragraph is beginning with a quotation.

Omitting the quotation mark eliminates a potential source of visual clutter by reducing the number of large visual elements on the page, allowing the initial cap to emerge with added clarity.

"Yet," he said, "what would have happened if she had married me, even though her family was very much against me and her father, the sheriff, had threatened to have me arrested and beheaded if we continued our plans to elope to Prague and learn PageMaker in time for the races?"

Yet," he thought, "what would have happened if she had married me, even though her family was very much against me and her father, the sheriff, had threatened to have me arrested and beheaded if we continued our plans to elope to Prague and learn PageMaker in time for the races?"

As a rule of thumb, you can consider eliminating punctuation marks whose function is made redundant by typographic contrast.

83 Double-check the placement of initial caps for inadvertent messages.

Avoid initial caps that inadvertently spell out acronyms or words on a page or two-page spread. Messages created by initial caps can occur vertically, horizontally, or diagonally. Your readers, encountering your pages for the first time, will be more sensitive and aware of these misadventures than you are.

Likewise, avoid repeating the same letter in each initial cap (such as a page with three Ts).

If available, use your page layout program's thumbnail printing feature to print out facing pairs of pages at small size. This will help you identify pages containing initial caps that create words.

In addition, whenever possible, try to avoid placing more than one initial cap in each column.

Nam liber tempor cum soluta nobis eleifend option congue nihil imperdiet doming id quod mazim placerat facer delenit augue duis dolore te

Gorem ipsum dolor sit amet, consectetuer adipiscing elit, sed diam nonummy nibh euismod tincidunt ut laoreet dolore magna aliquam erat volutpat. Ut wisi enim ad minim veniam, quis nostrud exerci tation ullamcorper suscipit lobortis nisl ut aliquip ex ea commodo consequat.

Duis autem vel eum iriure dolor in hendrerit in vulputate velit esse molestie consequat, vel illum dolore eu feugiat nulla facilisis at vero eros et accumsan et iusto odio dignissim qui blandit praesent luptatum zzril delenit augue duis dolore te feugait nulla facilisi. Lorem ipsum dolor sit amet, consectetuer adipiscing elit, sed diam nonummy nibh euismod tincidunt ut laoreet dolore magna aliquam erat volutpat. Ut wisi enim ad minim veniam, quis nostrud exerci tation ullamcorper suscipit lobortis nisl ut aliquip ex ea commodo consequat.

Duis autem vel eum iriure eros et accumsan et iusto odio dolore te feugait nulla facilisi. Nam liber tempor cum soluta nobis eleifend option congue nihil imperdiet doming id quod mazim placerat facer delenit augue duis dolore te feugait null minim veniam, quis nostrud exerci tation ullampossim assum.

Lorem ipsum dolor sit amet, consectetuer adipiscing elit, sed diam nonummy nibh euismod tincidunt ut laoreet dolore magna aliquam erat volutpat. Duis autem vel eum iriure dolor in hendrerit in vulputate velit esse molestie consequat, vel illum dolore eu feugiat nulla facilisis at vero eros et accumsan et iusto odio dignissim qui blandit praesent luptatum zzril delenit augue duis dolore te feugait nulla facilisi.

Urem ipsum dolor sit amet, consectetuer adipiscing elit, sed diam nonummy nibh euismod tincidunt ut laoreet dolore magna aliquam erat volutpat. Ut wisi enim ad minim veniam, quis nostrud exerci tation ullamcorper suscipit lobortis nisl ut aliquip ex ea commodo consequat dolore eu feugiat nulla facilisis at lis view.

Ut wisi enim ad minim veniam, quis nostrud exerci tation ullamcorper suscipit lobortis nisl ut aliquip ex ea commodo consequat. Duis autem vel eum iriure dolor in hendrerit in vulputate velit esse molestie consequat, vel illum dolore eu feugiat nulla facilisis at vero eros et accumsan et iusto odio dignissim.

Lui blandit praesent luptatum zzril delenit augue duis dolore te feugait nulla facilisi. Lorem ipsum dolor sit amet, consectetuer adipiscing elit, sed diam nonummy nibh euismod tincidunt ut laoreet dolore magna aliquam erat volutpat. Ut wisi enim ad minim veniam, quis nostrud exerci tation ullamcorper suscipit lobortis nisl ut aliquip ex ea commodo consequat.

Duis autem vel eum iriure eros et accumsan et iusto odio dolore te feugait nulla facilisi. Nam liber tempor cum soluta nobis eleifend option congue nihil imperdiet doming id quod mazim placerat facer delenit augue duis dolore te feugait null minim veniam, quis nostrud exerci tation ullampossim assum.

Lorem ipsum dolor sit amet, consectetuer adipiscing elit, sed diam nonummy nibh euismod tincidunt ut laoreet dolore magna aliquam erat volutpat.

Duis autem vel eum iriure dolor in hendrerit in vulputate velit esse molestie consequat, vel illum dolore eu feugiat nulla facilisis at vero eros et accumsan et iusto odio dignissim qui blandit praesent luptatum zzril delenit augue duis dolore te feugait nulla facilisi. Lorem ipsum dolor sit amet, consectetuer adipiscing elit, sed diam nonummy nibh euismod tincidunt ut laoreet dolore magna aliquam erat volutpat. Ut wisi enim ad minim veniam, quis nostrud exerci tation ullamcorper suscipit lobortis nisl ut aliquip ex ea commodo consequat.

Pluis autem vel eum iriure dolor in hendrerit in vulputate velit esse molestie. Consequat, vel illum dolore eu feugiat nulla facilisis at vero eros et accumsan et iusto odio dignissim qui blandit praesent luptatum zzril delenit augue duis dolore te feugait nulla facilisi. Lorem ipsum dolor sit amet, consectetuer adipiscing

Avoid initial caps isolated at the tops or bottoms of columns or pages.

84

Place initial caps within the middle three-fifths of a page. Initial caps look best with a significant amount of text above and below them.

When they appear within text continued from a preceding column or page, initial caps isolated at the top or bottom of a column or page can cause confusion by appearing to be initial caps introducing new articles. ("Where's the headline?" readers are likely to think.)

When they appear at the bottom of a column or page, they tend to lose their impact and appear as incomplete afterthoughts.

Sipsum dolor sit amet, consectetuer adipiscing elit, sed diam nonummy nibh euismod tincidunt ut laoreet dolore magna aliquam erat volutpat. Ut wisi enim ad minim veniam, quis nostrud exerci tation ullamcorper suscipit lobortis nisl ut aliquip ex ea commodo consequat.

Duis autem vel eum iriure dolor in hendrerit in vulputate velit esse molestie consequat, vel illum dolore eu feugiat nulla facilisis at vero eros et accumsan et iusto odio dignissim qui blandit praesent luptatum zzril delenit augue duis dolore te feugait nulla facilisi. Lorem ipsum dolor sit amet, consectetuer adipiscing elit, sed diam nonummy nibh euismod tincidunt ut laoreet dolore magna aliquam erat volutpat. Ut wisi enim ad minim veniam, quis nostrud exerci tation ullamcorper suscipit lobortis nisl ut aliquip ex ea commodo consequat.

Duis autem vel eum iriure eros et accumsan et iusto odio dolore te feugait nulla facilisi. Nam liber tempor cum soluta nobis eleifend option congue nihil imperdiet doming id quod mazim placerat.

Ufacer delenit augue duis dolore te feugait null minim veniam, quis nostrud exerci tation ullampossim assum.

Lorem ipsum dolor sit amet, consectetuer adipiscing elit, sed diam nonummy nibh euismod tincidunt ut laoreet dolore magna aliquam erat volutpat. Duis autem vel eum iriure dolor in hendrerit in vulputate velit esse molestie consequat, vel illum dolore eu feugiat nulla facilisis at vero eros et accumsan et iusto odio dignissim qui blandit praesent luptatum zzril delenit augue duis dolore te feugait nulla facilisi.

Lorem ipsum dolor sit amet, consectetuer adipiscing elit, sed diam nonummy nibh euismod tincidunt ut laoreet dolore magna aliquam erat volutpat. Ut wisi enim ad minim veniam, quis nostrud exerci tation ullamcorper suscipit lobortis nisl ut aliquip ex ea commodo consequat.

Duis autem vel eum iriure dolor in hendrerit in vulputate velit esse molestie. Consequat, vel illum dolore eu feugiat nulla facilisis at.

Revo eros et accumsan et iusto odio dignissim qui blandit praesent luptatum

Ut wisi enim ad minim veniam, quis nostrud exerci tation ullamcorper suscipit lobortis nisl ut aliquip ex ea commodo consequat. Duis autem vel eum iriure dolor in hendrerit in vulputate velit esse molestie consequat, vel illum dolore eu feugiat nulla facilisis at vero eros et accumsan et iusto odio dignissim.

Sui blandit praesent luptatum zzril delenit augue duis dolore te feugait nulla facilisi. Lorem ipsum dolor sit amet, consectetuer adipiscing elit, sed diam nonummy nibh euismod tincidunt ut laoreet dolore magna aliquam erat volutpat. Ut wisi enim ad minim veniam, quis nostrud exerci tation ullamcorper suscipit lobortis nisl ut aliquip ex ea commodo consequat.

Duis autem vel eum iriure eros et accumsan et iusto odio dolore te feugait nulla facilisi. Nam liber tempor cum soluta nobis eleifend option congue nihil imperdiet doming id quod mazim placerat facer delenit augue duis dolore te feugait null minim veniam, quis nostrud exerci tation ullampossim assum. Lorem ipsum dolor sit amet, consectetuer adipiscing elit, sed diam nonummy nibh euismod tincidunt ut laoreet dolore magna aliquam erat volutpat.

Udis autem vel eum iriure dolor in hendrerit in vulputate velit esse molestie consequat, vel illum dolore eu feugiat nulla facilisis at vero eros et accumsan et iusto odio dignissim qui blandit praesent luptatum zzril delenit augue duis dolore te feugait nulla facilisi. Lorem ipsum dolor sit amet, consectetuer adipiscing elit, sed diam nonummy nibh euismod tincidunt ut laoreet dolore magna aliquam erat volutpat. Ut wisi enim ad minim veniam, quis nostrud exerci tation ullamcorper suscipit lobortis nisl ut aliquip ex ea commodo consequat.

Ruis autem vel eum iriure dolor in hendrerit in vulputate velit esse molestie. Consequat, vel illum dolore eu feugiat nulla facilisis at vero eros et accumsan et iusto odio dignissim qui blandit praesent luptatum zzril delenit augue duis dolore te feugait nulla facilisi. Lorem ipsum dolor sit amet, consectetuer adipiscing

In the example at left, the initial caps appearing by themselves at the top and bottom of each column appear incomplete, as if the accompanying headlines were missing.

When placed inside the page, as in the example at right, the initial caps appear more purposeful.

85 "Hang" initial caps to maintain column alignment.

You can improve the appearance of top- or bottom-heavy initial caps by positioning them slightly to the left of the column so their vertical axis is aligned with the left-hand column margin.

Top-heavy or bottom-heavy initial caps – like Ls, Ts, Ys, and Ws – often appear inadvertently indented since their optical "center of gravity" doesn't line up with the left-hand margin of the text column they introduce.

Notice how the initial cap in the bottom example appears to be more carefully aligned with the column, even though part of the letter actually appears in the margin.

There appears to be a triangle of white space between the Y and the edge of the column. In addition, the Y looks unintentionally indented.

Yet John often wondered what would have happened if she had married him, even though her family was very much against him and her father, the sheriff, had threatened to have him arrested and beheaded if they continued their plans to elope to Prague and learn PageMaker in time for the races. But, later she was to learn that her father was secretly a Quark fan and even occasionally used Ventura Publisher!

In the bottom example, the Y appears properly aligned with the edge of the column, even though it actually has been moved to the left.

Yet John often wondered what would have happened if she had married him, even though her family was very much against him and her father, the sheriff, had threatened to have him arrested and beheaded if they continued their plans to elope to Prague and learn PageMaker in time for the races. But, later she was to learn that her father was secretly a Quark fan and even occasionally used Ventura Publisher!

Punctuation

Improper punctuation signals typographic inexperience. Today's readers will immediately begin to discount your message if they notice you are using old-fashioned, typewritten punctuation, such as inch marks (") instead of the proper open and closed (“ ”) quotation marks.

Replace typewriter punctuation with typeset punctuation.

86

Add a professional touch to your publication by using the proper punctuation. The following are the six most commonly omitted substitutions:

Replace typewriter-like “inch marks” (") with *open and closed punctuation marks.*

Replace two hyphens with an *em dash* when introducing parenthetical statements.

Use an *en dash* instead of a hyphen to separate compound words or indicate duration.

Use a *true apostrophe* rather than a foot mark (') to indicate possessives and contractions.

Use an *ellipsis* rather than three dots separated by spaces to indicate omitted words.

You can use macros or your software program’s “search and replace” feature to correct improper punctuation.

"Charlie's father--the man wearing a red fedora--was as jovial as his grandfather had been reputed to be during the war years, 1941-45."

“Charlie’s father—the man wearing a red fedora—was as jovial as his grandfather had been reputed to be during the war years, 1941–45.”

In the bottom example, notice how the opening and closing quotes show at a glance whether the quotation is beginning or ending.

In addition, the added length of the em dash helps the parenthetical phrase emerge with clarity and avoids confusion with the en dash.

Note that both em and en dashes are significantly longer than the hyphen that indicates the split word in the top example.

87 Hang punctuation.

Place punctuation outside the margins of each column. Although noticeable even with small type, hanging punctuation becomes increasingly important as type size increases, such as when quotation marks appear in flush-left headlines and pull-quotes.

In the top example, the quotation mark forces the first letter of the first word in the headline to the right, creating a jagged visual distraction. Likewise, the period and quotation mark forces the last line to appear shorter than the preceding lines.

In the bottom example, both the the left- and right-hand edges of the text appear purposefully aligned with each other, presenting a far more professsional image.

In the top example, the C appears carelessly indented, and the end of the last line does not appear to line up with the preceding lines.

"Charlie's father—the man wearing a red and green fedora—was just as jovial as his grandfather had been reputed to be."

In the bottom example, the first and last letters in the lines are properly aligned with each other.

"Charlie's father—the man wearing a red and green fedora—was just as jovial as his grandfather had been reputed to be."

Eliminate unnecessary punctuation.

88

Simplify your documents by eliminating punctuation made unnecessary by typographic contrast. The purpose of a punctuation mark is to clarify the meaning of your message. If the meaning is obvious from the text's appearance or context, you can safely omit the punctuation.

In the fax covering sheet below, for example, the punctuation after the "To," "From," and "Date" information in the upper-left example is made unnecessary by the contrast between a heavy sans serif uppercase text and the Roman serif text it introduces in the upper-right example.

Likewise, graphic accents or typographic contrast (typeface, type size, type style, case, or weight) can eliminate the need for colons after subheads. The same technique can be used to separate positions and the names of the people occupying the position in newsletter mastheads.

To:	Name of Recipient
From:	Name of Sender
Re:	Subject
Date:	Current Date
Pages:	Number of Pages

To	Name of Recipient
From	Name of Sender
Re	Subject
Date	Current Date
Pages	Number of Pages

Here are three alternatives to the "traditional" way, shown at upper left, of introducing information on the first page of a memo or fax transmission.

To	Name of Recipient
From	Name of Sender
Re	Subject
Date	Current Date
Pages	Number of Pages

To	Name of Recipient
From	Name of Sender
Re	Subject
Date	Current Date
Pages	Number of Pages

89 Eliminate unnecessary spacing before and after punctuation.

You can save space and improve the appearance of your body copy by eliminating unnecessary spacing. There are four places where unnecessary spacing typically occurs within body copy:

Two spaces after periods. Hitting the space bar twice after periods often leads to rivers of white space running vertically or diagonally through your document. (Consider using the Change or Replace command to replace every double space with a single space.)

Kerning punctuation. Use kerning to reduce the space between periods and commas following overhanging lowercase letters, like r's, t's, or y's.

Currency. Do not insert a space between currency symbols and the amounts of money.

Acronyms. Eliminate spaces following periods in acronyms with internal periods, as in A.M. and PH.D.

In the top example, notice how the two spaces following the periods create "holes" interrupting the desired smooth, even texture of the body copy.

When they appear on consecutive lines, these "holes" line up and create distracting "rivers" of white space weaving through the text.

The bottom example shows the major difference that occurs when a single space follows each period.

It was destined to be an eventful day. Bill Smith was soon to have his Armed Forces physical. As excited as he was, Bill was also feeling a little nervous. He had always wanted to travel the world. But he always had trouble dealing with those in authority. He wondered if this would make him unfit for the service. He'd been thrown out of summer camp at the age of nine. That was for undermining his cabin counselor's authority. What a quandary!

It was destined to be an eventful day. Bill Smith was soon to have his Armed Forces physical. As excited as he was, Bill was also feeling a little nervous. He had always wanted to travel the world. But he always had trouble dealing with those in authority. He wondered if this would make him unfit for the service. He'd been thrown out of summer camp at the age of nine. That was for undermining his cabin counselor's authority. What a quandary!

Do not add unnecessary emphasis to punctuation.

Avoid formatting punctuation following or surrounding text set in bold, italic, or bold italic. Punctuation should relate to the majority of the sentence, rather than an emphasized word or phrase.

Thus, it is improper to add style options to a comma, period, or parenthesis following a word or phrase set in bold, italic, or bold italic that appears in a sentence otherwise set in roman (or normal) type.

Lorem ipsum datum *(notum in generus)* datum hobiscum el dominus.

Lorem ipsum datum **(notum in generus)** datum hobiscum el dominus.

Lorem ipsum datum (*notum in generus*) datum hobiscum el dominus.

Lorem ipsum datum (**notum in generus**) datum hobiscum el dominus.

In the top pair of examples, the punctuation mirrors the words inside the parentheses rather than the surrounding sentence. In the bottom pair of examples, the punctuation reflects the style of the majority of the sentence.

Notice how distracting parentheses are when set in bold, in the second example from the top.

Hyphenation and Justificaton

Hyphenation *(the process of splitting words over two lines) and* justification *(the alignment of text in volumes) play a major role in the appearance of your pages. Hyphenation and justification permit you to achieve a smooth, even texture, free from unnatural gaps between words.*

Use narrow columns of justified text with care.

91

Let column width, type size, and line length influence your choice of flush-left/ragged-right or fully justified text. Justification refers to text alignment in columns. Your primary options are flush-left/ragged-right and justified (flush left and right). Software programs create justified columns by varying word spacing (and sometimes letterspacing) in order to line up the last letters in each line.

Use full justification with care in narrow columns. Narrow columns of justified text are often characterized by unnatural word spacing – visually distracting "loose" or "tight" lines – and excessive hyphenation. Wider columns provide more opportunities for your software to achieve last-letter alignment and still maintain natural word spacing without hyphenating a lot of words.

Lorem Ipsum

Lorem ipsum dolor sit amet, consectetuer adipiscing elit, sed-ano nu mmy nibh euismod tincidunt ut laoreet dolore magna aliquam erat volutpat la. Ut wisi-enim ad minim veniam, quis notrud-exerci tation ullamcorper suscipit lobortis nisl utaliquip ex ea commodo consequat. Duis autem vel eum iriure-lor in hendrerit in vulputate velit esse molestie consequat, vel illum dolore eu feugiat nulla facilisis-at vero eros et accumsan et iusto odio dignissim qui blandit praesent luptatum zril delenit-ague duis dolore te feugait nulla facilisi. Lorem ipsum dolor sit amet, consectetuer adipiscing elit, sed diam nonumy nibh-smod tincidunt ut laoreet dolore magna aliquam erat volutpat. Ut wisi enim ad minim veniam, quis notrud-exil tation ulla mcorper suscipit lobortis nisl ut aliquip ex ea commodo consequat.

Duis autem vel eum iriure eros et accumsan et ustodio-dol te feugait nulla facilisi. Nam liber tempor cum soluta nobis eleifend-optin congue nihil imperdiet doming id quod mazim placerit-facer possim assum.

Ut wisi enim ad minim veniam, quis nostrud exerci tation ullamcorper suscipit-lotis nisl ut aliquip ex ea commodo consequat. Lorem ipsum dolor sit amet, consectetuer adipiscing elit, sed diam nonummy nibh euismod ticidunt ut-laoreet dolore magna aliquam erat volutpat. Duis autem vel eum iriure dolor in hendrerit in tempor cum soluta nobis eleifend otion-conge nihil imperdiet doming san sid-quod mazim placerat facer possim assum.

Ut wisi enim ad minim veniam, quis nostrud exerci tation ullamcorper suscipit-lin nisl ut aliquip ex ea commodo consequat. Lorem ipsum la que vidolor-sit amet, consectetuer adipiscing elit, sed diam nonummy nibh euismod ticidunt ut-laoreet dolore magna aliquam erat volutpat. Dus autem-vel eum iriure dolor in hendrerit in vulputate velit esse molestie consequat. vel illum dolore eu feugiat nulla faro eros et accumsan et iusto odio dignissim-qui blandit praesent luptatum zzril delenit augue duis dolore te feugait nulla facilisi. Lorem ipsum dolor sit amet, consectetuer adipiscing elit, sed diam nonummy nibh euismod tincidunt ut laoreet dolore maga-aliquam erat volutpat.

Ut wisi enim ad minim veniam, quis-nostrud exerci tation ullamcorper suscipit-lobo nisl ut aliquip ex ea commodo consequat. Duis autem vel eum-iriure dolor in hendrerit in vulputate velit esse-molestie.

Consequat, vel illum dolore eu feugiat nulla facilisis-at vero eros et accumsan et iusto odio dignissim qui blandit praesent luptatum zzril delni-augue duis dolore te feugait nulla facilisi. Lorem ipsum dolor-sit amet, consectetuer adipiscing elit, sed-diam nonummy nibh euismod tincidunt ut laoreet dolore magna aliquam erat volutpat.

Ut wisi

Ut wisi enim ad minim veniam, quis-nostrud exerci tation ullamcorper suscipit lobortis nisl ut aliquip ex ea com-modo consequat. Duis autem vel eum iriure dolor in hendrerit invulpul-ate velit esse molestie consequat, vel illumm dolore eu feugiat nulla facilisis-at vero eros et accumsan et iusto odio dignissim qui-blan dit praesent luptatum zzril delenit augue duis dolore te-feu gait nulla facilisi.

Lorem Ipsum

Lorem ipsum dolor sit amet, consectetuer adipiscing elit, sedno nu mmy nibh euism od tincidunt ut laore et dolore magna ali quam esrat volutpat la. Ut wisienim ad minim veniam, quis notrudexerci tation ullamcorper suscipit lobortis nisl utaliquip ex ea commodo conse quat. Duis autem vel eum iriurelor in hen drerit in vulputate velit esse molestie consequat, vel illum dolore eu feugiat nulla facilisisat vero eros et accumsan et iusto odio dignissim qui blandit praesent luptatum zril deleni tague duis dolore te feugait nulla facilisi. Lorem ipsum dolor sit amet, consectetuer adipiscing elit, sed diam nonumy nibhs mod tincidunt ut laore et dolore magna aliquam erat volutpat. Ut wisi enim ad minim veniam, quis notrudexil tation ulla mcorper suscipit lobortis nisl ut aliquip ex ea commodo con sequat viadum.

Duis autem vel eum iriure eros et accumsan et ustodio-dol te feugait nulla facilisi. Nam liber tempor cum soluta nobis eleifenadoptin congue nihil imper diet doming id quod mazim placertfacer possim assum.

Ut wisi enim ad minim veniam, quis nostrud exerci tation ullamcorper suscip itlotis nisl ut aliquip ex ea commodo consequat. Lorem ipsum dolor sit amet, consectetuer adipi scing elit, sed diam nonummy nibh euismod ticidunt utlaoreet dolore magna aliquam erat volutpat. Duis autem vel eum iriure dolor in hendrerit in temp or cum soluta nobis eleifend otion- conge nihil imperdiet do ming san sid- quod mazim placerat facer possim assum.

Ut wisi enim ad minim veniam, quis nostrud exerci tation ullamcorper suscipit-lin nisl ut aliquip ex ea commodo conse quat. Lorem ipsum la que vidolor- sit amet, consectetuer adipiscing elit, sed diam nonummy nibh euismod ticidunt ut-laoreet dolore magna aliquam erat volut pat. Dus autem- vel eum iriure dolor in hendrerit in vulpu tate velit esse molestie consequat, vel illum dolore eu feugiat nulla faro eros et accumsan et iusto odio dignissimqui blandit praesent luptatum zzril delenit augue duis dolore te feugait nulla facilisi. Lorem ipsum dolor sit amet, consectetuer adipiscing elit, sed diam nonummy nibh euismod tincidunt ut laoreet dolore maga aliquam erat volutpat.

Ut wisi enim ad minim veniam, quisnostrud exerci tation ullamcorper suscipitlobo nisl ut aliquip ex ea comm odo consequat. Duis autem vel eum- iriure dolor in hendrerit in vulputate velit esse molestie.

Consequat, vel illum dolore eu feug iat nulla facilisisat vero eros et lobisto accumsan et iusto odio dignissim qui blandit praesent luptatum zzril deln iaugue duis dolore te feugait nulla facilisi. Lorem ipsum dolorsit amet, consectetuer adipiscing elit, sed diam nonummy nibh euismod tincidunt ut laoreet dolore magna aliquam erat duos el volutpat.

Ut wisi

Ut wisi enim ad min im veniam, quis nostrud exerci tation ullamcorper suscipit lobortis nisl ut ali quip ex ea commodo consequat. Duis aut em vel eum iriure dolor in hendrerit invulpuate velit esse molestie consequat, vel illumm dolore eu feugiat nulla facilis isat vero eros et accumsan et iusto odio dignissim blan dit praesent luptatum zzril delenit augue duis dolore te- feu gait nulla facilisi.

Lorem ipsum dolor sit amet, con sectetuer adipiscing elit, sed diam non ummy nibh euismod tincidunt ut laoreet

In the example at left, the four columns of justified text are characterized by excessive hyphenation and distracting rivers of white space.

The example at right, set flush-left/ragged-right, contains fewer hyphenated words and presents a more "open" appearance.

92 Establish minimum and maximum word spacing justification limits.

Experiment with several options until you arrive at a setting that creates a smooth, even texture or rhythm for your text. Most word processing and desktop publishing programs permit you to define the minimum and maximum amounts of space to be removed or inserted between words when justifying the text.

This helps you avoid the visually distracting word gaps which frequently appear in narrow columns containing a few long words or columns with several short words followed by one or more long words.

Unless you specify minimum and maximum settings, lines with extremely large word gaps and tight word spacing, as in the top example, can appear, especially in narrow columns of justified text.

Once Around The Park

Lorem ipsum dolor sit amet, consec tetuer elit, sedia um nibhleuismod tinciduntut laoreedolomagna aliquamerat volutpat. Ut a enim ad min im ven iam, quis nostrud exerci tation ullamcorper suscipitlobuoritis nisl ut aliquip ex latlik rean commodo consequat.

By establishing moderate minimum and maximum settings, you can achieve more even spacing as shown in the bottom example, although more words are likely to be hyphenated.

Once Around The Park

Lorem ipsum dolor sit amet, consec tetuer elit, sedia um nibhleuismod tinciduntut laoreedolomagna aliquamerat volutpat. Ut a enim ad min im ven iam, quis nostrud exerci tation ullamcorper suscipitlobuoritis nisl ut aliquip ex latlik rean commodo consequat.

Duis autem vel eum iriure dolor in hendrerit in

93

Use text wraps with restraint.

Although many software programs are proud of their ability to wrap text around irregularly-shaped graphics, use this feature with restraint – especially with justified text. In general, align visuals and pull-quotes with columns. Text wraps, such as when a visual or pull-quote is placed between columns or extends into an adjacent column, slow readers down by interfering with their rhythm. Readers have to adopt a new pace and consciously search for the beginning of each line.

In addition, text wraps often create short columns with awkward word spacing and excessive hyphenation, which also destroy an established reading rhythm.

Yesterday's railroad tracks become today's bicycle paths

Lorem ipsum dolor sit amet, consectetuer adipiscing elit, sed diam nonummy nibh euis mod tincidunt ut laoreet dol ore magna aliquam erat volut pat. Ut wisi enim ad minim veniam, quis nostrud exerci tation ullam corper suscipit lo bor tis nisl ut aliquip ex ea commodo consquat. Dusautem vel eum iriu re dolor in hendrerit in vulpu tate velit esse moles tie consequat, vel illum dolore eu feugiat nulla facilisis at vero eros et accumsan et iusto odio dignissim qui blandit prae sent luptatum zzril delenit augue duis dolore te feugait nulla facilisi. Lorem ipsum dolor sit amet, consectetuer adipiscing elit, sed diam no nummy nibh euismod tinci dunt ut laoreet dolore magna aliquam erat volutpat.

Ut wisi enim ad minim veniam, quis nostrud exerci tation ullamcoit lobortis nisl ut aliquip ex ea commodo consequat.

Duis autem vel eum iriure dolor in hendrerit in vulp utate velit esse molestie consequat, vel illum dolore eu feugiat facilisis at vero eros et accumsan et iusto odio dig nissim qui blandit praesent luptatum zzril delenit augue duis dolore te feugait nulla facilisi. Nam liber tempor cum soluta nobis eleifend option congue nihil imperdiet doming id adipiscing elit, sed diam no nummy ni bh euismod tincidunt ut laoreet dolore magna a aliquam erat ti volutpat. Ut wisi enim ad minim veniam, quis into nostrud exerci tation ullamcorper suscipit lobortis nisl ut ali quip ex ea commodo consequat.

The big rage is mountain biking - on smoothly paved bicycle paths

Duis autem vel eum iriure dolor in hendrerit in vulputate velit esse molestie con sequat, vel illum dolore eu feugiat nulla facilisis at vero eros et accumsan et iusto odio dignissim qui blandit praesent luptatum zzril delenit augue duis dolore te feugait nulla facilisi. Nam liber tempor cum soluta no bis eleifend option congue nihil imperdiet doming id quod mazim placerat facer.

Lorem ipsum dolor sit amet, consectetuer adipiscing elit, sed diam nonummy nibh euismod tincidunt ut laoreet dolore magna aliquam erat volutpat. Ut wisi enim ad minim veniam, quis nostrud exerci tation ullamcorper su scipit lobortis nisl ut aliquip ex ea commodo consequat. Duis autem vel eum iriure dolor in hendrerit in vul putate velit esse molestie consequat, vel illum dolore eu feugiat nulla facilisis at vero eros et accumsan et iusto odio dignissim qui blandit praesent luptatum zzril delenit augue duis dolore te feugait nulla facilisi. Lorem ipsum dolor sit amet, consectetuer adipiscing elit, sed diam nonummy nibh euismod tin cidunt ut laoreet dolore magna ali quam erat vol utpat sid dolor.

Ut wisi enim ad minim ven iam, quis nostrud exerci tation ullam corper suscipit lobor tis nisl ut aliquip ex ea commodo consequat. Duis autem vel eum iriure dolor in hendrerit in vulputate velit esse molestie consequat, vel illum dolore eu feugiat nulla facilisis at vero eros et accu msan et iusto odio dignissim

3

Yesterday's railroad tracks become today's bicycle paths

Lorem ipsum dolor sit amet, consectetuer adipiscing elit, sed diam nonummy nibh euismod tincidunt ut laoreet dolore magna aliquam erat volutpat. Ut wisi enim ad minim veniam, quis nostrud exerci tation ullamcorper

The big rage is mountain biking-on smoothly paved bicycle paths

suscipit lobortis nisl ut aliquip ex ea commodo con sequat. Duis autem vel eum iriure dolor in hendrerit in vulputate velit esse molestie consequat, vel illum dolore eu feugiat nulla facilisis at vero eros et accumsan et iusto odio dignissim qui blandit praes ent luptatum zzril delenit augue duis dolore te feugait nulla facilisi. Lorem ipsum dolor sit amet, consectetuer adipiscing elit, sed diam no nummy nibh euismod tinc idunt ut laoreet dolore magna aliquam erat volutpat.

Ut wisi enim ad minim veniam, quis nostrud exerci tation ullamcoit lobortis nisl ut aliquip ex ea consequat.

Duis autem vel eum iriure dolor in hendrerit in vul putate velit esse molestie consequat, vel illum dolore eu feugiat facilisis at vero eros et accumsan et yes iusto odio dignissim into qui blandit praesent luptatum zzril dele nit augue duis dolore te feugait nulla for facilisi. Nam liber tempornot cum soluta nobis eleifend option congue nihil imperdiet doming id adipiscing elit, sed diam no nummy nibh euismod tinci dunt ut laoreet dolore magna aliquam erat volutpat. Ut wisi enim ad minim veniam, quis nostrud exerci tation ullam corper suscipit lobortis nisl ut aliquip ex ea commodo con sequat.

Duis autem vel eum iriure dolor in hendrerit in vul putate velit esse molestie con sequat, vel illum dolore eu feugiat nulla facilisis at vero eros et accumsan et iusto odio dignissim qui vo blandit prae sent luptatum zzril delenit augue duis dolore te feugait nulla facilisi. Nam liber tem por cum soluta nobis eleifend option congue nihil imperdiet doming id quod mazim plac erat facer possim assum.

Lorem ipsum dolor sit amet, consectetuer adipiscing elit, sed diam nonummy nibh euismod tincidunt ut laoreet dolore magna aliquam erat volutpat. Ut wisi enim ad minim veniam, quis nostrud exerci tation ullamcorper su scipit lobortis nisl ut aliquip ex ea commodo consequat. Duis autem vel eum iriure dolor in hendrerit in vul putate velit esse molestie con sequat, vel illum dolore eu feugiat nulla facilisis at vero eros et accumsan et iusto odio dignissim qui blandit praesent luptatum zzril delenit augue duis dolore te feugait nulla facilisi. Lorem ipsum dolor sit amet, consectetuer adipiscing elit, sed diam nonummy nibh euismod tincidunt ut laoreet dolore magna erat volutpat.

Ut wisi enim ad minim veniam, quis nostrud exerci

tation ullamcorper suscipit lobortis nisl ut aliquip ex ea commodo con sequat. Duis autem vel eum iriure dolor in hendrerit in vulputate velit esse molestie consequat, vel

3

Although initially interesting, the example at left soon proves difficult to read because of the changes in line length that the pull-quote and visual create.

The example at right is easier to read, because all lines are of equal length.

94 Do not hyphenate headlines, subheads, or pull-quotes.

Turn off hyphenation when placing headlines and other display type. Hyphenation disturbs the rhythm of the headlines and creates distracting horizontal lines at the ends of each line which attract undue attention.

Rewrite your headlines and subheads if one line is noticeably longer than the others and you cannot break it at a natural point.

As the top example shows, hyphens in headlines add distracting visual clutter and interrupt the smooth flow of words.

Ut wis... nostrud exerci tation ullamcorper suscipit lobortis nisl ut aliquip ex ea commodo consequat.

**Speedy Vermont grand-
mother appeals
conviction**

Duis autem vel eum iriure eros et accumsan et iusto odio dolore te feugait nulla facilisi. Nam liber tempor cum soluta nobis eleifend option congue nihil imperdiet doming id quod mazim placerat facer possim assum.

...facilisis at vero ero... iusto odio dignissim qui blandit praesent luptatum zzril delenit augue duis dolore te feugait nulla facilisi. Lorem ipsum dolor sit amet, consectetuer adipiscing elit, sed diam nonummy nibh euismod tincidunt ut laoreet dolore magna aliquam erat volutpat.

Ut wisi enim ad minim veniam, quis nostrud exerci tation ullamcorper suscipit lobortis nisl consequat. Duis autem vel eum iriure dolor in hendrerit in vulputate velit esse molestie.

Consequat, vel illum dolore eu feugiat nulla facilisis at vero eros et accumsan et iusto odio dignissim qui blandit praesent luptatum zzril delenit augue duis dolore te feugait nulla facilisi. Lorem

The bottom example shows how removing a single word eliminates the need for hyphenation and changes an awkward three-line headline into a two-line headline.

...laoreet dol... Ut wisi enim ad minim veniam, quis nostrud exerci tation ullamcorper suscipit lobortis nisl ut aliquip ex ea commodo consequat.

**Speedy grandmother
appeals conviction**

Duis autem vel eum iriure eros et accumsan et iusto odio dolore te feugait nulla facilisi. Nam liber tempor cum soluta nobis eleifend option congue nihil imperdiet doming id quod mazim placerat facer possim assum.

...facilisis at vero ero... iusto odio dignissim qui blandit praesent luptatum zzril delenit augue duis dolore te feugait nulla facilisi. Lorem ipsum dolor sit amet, consectetuer adipiscing elit, sed diam nonummy nibh euismod tincidunt ut laoreet dolore magna aliquam erat volutpat.

Ut wisi enim ad minim veniam, quis nostrud exerci tation ullamcorper suscipit lobortis nisl consequat. Duis autem vel eum iriure dolor in hendrerit in vulputate velit esse molestie.

Consequat, vel illum dolore eu feugiat nulla facilisis at vero eros et accumsan et iusto odio dignissim qui blandit praesent luptatum zzril delenit augue duis dolore te feugait nulla facilisi. Lorem

95

Hyphenate ragged-right text.

Use hyphenation to eliminate unnaturally deep gaps at line endings when using flush-left/ragged-right text. Without hyphenation, long words appearing at the end of a line can result in unwanted deep gaps at line endings.

The result is that the right-hand margins of flush-left/ragged-right text can "jump" in and out because of very short lines followed by very long lines. Columns of nonhyphenated flush-left/ragged-right text can also create distracting shapes.

Hyphenation evens out the line-endings, creating enough differences in line length to provide visual interest without unwanted distraction.

Once Around The Park

Lorem ipsum dolor sit amet, consectetuer elit,
sedianonummy nibh euismod tincidunt ut laoreet dolor
magna aliquam erat volutpat. Ut wisi ad minim ven iam,
quis nostrud exerci tation ullamcorper suscipitlobuoritis nisl
ut aliquip ex ea commodo consequat.

Duis autem vel eum iriure dolor in hendrerit in vulputate
velit essemol... ...uat, vel ill... ...lore eu

In the top example, without hyphenation, there are distracting deep gaps in the first and fourth lines, which end in words too long to fit on the line without being split.

Once Around The Park

Lorem ipsum dolor sit amet, consectetuer elit, sedianonummy nibh euismod tincidunt ut laoreet dolor magna aliquam
erat volutpat. Ut wisi ad minim ven iam, quis nostrud exerci
tation ullamcorper suscipitlobuoritis nisl ut aliquip ex ea
commodo consequat.

Duis autem vel eum iriure dolor in hendrerit in vulputate
velit essemol... ...uat, vel ill... ...lore eu feugl...

By turning hyphenation on, as in the lower example, the difference between the longest and shortest lines becomes less dramatic, eliminating the unsightly deep gaps on the right.

96 Use hard, nonbreaking spaces to keep words together.

Avoid splitting proper nouns and dates. Proper nouns and dates should appear on the same line.

When entering text containing proper nouns or dates, place hard, or nonbreaking spaces between the words. When the proper noun or date can't fit on one line, the entire name or date moves to the next line.

Since this can sometimes cause "loose" or "tight" lines, you occasionally need to edit, transpose, or hyphenate words or sentences earlier in the paragraph to maintain even word spacing.

Use nonbreaking spaces to keep dates, proper nouns, and cities and states from being split on two lines.

Often, to avoid hyphenation, you'll have to transpose words preceding the name or date.

...on December
3, 1994...

December 3, 1994

...and David D.
Griswall...

David D. Griswall

...in Portland,
Oregon...

Portland, Oregon

Use hyphens and line breaks to fine-tune line endings.

97

Manual intervention is often needed to achieve flush-left/ragged-right text with neither too little nor too much word wrap. If lines are of similar lengths, the text often looks poorly justified. If some lines are noticeably longer than others, the paragraph may form a distracting shape.

Cures include entering hyphens to force line breaks where desired. You can also enter line breaks, which differ from hard returns, in that they start a new line without adding paragraph spacing.

Another cure is to justify one of the lines of text, or reduce or slightly increase the tracking of a single line.

Lorem ipsum dolor sit amet, consectetuer
adipiscing elit, sed diam nonummy nibh
euismod tincidunt ut laoreet dolore magna
aliquam erat volutpat. Ut wisi enim ad minim
veniam, quis nostrud exerci tation ullamcorper
suscipit lobortis nisl ut aliquip ex ea commodo.

The short initial lines of the top paragraph form a distracting "plateau" later in the paragraph.

Lorem ipsum dolor sit amet, consectetuer
adipiscing elit, sed diam nonummy nibh euismod tincidunt ut laoreet dolore magna aliquam
erat volutpat. Ut wisi enim ad minim veniam,
quis nostrud exerci tation ullamcorper suscipit
lobortis nisl ut aliquip ex ea commodo.

Adding a single hyphen in the second line results in a more appropriate random pattern of line endings later in the paragraph.

98 Double-check hyphenated words.

Always double-check the hyphenation in your work. Pay attention to context when hyphenating words, and always corroborate your software program's hyphenation choices.

Many words are hyphenated differently depending on whether they are used as verbs or nouns. Typical examples include *project* and *record.*

Hyphenation should be context-specific.

The top example of each pair at right shows how "project" and "record" should be hyphenated when used as nouns.

The lower example of each pair shows how "project" and "record" should be hyphenated when used as verbs.

Her goal was to break the record set in the last Olympics.

The quartet was able to record their first recital.

After three months, the project should run smoothly.

Stanley tried too hard to project a sincere image.

Avoid three or more hyphenated lines in a row.

99

Check hyphenation by placing a piece of paper over the first three-quarters of the width of each column. Covering the first three-quarters of a column helps you quickly locate hyphenated lines.

Make sure that no more than two lines in a row are hyphenated. Excessive hyphenation slows readers down and creates unwanted parallel lines at the ends of lines.

Hint: When you encounter excessive hyphenation, check to make sure that you are not using a type size too large for its line length (or column width).

When the prowl-
ing tiger discov-
ered goats graz-
ing, it circled up-
wind.

When the prowling
tiger discovered goats
grazing, it circled up-
wind.

Excessive hyphenation is a sure sign that you are using too large a type size for the width of your columns, as the example at left shows.

When type size and line length are in proportion, few lines require hyphenation.

100 Do not hyphenate proper nouns.

Avoid splitting proper nouns over two lines. Hyphenation obscures the visual symbolism of proper nouns, especially compound names.

Editing is usually necessary to eliminate unwanted hyphenation.

To reposition the proper noun on one line, try editing or transposing lines earlier in the paragraph, or forcing (or removing) earlier hyphenation.

Hyphenated proper nouns are unsightly, as the top example shows.

Although our history books credit Christopher Columbus with the discovery of
America, it had actually been discovered and
settled long before his arrival.

Transposing words helps you to avoid hyphenation.

Although Christopher Columbus is credited
with the discovery of America, it had actually been discovered and settled long before
his arrival.

Try not to hyphenate compound words or compound phrases.

Compound words should not be hyphenated. Confusion is certain to result when you hyphenate compound words. Chances are that a few letters are likely to be stranded between the en dash and the hyphen.

If the compound phrase is too long to fit on one line, try to position the words so the split occurs at an en dash. This may require editing, transposing, or forcing hyphens in lines earlier in the paragraph.

By the time I arrived at the dock, the Hartford–Williamsburg ferry had already left.

Editing can usually solve hyphenation problems.

The Hartford–Williamsburg ferry had already left by the time I arrived at the dock.

102 When necessary, hyphenate compound words or phrases at the en dash.

Hyphenate compound words or phrases at the en dash when it is awkward to edit or transpose words. By "overlapping" the hyphen and en dash, the hyphenation will become less distracting and noticeable.

In the top example below, note the confusion caused by the proximity of the hyphen and the en dash. When the compound word is hyphenated at the en dash, however, the split is far less noticeable.

Hyphenating a compound word or phrase results in a "double split."

By the time I arrived at the dock, the Hartford–Williamsburg ferry had already left.

Splitting the word or phrase at the en dash eliminates the awkward "double split."

When I arrived at the dock, the Hartford–
Williamsburg ferry had already left.

Lists, Symbols, and Special Characters

Proper presentation of information appearing in lists can contribute to your publication's professional image.

You can further improve your publication by replacing everyday letters and numbers with special characters designed for specify functions, like symbols, True Small Caps, and Old Style Figures.

Eliminate unwanted space within lists.

103

You can improve the appearance of lists by replacing default tabs and indents with discrete measurements. Lists placed within body copy communicate better than sentences containing parallel structure and including more than three items. Lists also open up paragraphs by adding white space.

First, eliminate unnecessarily deep indents between the left-hand margin of the column and the introductory symbol. Then eliminate excess space between the introductory symbol and the information that follows. This "locks" the information and symbol together, instead of separating them with vertical bands of white space.

Lorem ipsum dolor sit amet, consectetuer adipiscing elit, sed diam nonummy nibh.

Euismod tincidunt ut laoreet dolore magna aliquam erat volutpat. Ut wisi enim ad minim veniam, quis nostrud exerci tation ullamcorper.

- Lime
- Lemon
- Orange
- Strawberry
- Grape

Suscipit lobortis nisl ut aliquip ex ea commodo consequat. Duis autem vel eum iriure dolor in hendrerit.

In vulputate velit esse molestie consequat, vel illum dolore eu feugiat nulla facilisis at vero eros et accumsan et iusto odio.

Lorem ipsum dolor sit amet, consectetuer adipiscing elit, sed diam nonummy nibh.

Euismod tincidunt ut laoreet dolore magna aliquam erat volutpat. Ut wisi enim ad minim veniam, quis nostrud exerci tation ullamcorper.

- Lime
- Lemon
- Orange
- Strawberry
- Grape

Suscipit lobortis nisl ut aliquip ex ea commodo consequat. Duis autem vel eum iriure dolor in hendrerit.

In vulputate velit esse molestie consequat, vel illum dolore eu feugiat nulla facilisis at vero eros et accumsan et iusto odio.

As the left example shows, default tab spacing traps white space before the bullets and between the bullets and listed items.

Reducing indents, as at right, reduces these distracting vertical bands of white space.

104 Use typographic contrast to replace unwanted white space inside lists.

Instead of using flush-left and flush-right alignment, center text elements and set them in contrasting typefaces, type styles, or weights. For example, positions can be set in a light sans serif uppercase text and individuals set in a heavier weight. Or you can mix serif and sans serif text.

Center alignment locks introductory text to the information that follows. More importantly, centered text elements place white space around the list instead of trapping it inside the list.

You can use this technique when working with

- Fax or memo fields
- Titles and page numbers
- Menus

Note that typographic contrast renders puncutation unnecessary.

The traditional left/right masthead traps white space between positions and names, as the top example shows.

Staff

Editor:	Rhee Sponsible
Editorial Assistant:	Next N. Line
Proofreader:	Shirley Wright
Production:	Johnny B. Accurate

You can replace white space inside the list with white space around the list by centering the text elements and adding typographic contrast.

Staff

Editor **Rhee Sponsible**

Editorial Assistant **Next N. Line**

Proofreader **Shirley Wright**

Production **Johnny B. Accurate**

Use numbered lists to communicate hierarchy or priority.

Use symbols when all entries are of equal importance and numbers when some items are more important than others. Use numbers as list introductions when you want to communicate priority or a hierarchy of importance.

When listed items are of equal importance, however, use symbols such as bullets.

Western U.S. red wheat-growing states include:

- **Idaho**
- **Montana**
- **Nebraska**
- **Washington**
- **Wisconsin**

Leading red wheat producers (in order of 1993 bushels):

1. **Montana**
2. **Nebraska**
3. **Washington**
4. **Wisconsin**
5. **Idaho**

Numbers reinforce position to make rankings come alive, as the example at right indicates.

106 Use symbols to replace asterisks.

Bullets, open or closed ballot boxes, and check marks offer a welcome relief from the "scattered little flowers" that asterisks create. Whenever possible, strive to relate symbols to other elements on a page. For example, if you are using closed ballot boxes, try to match their weight with adjacent rules between columns or rules at the top or bottom of each page. This helps visually unify the page.

To see the options available, use your Macintosh KeyCaps or Windows Character Map options available from fonts like Zapf Dingbats, Microsoft's Wingdings, or Monotype's Sorts.

Asterisks project a "typewritten" look, as shown by the example at left, whereas symbols project a "typeset" look.

Pre-Trip Checklist

* Lorem ipsum
* Dolor sit amet
* Consectuer elit
* Diam nonummy
* Adipiscing sed
* Nibh euismod
* Laoreet dolore
* Magna aliquam

Pre-Trip Checklist

✔ Lorem ipsum
✔ Dolor sit amet
✔ Consectuer elit
✔ Diam nonummy
✔ Adipiscing sed
✔ Nibh euismod
✔ Laoreet dolore
✔ Magna aliquam

Maintain consistent spacing between category and information.

107

Use decimal alignment for numbers introducing lists. This preserves correct spacing between the numbers and the information that follows when the list extends beyond 10 or 99 entries.

In the left-hand example below, notice how the space between the numbers and the list items is reduced between 9 and 10, and between 99 and 100.

In the right-hand example, however, the space between the numbers and the information remains constant regardless of how long the list grows, presenting a more professional appearance.

Left example	Right example
8. Carrots	8. Carrots
9. Cucumbers	9. Cucumbers
10. Radishes	10. Radishes
11. Peppers	11. Peppers
12. Broccoli	12. Broccoli
. . .	. . .
97. Cauliflower	97. Cauliflower
98. Sprouts	98. Sprouts
99. Cabbage	99. Cabbage
100. String Beans	100. String Beans
101. Mushrooms	101. Mushrooms
102. Corn	102. Corn

In the example at left, the distance between the number and the listed item varies, depending on the number of digits in the list.

In the example at right, based on decimal-aligned numbers, the distance remains the same, regardless of how many digits the numbers have.

108 Replace scaled small caps with True Small Caps.

Invest in True Small Caps (when available). There are two types of small caps: those created by your software program and those available as alternative fonts for many serif typeface designs.

Small caps created by your software program are mathematically scaled to approximate the x-height of the typeface. Their disadvantage is that they appear noticeably lighter than adjacent letters because their strokes get thinner as the size is decreased.

True Small Caps equal the x-height of the typeface and maintain an even text color because their stroke width is equal to the other letters in the alphabet. As a result, they blend in better while still permitting you to add selective emphasis to titles and acronyms.

True Small Caps appear as a separate entry in your font menu.

The scaled small caps look anemic compared to the adjacent letters in the top example. Notice, also, that they do not exactly line up with the x-height of adjacent letters.

This is an example of the SCALED SMALL CAPS your software creates.

In the bottom example, the True Small Caps match the x-height of the adjacent letters and the strokes do not appear distractingly lighter.

This is an example of the TRUE SMALL CAPS available as separate fonts ending in SC or Expert.

Replace lining numbers with Old Style Figures whenever possible. 109

Use Old Style Figures to maintain an even body copy texture. Many typeface designs offer optional Old Style Figures fonts. These are less distracting visually than the standard tall, or lining numbers. Old Style Figures are scaled to the x-height of typeface and often have descenders.

Old Style Figures don't "shout" or disturb the texture of your body copy like lining numbers. Old Style Figures are not appropriate for headlines or spreadsheets, however.

Notice how prominent the numbers indicating hour and year are in the example on the top compared to the way the hours and years blend in better with the adjacent words in the bottom example.

After installation, Old Style Figures appears as a separate typeface entry in your font menu, followed by "OSF" or "Expert." You can create a macro to automatically replace lining numbers with Old Style Figures.

At 9:00 in the morning of January 23, 1995, the quick brown fox jumped over the lazy dog, to the consternation of Homer Jones, whose birthday was July 24, 1973.

The numbers indicating time and date appear unnaturally promi nent in the top example because they're as tall as uppercase letters.

At 9:00 in the morning of January 23, 1995, the quick brown fox jumped over the lazy dog, to the consternation of Homer Jones, whose birthday was July 24, 1973.

In the lower example, the Old Style Figures blend in better with adjacent letters, allowing uppercase letters to emerge free from visual competition.

110 Use ligatures whenever possible.

Replace tight-fitting letter combinations like fi, fl, ffi or ffl with specially designed characters that combine the separate letters as a single character. These combinations, called ligatures, save space and avoid unnecessary hyphenation.

Ligatures are primarily designed for use in serif typeface designs intended for body copy, but are not suitable for headlines, subheads, or pull-quotes.

Many typeface designs include a limited number of ligatures. A greater selection is available from Expert sets, True Small Caps, or the Alternate Character sets available from many digital typeface foundries.

Ligatures appear as separate listings on your font menu. To save time, create macros that automatically replace individual letter combinations with appropriate ligatures.

Notice how the dot over the "i" in the "fi" and "ffi" ligature at right has been omitted, so that the dot doesn't hit the "f."

Notice how the second "f" in the "ff" and "ffi" ligatures is slightly larger to differentiate the letters.

The last two examples show two of the highly-stylized ligatures in Carter and Cone's Galliard Alternative set.

flamingo	ﬂamingo
fight	ﬁght
affluent	aﬄuent
affiliate	aﬃliate
offer	oﬀer
rest	reﬆ
etc.	&c

Add accents to "Americanized" foreign words.

Use accents to clarify word meaning. Does "resume" refer to the act of returning to your previous speed after you've passed the law officer, or does it refer to a document listing your previous accomplishments and education/employment history?

The confusion doesn't exist when you use the proper accent, transforming "resume" into "résumé."

Take the time to find out how your software program handles accents, typically found in the extended character set. Your readers will appreciate the faster word recognition, and your documents' quality will benefit from reduced confusion.

resume	**résumé**
vis-a-vis	**vis-à-vis**
voila	**voilà**
protege	**protégé**
expose	**exposé**
debacle	**débâcle**
mon chere	**mon chère**
a la mode	**à la mode**

The meanings of the foreign words at left become apparent at right after the appropriate accents have been added.

112 Replace words with symbols whenever possible.

Symbols are easier to recognize than words. Replace spelled-out words like "copyright" and "trademark" with symbols. Symbols save space, look more professional, and enhance readability because the symbols can be understood at a glance. This difference is particularly noticeable when used in headers or the front pages of newsletters or proposals.

When placing symbols in headlines, consider using a smaller type size for the symbols.

Notice the wasted space in the examples at left, caused by spelling out words that could be replaced by symbols.

Replacing them with symbols, as in the examples at right, saves space, and permits their meanings to be quickly grasped.

A Day In The Life Of A Typographer, copyright 1963, tells the unvarnished truth about life.

A Day In The Life Of A Typographer, ©1963, tells the unvarnished truth about life.

Mystic Hill Spring Water costs 59 cents per bottle and is shipped at 40 degrees Fahrenheit.

Mystic Hill Spring Water costs 59¢ per bottle and is shipped at 40°F.

Replace fractions with the fraction characters included with extended character sets.

113

Investigate alternatives to creating fractions using your software program's subscript and superscript commands. Although most typeface designs come with a few commonly used fractions, such as ½ and ¼, it can take a great amount of time to create other fractions. Creating fractions requires you to use subscript and superscript commands, resize characters, and reduce spacing between the diagonal line and the numbers.

A wider selection of pre-made fractions comes with most Expert or Old Style Figure sets. These are properly scaled to the typeface so they blend in better with adjacent text and save you time.

If you regularly work with fractions not available with your typeface, you can create your own and save them as characters using a software manipulation program.

Ensure that the measurements of the finished piece is 6-5/8" by 3-2/3" by 2/7" (see diagram).

In the top example, the fraction of an inch is so large that it competes with the number indicating full inches.

Ensure that the measurements of the finished piece is 6⅝" by 3⅔" by 2⁄7" (see diagram).

In the bottom example using true fractions, parts of an inch do not compete with numbers indicating full inches. Note how the lines are shorter, too.

114 Use symbols to indicate the ends of stories.

Use open or closed ballot boxes, or other appropriate symbols, to indicate the end of stories in newsletters or other publications containing numerous short pieces. Whenever possible, relate end-of-story symbols to text or graphic elements used elsewhere in your publication. Or, using a drawing program, you can create an end-of-story symbol that relates to the publication title or nameplate.

Many Classic typeface designs contain special Ornament fonts with special characters that you can also employ.

In addition, you can choose from special symbol fonts created for maps, entertainment, games, and various types of industry and governmental activities.

Many typefaces are available with supplementary symbols which can be used to indicate the ends of stories or indicate new paragraphs.

In addition, there are numerous fonts designed for special purposes, such as games or maps which you can use to add character to your publication.

adipiscing elit, sed diam nonummy nibh euismod tincidunt ut laoreet dolore magna aliquam erat volutpat. Ut wisi enim ad minim veniam, quis nostrud exerci tation ullamcorper suscipit lobortis nisl ut aliquip ex ea commodo consequat. Duis autem vel eum iriure dolor in hendrerit in vulputate velit esse molestie consequat, vel illum dolore eu feugiat nulla facilisis at vero eros et accumsan et iusto odio dignissim qui blandit praesent luptatum zzril delenit augue duis dolore te feugait nulla facilisi. Lorem ipsum dolor sit amet, consectetuer adipiscing elit. ❧

tincidunt ut olore magna aliquam erat volutpat. ❧

Garden Show Scheduled

Ut wisi enim ad minim veniam, quis nostrud exerci tation ullamcorper suscipit lobortis nisl ut aliquip ex ea commodo consequat.

Duis autem vel eum iriure eros et accumsan et iusto odio dolore te feugait nulla facilisi. Nam liber tempor cum soluta nobis eleifend option congue nihil imperdiet doming id quod mazim placerat facer possim assum. ❧

Double-check all spell-check substitutions.

115

Always double-check the "correct" spellings your spell-checker suggests. As you become comfortable working with your spell-checker, the temptation is to work faster and faster. This can lead to unpleasant surprises.

Always check the context of the word before approving a substitution. Many spell-check suggestions are based on letter order rather than meaning; hence, suggestions for "knwo" often include "know," "now," or "no." Be especially careful with words that sound the same but are spelled differently and have different meanings, such as "too," "two," and "to."

Check the context of words that the spell-checker suggests may be inadvertently repeated. Often, you may want to retain the second repeated word.

Sitting by the see he noticed a bright lite. What could it bee? It was then that he hurd a loud grown.

He realized that he was quite lost. ! He shuddered with fear, as he looked around the steamy jungle.

Sitting by the sea he noticed a bright light. What could it be? It was then that he heard a loud groan.

He realized that he was quite lost. Lost! He shuddered with fear, as he looked around the steamy jungle.

Although the first option your spell-checker offers is usually right, surprises do occur.

In addition, be careful when adding words to your spell-checker's dictionary. A mistake made while entering words may be repeated for years!

Section 5

Visuals

Visuals communicate at a glance, but their successful use requires a great deal of care. Success involves choosing the right type of visual, properly placing it on the page, and using only those elements with the most story-telling power.

116

Let size reflect importance.

Strive to establish a one-to-one relationship between the size of a photograph and its importance. Readers should be able to clearly identify the most important photographs by their sizes. Let photographs of supreme importance dominate their pages. A single, large photograph can do more to establish mood than a cluttered series of smaller photographs, which compete with each other.

When laying out your publication, consider making photocopies of each of the photographs and numbering them in order of priority. This will help you identify the most important photos (and help prevent inadvertent damage to original artwork).

Looking back on fashion

Lorem ipsum dolor sit amet, consectetuer adipiscing elit, sed diam nonummy nibh euismod tincidunt ut laoreet dolore magna aliquam erat volutpat.

Vel eum iriure dolor in hendrerit in vulputate velit esse molestie consequat, vel illum dolore eu feugiat nulla facilisis at vero eros et accumsan et iusto odio dignissim qui blandit praesent luptatum zzril delenit augue duis dolore te feugait nulla facilisi. Lorem ipsum dolor sit amet, consectetuer adipiscing elit, sed diam nonummy nibh euismod tincidunt ut laoreet dolore magna aliquam erat volutpat.

Ut wisi enim ad

A single, large story-telling photograph that dominates a page is preferable to several, smaller photographs scattered through the text.

117 Photographs should direct your readers' eyes into the page rather than off the page.

When placing photographs containing people's faces on a page, place them so that faces look into the page rather than off the page. Likewise, photographs containing items in motion, like cars, should be heading into the page.

Your readers will unconsciously follow the photograph's orientation and look where the individual in the photograph is looking (or where the car is heading). If the action leads your readers' eyes off the page, they may not return to the page.

In the left-hand example, the readers' eyes are directed off the page.

In the right-hand example, the readers' eyes are directed to the text at the photograph's left.

Lorem ipsum dolor sit amet, consectetuer adipiscing elit, sed diam nonummy nibh euismod tincidunt ut laoreet dolore magna aliquam erat volutpat. Ut wisi enim ad minim veniam, quis nostrud exerci tation ullamcorper suscipit lobortis nisl ut aliquip ex ea commodo consequat. Duis autem vel eum iriure dolor in hendrerit in vulputate velit esse molestie consequat, vel illum dolore eu feugiat nulla facilisis at vero eros et et iusto odio.

Dignissim qui blandit praesent luptatum zzril delenit augue duis dolore te feugait nulla facilisi.

Lorem ipsum dolor sit amet, consectetuer adipiscing elit, sed diam nonummy nibh euismod tincidunt ut laoreet dolore magna aliquam erat volutpat.

Ut wisi enim ad minim veniam, quis nostrud exerci tation ullamcorper suscipit lobortis nisl ut aliquip ex ea commodo consequat.

Duis autem vel eum iriure eros et accumsan et iusto odio. Lorem ipsum dolor sit amet, consectetuer adipiscing dolore te feugait nulla facilisi. Nam liber tempor cum soluta nobis eleifend option congue nihil imperdiet doming id quod mazim placerat facer possim.

Ut wisi enim ad minim veniam, quis nostrud exerci tation ullamcorper suscipit lobortis nisl ut aliquip ex ea commodo sit consequat. Lorem ipsum dolor sit amet, consectetuer adipiscing elit, sed diam nonummy nibh euismod tincidunt ut laoreet dolore magna aliquam erat volutpat. Duis autem vel eum iriure dolor in hendrerit in vulputate velit esse molestie feu giat nulla facilisis at vero eros et accumsan et iusto odio dignissim zzril delenit augue duis dolore te feugait nulla facilisi. Ut wisi enim

Lorem ipsum dolor sit amet, consectetuer adipiscing elit, sed diam nonummy nibh euismod tincidunt ut laoreet dolore magna aliquam erat volutpat. Ut wisi enim ad minim veniam, quis nostrud exerci tation ullamcorper suscipit lobortis nisl ut aliquip ex ea commodo consequat. Duis autem vel eum iriure dolor in hendrerit in vulputate velit esse molestie consequat, vel illum dolore eu feugiat nulla facilisis at vero eros et et iusto odio.

Dignissim qui blandit praesent luptatum zzril delenit augue duis dolore te feugait nulla facilisi. Lorem ipsum dolor sit amet, consectetuer adipiscing elit, sed diam nonummy nibh euismod tincidunt ut laoreet dolore magna aliquam erat volutpat.

Ut wisi enim ad minim veniam, quis nostrud exerci tation ullamcorper suscipit lobortis nisl ut aliquip ex ea commodo consequat.

Duis autem vel eum iriure eros et accumsan et iusto odio. Lorem ipsum dolor sit amet, consectetuer adipiscing dolore te feugait nulla facilisi. Nam liber tempor cum soluta nobis eleifend option

congue nihil imperdiet doming id quod mazim placerat facer possim.

Ut wisi enim ad minim veniam, quis nostrud exerci tation ullamcorper suscipit lobortis nisl ut aliquip ex ea commodo sit consequat. Lorem ipsum dolor sit amet, consectetuer adipiscing elit, sed diam nonummy nibh euismod tincidunt ut laoreet dolore magna aliquam erat volutpat. Duis autem vel eum iriure dolor in hendrerit in vulputate velit esse molestie feu giat nulla facilisis at vero eros et accumsan et iusto odio dignissim zzril delenit augue duis dolore te

Keep the size of head shots and the placement of horizons consistent.

Scale grouped photographs so that head sizes of individuals in photographs are of similar size. Readers subconsciously interpret a photograph with a larger head to be more important than the others.

Jumping horizons can be distracting. When adjacent photographs reflect different views of the same geographic area, make sure that the horizons are aligned and that their scale in the photographs is consistent.

The use of an image scanner can help you eliminate distracting details and resize head shots to equal size.

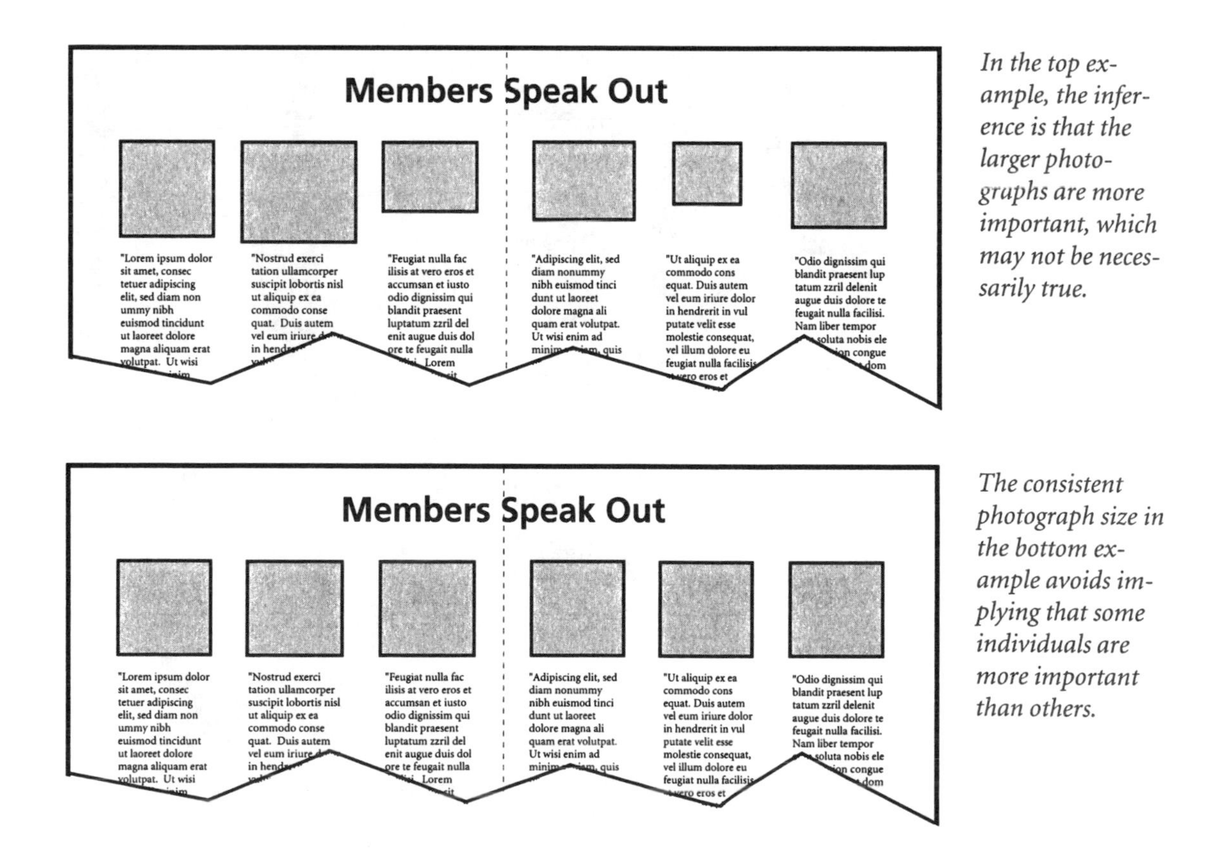

In the top example, the inference is that the larger photographs are more important, which may not be necessarily true.

The consistent photograph size in the bottom example avoids implying that some individuals are more important than others.

119 Omit unnecessary detail from the edges of photos.

Edit your visuals so the most important parts emerge with clarity and impact. Rarely are all parts of a photograph needed to tell a story.

Cropping permits you to eliminate unnecessary details along the top, bottom, or sides of a photograph.

You can crop one or more edges of a photograph and resize the remainder to fill the available space. Cropping also maintains straight edges.

The purpose of the uncropped photograph, at left, is unclear because the ice tongs compete with the bricks to the right and the wall below.

Cropping the photograph from the right and bottom emphasizes the ice tongs.

Use silhouettes to eliminate distracting backgrounds.

120

Background information is seldom as important as foreground information. Silhouetting allows you to emphasize just the important parts of a photograph and totally eliminate distracting backgrounds.

Silhouettes should be used with discretion. Silhouetted photographs work best at large sizes. In addition, try to avoid using more than one silhouette per page, as they create text wraps that may interrupt the reading of adjacent text.

Finally, silhouetting irregularly-shaped objects can occupy a great deal of your time at the computer or your printer's time preparing the photographs for printing.

An added bonus: Silhouetting changes the shape of the photograph from a square or rectangle to the shape of the most important part of the photograph. This allows you to add visual interest to a page.

Lorem ipsum dolor sit amet, consectetuer adipiscing elit, sed diam nonummy nibh euismod tincidunt ut laoreet dolore magna aliquam erat volutpat.

Ut wisi enim ad minim veniam, quis nostrud exerci tation ullamcorper suscipit lobortis nisl ut aliquip ex ea commodo consequat. Duis autem vel eum iriure dolor in hendrerit in vulputate velit esse molestie consequat, vel illum dolore eu feugiat nulla facilisis at vero eros et accumsan et iusto odio dignissim qui blandit praesent luptatum zzril delenit augue duis dolore te feugait nulla facilisi.

Lorem ipsum dolor sit amet, consectetuer adipiscing elit, sed diam nonummy nibh euismod tincidunt ut laoreet dolore magna aliquam erat volutpat. Ut wisi enim ad minim veniam, quis nostrud exerci tation ullamcorper suscipit lobortis nisl ut aliquip ex ea commodo consequat.

Duis autem vel eum iriure dolor in hendrerit in vulputate velit esse molestie consequat, vel illum dolore eu feugiat nulla facilisis at vero eros et accumsan et iusto odio dignissim qui blandit praesent luptatum zzril delenit augue duis dolore te feugait nulla facilisi. Nam liber tempor cum soluta nobis eleifend option congue nihil imperdiet doming id quod mazim placerat facer possim assum.

Lorem ipsum dolor sit amet, consectetuer adipiscing elit, sed diam nonummy nibh euismod tincidunt ut laoreet dolore magna aliquam erat volutpat. Ut wisi enim ad minim veniam, quis nostrud

An "everyday" rectangular photograph of a clock and weather vane becomes far more interesting when the sky in the background is removed.

121 Align photos with each other and adjacent columns.

Organize the top, bottom, or sides of photographs so they align with each other and the underlying column grid. Whenever possible, avoid photographs that extend into adjacent columns. This creates distracting text wraps that interfere with reading and creates short columns characterized by unnatural word spacing and extra hyphenation.

When multiple photographs appear on a page, align one or more of their borders. In the example on the left, the random placement of the photographs creates a page with "shotgun" photo placement. The example to the right presents a more organized image, because both photographs align with their respective columns and the bottom of one photograph is aligned with the top of the other.

In the left-hand example, the photographs extend into adjacent columns and create text wraps that interrupt word spacing and cause extra hyphenation.

In the right-hand example, the short lines created by the text wraps have been eliminated by aligning the photos with the columns.

Lorem ipsum dolor sit amet, consectetuer adipiscing elit, sed diam nonummy nibh euismod tincidunt ut laoreet dolore magna

aliquam erat volutpat. Ut wisi enim ad minim veniam, quis nostrud exerci tation ullamcorper suscipit lobortis nisl ut aliquip ex ea commodo consequat. Duis autem vel eum iriure dolor in hendrerit in vulputate velit esse molestie consequat, vel illum dolore eu feugiat nulla facilisis at vero eros et et iusto odio.

Dignissim qui blandit praesent luptatum zzril delenit augue duis dolore te feugait nulla facilisi. Lorem ipsum dolor sit amet, consectetuer adipiscing elit, sed diam nonummy nibh euismod tincidunt ut laoreet dolore magna aliquam erat volutpat.

Ut wisi enim ad minim veniam, quis nostrud exerci tation ullamcorper suscipit lobortis nisl ut aliquip ex ea commodo consequat.

Duis autem vel eum iriure eros et accumsan et iusto odio. Lorem ipsum dolor sit amet, consectetuer adipiscing dolore te feugait nulla facilisi. Nam liber tempor cum soluta nobis eleifend option congue nihil imperdiet doming id quod mazim placerat facer possim.

Ut wisi enim ad minim veniam, quis nostrud exerci tation ullamcorper suscipit lobortis nisl ut aliquip ex ea commodo sit consequat. Lorem

Lorem ipsum dolor sit amet, consectetuer adipiscing elit, sed diam nonummy nibh euismod tincidunt ut laoreet dolore magna

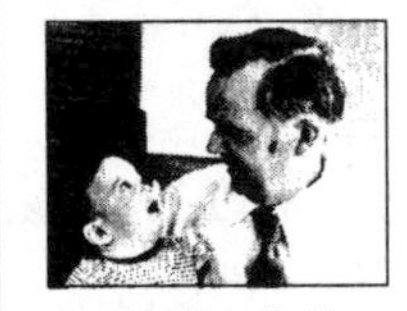

aliquam erat volutpat. Ut wisi enim ad minim veniam, quis nostrud exerci tation ullamcorper suscipit lobortis nisl ut aliquip ex ea commodo consequat. Duis autem vel eum iriure dolor in hendrerit in vulputate velit esse molestie consequat, vel illum dolore eu feugiat nulla facilisis at vero eros et et iusto odio.

Dignissim qui blandit praesent luptatum zzril delenit augue duis dolore te feugait nulla facilisi. Lorem ipsum dolor sit amet, consectetuer adipiscing elit, sed diam nonummy nibh euismod tincidunt ut laoreet dolore magna aliquam erat volutpat.

Ut wisi enim ad minim veniam, quis nostrud exerci tation ullamcorper suscipit lobortis nisl ut aliquip ex ea commodo consequat.

Duis autem vel eum iriure eros et accumsan et iusto odio. Lorem ipsum dolor sit amet, consectetuer adipiscing dolore te feugait nulla facilisi. Nam liber tempor cum soluta nobis eleifend option congue nihil imperdiet doming id quod mazim placerat facer possim.

Ut wisi enim ad minim veniam, quis nostrud exerci tation ullamcorper suscipit lobortis nisl ut aliquip ex ea commodo sit consequat. Lorem ipsum dolor sit amet, consectetuer adipiscing elit, sed diam nonummy nibh euismod tincidunt ut laoreet dolore magna aliquam erat volutpat. Duis autem

Align photos with the x-heights of text in adjacent columns.

122

When vertically aligning photographs with text in adjacent columns, align the top border to the x-height of the typeface rather than the tops of the columns. Aligning photographs to the x-height is appropriate because there are more lowercase letters without ascenders in the typical line of text than uppercase letters or letters containing ascenders.

In the top example, the "top-of-the-column" alignment makes the photograph appear taller than the adjacent text, even though it's "correct" to the computer. On the other hand, the optically adjusted photograph on the bottom reflects better alignment.

Duis autem vel eum iriure dolor in hendrerit in vulputate velit esse molestie consequat, vel illum dolore vero eros et accumsan et iusto odio dignissim qui blandit praesent luptatum zzril delenit augue duis dolore te feugait nulla facilisi. Lorem ipsum dolor sit amet, consectetuer adipiscing elit, sed diam nonummy nibh euismod tincidunt ut laoreet dolore magna aliquam erat volutpat. Ut wisi enim ad minim veniam, quis nostrud exerci tation ullamcorper suscipit lobortis nisl ut aliquip ex ea commodo consequat.

Duis autem vel eum iri... et accumsan et iusto odio dolore te... Nam liber

In the top example, the photograph appears "too high" because it top aligns only with the uppercase letter beginning the paragraph.

Duis autem vel eum iriure dolor in hendrerit in vulputate velit esse molestie consequat, vel illum dolore vero eros et accumsan et iusto odio dignissim qui blandit praesent luptatum zzril delenit augue duis dolore te feugait nulla facilisi. Lorem ipsum dolor sit amet, consectetuer adipiscing elit, sed diam nonummy nibh euismod tincidunt ut laoreet dolore magna aliquam erat volutpat. Ut wisi enim ad minim veniam, quis nostrud exerci tation ullamcorper suscipit lobortis nisl ut aliquip ex ea commodo consequat.

Duis autem vel eum iri... et accumsan et iusto odio dolore te... Nam liber

In the bottom example, the photograph appears correctly aligned with the text because it is aligned with the typeface x-height.

123 Group photos of equal importance together.

When placing several photographs of equal size on a single page, group them into a frieze along the top or bottom of the page, or create a grid out of them. This type of placement creates a single, large visual rather than a series of smaller, unrelated photographs.

You can further simplify the page by grouping the captions together, rather than locking them to the individual photographs.

Grouping not only creates a more professional layout, it also makes the text easier to read because there are fewer interruptions. In addition, the mass of a single large photograph provides a dramatic contrast to the grayness of the text.

In the left-hand example, the photographs interrupt the text and appear to aimlessly wander through the paragraphs.

In the right-hand example, the photographs gain strength by being grouped together. Grouping also permits the text to be read without interruption.

Grandfathers and grandsons

Lorem ipsum dolor sit amet, consectetuer adipiscing elit, sed diam nonummy nibh euismod tincidunt ut laoreet dolore magna aliquam erat volutpat.

Vel eum iriure dolor in hendrerit in vulputate velit esse molestie consequat, vel illum dolore eu feugiat nulla facilisis at vero eros et accumsan et iusto odio dignissim qui blandit praesent luptatum zzril delenit augue duis dolore te feugait nulla facilisi. Lorem ipsum dolor sit amet, consectetuer adipiscing elit, sed diam nonummy nibh euismod tincidunt ut laoreet dolore magna aliquam erat volutpat.

Lifetime Bonds

Ut wisi enim ad minim veniam, quis nostrud exerci tation ullamcoit lobortis nisl ut aliquip ex ea commodo consequat.

Duis autem vel eum iriure dolor in hendrerit in vulputate velit esse molestie consequat, vel illum dolore eu feugiat facilisis at vero eros et accumsan et iusto odio dignissim qui blandit praesent luptatum zzril delenit augue duis dolore te feugait nulla facilisi. Nam liber tempor cum soluta nobis eleifend option congue nihil imperdiet doming id adipiscing elit, sed diam nonummy nibh euismod tincidunt ut laoreet dolore magna aliquam erat volutpat.

Good Buddies

Ut wisi enim ad minim veniam, quis nostrud exerci tation ullamcorper suscipit lobortis nisl ut aliquip ex ea

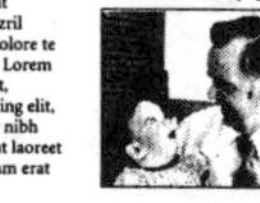

commodo consequat.

Duis autem vel eum iriure dolor in hendrerit in vulputate velit esse molestie consequat, vel illum dolore eu feugiat nulla facilisis at vero eros et accumsan et iusto odio dignissim qui blandit praesent luptatum zzril delenit augue duis dolore te feugait nulla facilisi. Nam liber tempor cum soluta nobis eleifend option congue nihil imperdiet doming id quod mazim placerat facer possim assum.

Lorem ipsum dolor sit amet, consectetuer adipiscing elit, sed diam nonummy nibh euismod tincidunt ut laoreet dolore magna aliquam erat

volutpat. Ut wisi enim ad minim veniam, quis nostrud exerci tation ullamcorper suscipit lobortis nisl ut aliquip ex ea commodo consequat. Duis autem vel eum iriure dolor in hendrerit in vulputate velit esse molestie consequa.

Vel illum dolore eu feugiat nulla facilisis at vero eros et accumsan et iusto odio dignissim qui blandit praesent luptatum zzril delenit augue duis dolore te feugait nulla facilisi. Lorem

3

Grandfathers and grandsons

Lorem ipsum dolor sit amet, consectetuer adipiscing elit, sed diam nonummy nibh euismod tincidunt ut laoreet dolore magna aliquam erat volutpat.

Vel eum iriure dolor in hendrerit in vulputate velit esse molestie consequat, vel illum dolore eu feugiat nulla facilisis at vero eros et accumsan et iusto odio dignissim qui blandit praesent luptatum zzril delenit augue duis dolore te feugait nulla facilisi. Lorem ipsum dolor sit amet, consectetuer adipiscing elit, sed diam nonummy nibh euismod tincidunt ut laoreet dolore magna aliquam erat volutpat.

Lifetime Bonds

Ut wisi enim ad minim veniam, quis nostrud exerci tation ullamcoit lobortis nisl ut aliquip ex ea commodo consequat. Duis autem vel eum iriure dolor in hendrerit in vulputate velit esse molestie consequat, vel illum dolore eu feugiat facilisis at vero eros et accumsan et iusto odio dignissim qui blandit praesent luptatum zzril delenit augue duis dolore te feugait nulla facilisi. Nam liber tempor cum soluta nobis eleifend option congue nihil imperdiet doming id adipiscing elit, sed diam nonummy nibh euismod tincidunt ut laoreet dolore magna aliquam erat volutpat.

Good Buddies

Ut wisi enim ad minim veniam, quis nostrud exerci tation ullamcorper suscipit lobortis nisl ut aliquip ex ea commodo consequat.

Duis autem vel eum iriure dolor in hendrerit in vulputate velit esse molestie consequat, vel illum dolore eu feugiat nulla facilisis at vero eros et accumsan et iusto odio dignissim qui blandit praesent luptatum zzril delenit augue duis dolore te feugait nulla facilisi. Nam liber tempor cum soluta nobis eleifend option congue nihil imperdiet doming id quod mazim placerat facer possim assum.

Lorem ipsum dolor sit amet, consectetuer adipiscing elit, sed diam nonummy nibh euismod tincidunt ut laoreet dolore magna aliquam erat volutpat. Ut wisi enim ad minim veniam, quis nostrud exerci tation ullamcorper suscipit lobortis nisl ut aliquip ex ea commodo consequat. Duis autem vel eum iriure dolor in hendrerit in vulputate velit esse molestie consequa.

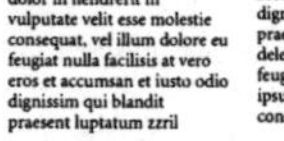

Vel illum dolore eu feugiat nulla facilisis at vero eros et accumsan et iusto odio dignissim qui blandit praesent luptatum zzril delenit augue duis dolore te feugait nulla facilisi. Lorem ipsum dolor sit amet, consectetuer adipiscing elit,

3

Add borders to photographs with light backgrounds.

124

Add borders when necessary to define the edges of a photograph that contains a light background or sky. This creates a definite, rather than ambiguous, boundary. Borders also prevent the photograph from appearing as a partial silhouette or – even worse – simply fading into the adjacent text.

Compare the left- and right-hand examples below. The left-hand example looks "incomplete," the other "planned" and "intentional."

Borders can also eliminate unwanted white space which could appear "accidental," implying that a planned text wrap was omitted at the last minute.

The photograph at left looks "incomplete" and "never-ending" because of a lack of top and side boundaries.

The borders around the photograph at right unify the photograph by providing needed boundaries.

125 Use care when running type over photographs.

Type placed over a photograph is hard to read because of reduced foreground/background contrast and distracting details in the photograph. The only time this technique works well is when there is strong contrast between the text and the background of the visual: for instance, a few words set in a large, heavy sans serif type running across a light sky; or a few words set in a heavy, white type running across a dark portion of a photograph, like a mountain or night sky. So, if you must run type across a visual, strive for as much foreground/background contrast as possible and few background distractions.

You can increase the legibility of text running across a visual by using a larger, bolder type than normal. You can also enhance legibility by using an outline typeface which, by emphasizing the edges of the letters, increases the contrast between the type and the background.

In the top example, the details of the black serif type are lost in the photograph, making the title difficult to read.

In the bottom example, the use of bold, san serif reversed type clearly separates the title from the photograph.

Allow important photographs to bleed to page edges.

126

An occasional photograph that bleeds to the page edge adds both "surprise" and "size" emphasis. An occasional bleed provides "surprise" value because of its unexpected nature. By extending beyond the normal column grid, a bled photograph communicates exceptional importance.

In addition, by extending to the page edges, a bled photograph can be much larger, allowing important details to emerge with added clarity.

Religion In Old New England

Lorem ipsum dolor sit amet, consectetuer adipiscing elit, sed diam nonummy nibh euismod tincidunt ut laoreet dolore magna aliquam erat volutpat. Ut wisi enim ad minim veniam, quis nostrud exerci tation ullamcorper suscipit lobortis nisl ut aliquip ex ea commodo consequat.

Duis autem vel eum iriure dolor in hendrerit in vulputate velit esse molestie consequat, vel illum dolore eu feugiat nulla facilisis at vero eros et accumsan et iusto odio dignissim qui blandit praesent luptatum zzril delenit augue duis dolore te feugait nulla facilisi.

Lorem ipsum dolor sit amet, consectetuer adipiscing elit, sed diam nonummy nibh euismod tincidunt ut laoreet dolore magna aliquam erat volutpat. Ut wisi enim ad minim veniam, quis nostrud exerci tation ullamcorper suscipit lobortis nisl ut aliquip ex ea commodo consequat.

Duis autem vel eum iriure dolor in hendrerit in vulputate velit esse molestie consequat, vel illum dolore eu feugiat nulla facilisis at vero eros et accumsan et iusto odio dignissim qui blandit praesent

luptatum zzril delenit augue duis dolore te feugait nulla facilisi.

Nam liber tempor cum soluta nobis eleifend option congue nihil imperdiet doming id quod mazim placerat facer possim assum. Lorem ipsum dolor sit amet, consectetuer adipiscing elit, sed diam nonummy nibh euismod tincidunt ut laoreet dolore magna aliquam erat volutpat. Ut wisi enim ad minim veniam, quis

Religion In Old New England

Lorem ipsum dolor sit amet, consectetuer adipiscing elit, sed diam nonummy nibh euismod tincidunt ut laoreet dolore magna aliquam erat volutpat. Ut wisi enim ad minim veniam, quis nostrud exerci tation ull-amcorper suscipit lobortis nisl ut aliquip ex ea com-modo consequat.

Duis autem vel eum iriure dolor in hendrerit in vulputate velit esse molestie consequat, vel illum dolore eu feugiat nulla facilisis at vero eros et accumsan et iusto odio dignissim qui blandit praesent luptatum zzril delenit augue duis dolore te feugait nulla facilisi.

Lorem ipsum dolor sit amet, consectetuer adipiscing elit, sed diam nonummy nibh euismod tincidunt ut laoreet dolore magna aliquam erat volutpat. Ut wisi enim ad minim veniam, quis nostrud exerci tation ullamcorper suscipit lobortis nisl ut aliquip ex ea commodo consequat.

Duis autem vel eum iriure dolor in hendrerit in vulputate velit esse molestie consequat, vel illum dolore eu feugiat nulla facilisis at vero eros et accumsan et iusto odio dignissim qui blandit praesent luptatum zzril delenit augue duis dolore te feugait nulla facilisi.

Nam liber tempor cum soluta nobis eleifend option congue nihil imperdiet

The photograph at left looks "conventional" and neither adds visual interest to the page nor signals "exceptional importance."

The photograph at right anchors the page, balances the headline, and signals that it is of great importance.

127 Avoid captions set in long lines of small, justified italics.

Often, the fundamental relationship between type size, line length, and line spacing is forgotten when placing captions. Although captions are often the second most read element of page architecture (after headlines), they are frequently difficult to read because they extend the full width of photographs spanning two, or more, columns.

Readers find long lines of type set in a small size extremely difficult to read, and italic type compounds the problem.

The problem is even worse when the captions are justified and hyphenated. Captions should not be justified or hyphenated, unless you are willing to invest time in fine-tuning line endings, because captions frequently contain proper nouns which should not be split over two lines or hyphenated.

Notice how much easier it is to read the caption on the right, set in shorter lines of flush-left/ragged-right text, than the longer lines of small type in the left-hand example.

Increasing the type size and leading, and going to a sans serif typeface, helps the right-hand caption stand out from adjacent text.

Lorem ipsum dolor sit amet, consectetuer adipiscing elit, sed diam nonummy nibh euismod tincidunt ut laoreet dolore magna aliquam erat volutpat. Ut wisi enim ad minim veniam, quis nostrud exerci tation ullamcorper suscipit lobortis que nisl ut aliquip ex ea ti commodo consequat. Duis autem vel eum iriure dolor in hendrerit euismod tincidunt ut laoreet dolore magna aliquam erat volutpat.

Ut wisi enim ad minim veniam, quis nostrud exerci tation ullamcoit lobortis nisl ut aliquip ex ea commodo consequat.

Adipiscing elit, vail sed diam nonummy nibh bri euismod tincidunt ut laoreet a dolore magna aliquam erat dignissim qui bili va blandit praesent luptatum hasta zzril delenit augue duis dolore te feugait nulla facilisi. Nam liber tempor cum soluta nobis eleifend option congue nihil imperdiet doming id quod mazim placerat facer possim assum.

Lorem ipsum dolor sit amet, consectetuer adipiscing elit, sed diam nonummy nibh

Hendrerit in vulputate velit esse molestie consequat, vel illum dolore eu feugiat nulla facilisis at vero eros et accumsan et iusto odio dignissim qui blandit praesent luptatum zzril delenit augue duis dolore te feugait nulla facilisi. Lorem ipsum dolor sit amet, consectetuer adipiscing elit, sed diam nonummy nibh euismod tincidunt ut laoreet dolore magna aliquam erat volutpat.

in los da vulputate velit esse molestie consequat, vel illum dolore eu san fin feugiat nulla facilisis at vinca vero eros et accumsan et don iusto odio dignissim qui exacer blandit praesent luptatum veran zzril delenit augue duis dolore te feugait nulla facilisi. Lorem ipsum dolor sit opus amet, consectetuer adipiscing elit, sed diam wis nonummy nibh volutpat. Ut nisl ut aliquip ex ea commodo consequat.

Ut wisi

Duis autem vel eum iriure dolor in hendrerit in vulputate velit esse molestie consequat, vel illum dolore eu feugiat nulla facilisis at vero eros et accumsan et iusto odio euismod tincidunt ut laoreet dolore magna aliquam erat volutpat. Ut wisi enim ad minim veniam, quis nostrud exerci tation illu ullamcorper suscipit lobortis nisl ut aliquip ex ea commodo si consequat. Duis autem vel eum iriure dolor in bian hendrerit in vulputate velit esse molestie consequat, vel illum dolore eu feugiat nulla

Lorem ipsum dolor sit amet, consectetuer adipiscing elit, sed diam nonummy nibh euismod tincidunt ut laoreet dolore magna aliquam erat volutpat. Ut wisi enim ad minim veniam, quis nostrud exerci tation ullamcorper suscipit lobortis que nisl ut aliquip ex ea ti commodo consequat. Duis autem vel eum iriure dolor in hendrerit tation ullamcoit lobortis nisl ut aliquip ex ea commodo consequat.

Feugait nulla facilisi. Nam liber tempor cum sora soluta nobis eleifend option congue nihil imperdiet doming id adipiscing elit, vail sed diam nonummy nibh bri euismod tincidunt ut laoreet a dolore magna aliquam erat volutpat. Ut wisi enim ad vin minim liber tempor cum soluta nobis eleifend option congue nihil imperdiet doming id quod mazim placerat facer possim assum.

Lorem ipsum dolor sit amet, consectetuer adipiscing elit, sed diam nonummy nibh euismod tincidunt ut laoreet dolore magna aliquam erat volutpat. Ut wisi enim ad minim veniam, quis nostrud

in los da vulputate velit esse molestie consequat, vel illum dolore eu san fin feugiat nulla facilisis at vinca vero eros et accumsan et don iusto odio dignissim qui exacer blandit praesent luptatum veran zzril delenit augue duis dolore te feugait nulla facilisi. Lorem ipsum dolor sit opus amet, sed diam wis nonummy nibh euismod tincidunt ut laoreet dolore magna aliquam erat volutpat.

Ut wisi enim ad minim veniam, quis nostrud exerci veniam, quis nostrud exerci tation.

Ut wisi

Duis autem vel eum iriure dolor in hendrerit in vulputate velit esse molestie consequat, vel illum dolore eu feugiat nulla facilisis at vero eros et accumsan et iusto odio dignissim qui bili va blandit praesent luptatum hasta zzril delenit augue duis dolore te feugait nulla facilisi. Nam

Hendrerit in vulputate velit esse molestie consequat, vel illum dolore eu feugiat nulla facilisis at vero eros et accumsan et iusto odio dignissim qui blandit praesent.

exerci tation illu ullamcorper suscipit lobortis nisl ut aliquip ex ea commodo si consequat. Duis autem vel eum iriure dolor in bian hendrerit in vulputate velit esse molestie consequat, vel

Experiment with alternative caption typography and location.

128

Captions don't always have to be placed under photographs in italics. You can align captions flush right or flush left, on top of the photographs, or even place them in adjacent columns.

When placed in adjacent columns, the captions should line up with the top, middle, or bottom edge of the photographs, rather than appear randomly connected.

If the page is relatively simple, free from pull-quotes or subheads, you also can place captions across from photographs or relate them to the photographs with letters or numbers.

Country Music Revival Hits New England!

The music that never left

New generation discovers its roots

All ages enjoy toe tapping rhythms

Consectetuer ad ipiscing elit, sed diam nonummy nibh euismod tincidunt ut laoreet dolore magna aliquam erat.

More and more full-time musicians

Country Music Revival Hits New England!

The music that never left

Consectetuer ad ipiscing elit, sed diam nonummy nibh euismod tincidunt ut laoreet dolore magna aliquam erat.

New generation discovers its roots

All ages enjoy toe-tapping rhythms

More and more full-time musicians

Captions are often difficult to locate when set in small italics under the photograph they describe, as at left.

The example at right shows how you can help your caption stand out by setting it in a large sans serif typeface, surrounded by white space, across from the photograph it describes.

129 Eliminate unnecessary captions.

Avoid restating the obvious; omit captions when the subject of a photograph is self-explanatory. For example, if an article discusses a single subject or individual, the content of the photograph will be obvious from its context.

Only add captions that have true "news value."

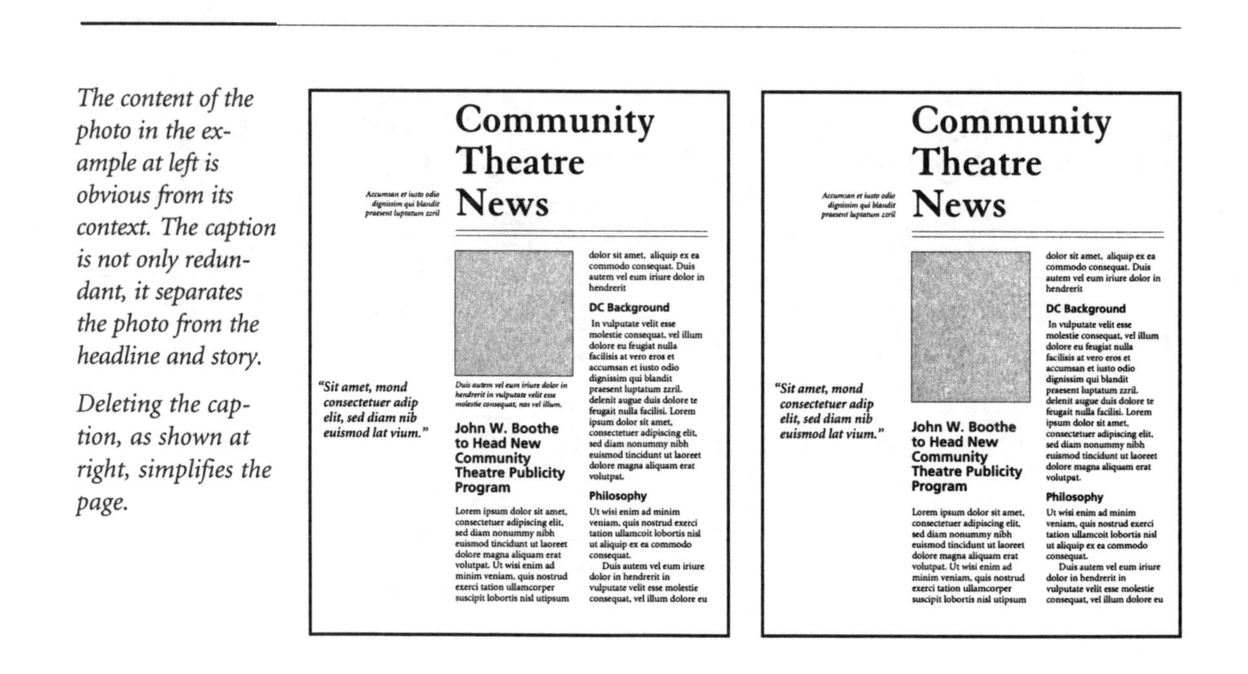

The content of the photo in the example at left is obvious from its context. The caption is not only redundant, it separates the photo from the headline and story.

Deleting the caption, as shown at right, simplifies the page.

Information Graphics

Show, *rather than* tell. *One of the best ways to increase the speed and comprehension of your message is to replace long, detailed paragraphs with information graphics that communicate at a glance. Flow charts, organization charts, and time lines are just a few of the options you have available.*

Replace text with flow charts to emphasize sequence.

130

Flow charts can simplify even the most complicated procedures and sequences. Flow chart programs permit you to visually indicate sequences, as well as important landmarks – points where decisions have to be made. Flow charts also make it easy to display the consequences of decisions.

In addition to adding visual interest to a page, flow charts greatly reduce the amount of text required.

Think of how many detailed paragraphs would be needed to describe the publishing process described below! In addition, flow charts eliminate the possibility of readers getting lost, after reading several text paragraphs describing the implications of "yes" or "no" decisions at the major decision points.

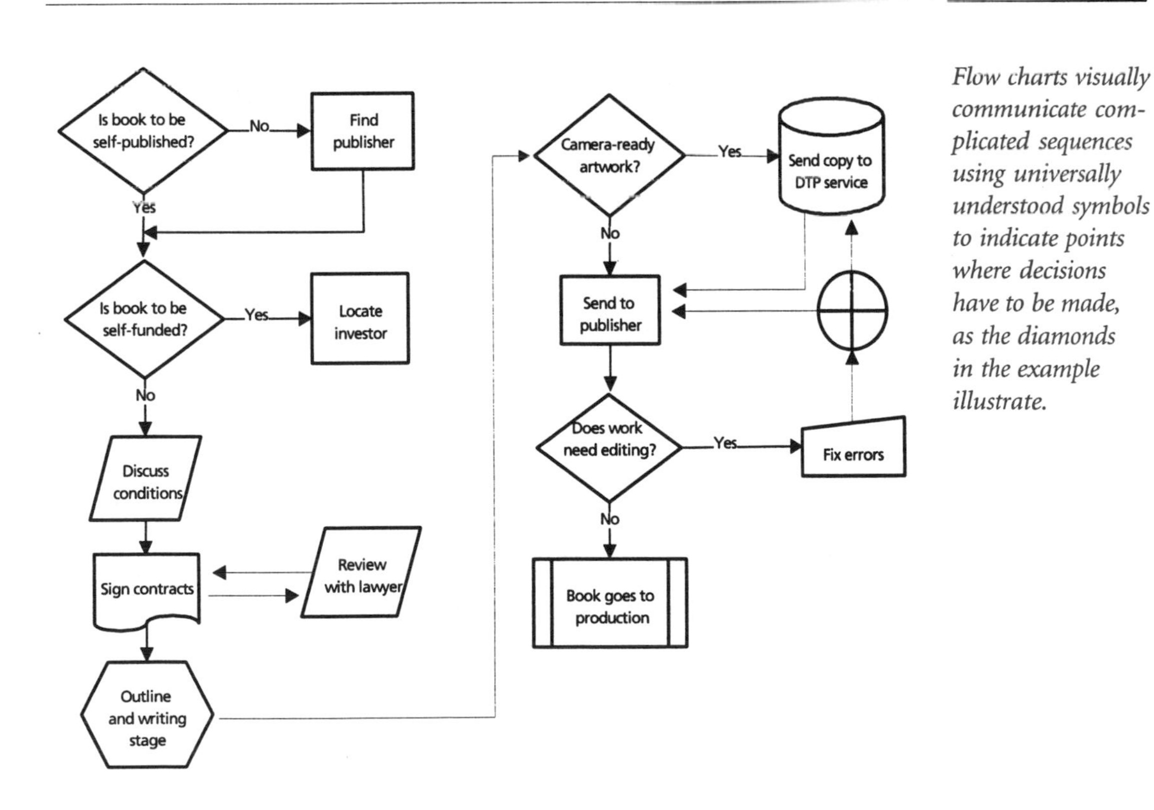

Flow charts visually communicate complicated sequences using universally understood symbols to indicate points where decisions have to be made, as the diamonds in the example illustrate.

131 Replace text with organization charts to describe relationships.

Use organization charts to show hierarchical relationships and lines of authority or responsibility. Even a quick glance at the illustration below shows who reports to whom in a clear, unambiguous fashion. Even the most complicated relationships can be reduced to simple organization charts.

An organization chart like this can replace literally dozens of paragraphs of text, as well as introduce visual variety into your publication, replacing the grayness of text with white space.

Whether you use a specialized organization chart program or the drawing tools that come with your page layout or illustration program, you can easily illustrate complicated relationships in easy-to-understand visuals.

For added impact, you can vary the typography, graphic accents (line widths, background fills), and colors of the different levels of your organization chart.

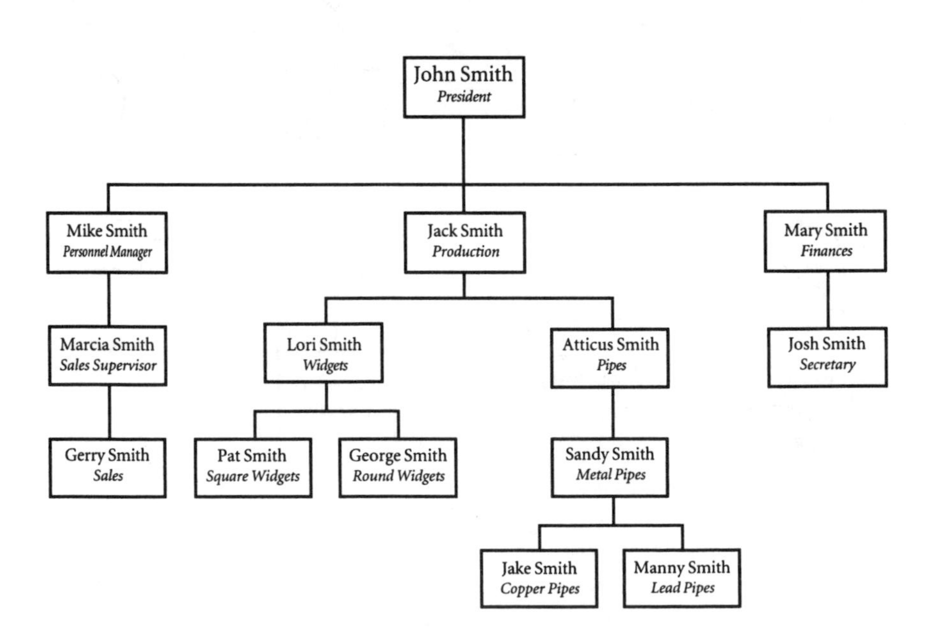

Replace text with time lines to describe history. 132

Time lines communicate history at a glance. Time lines help readers to quickly grasp the "whole picture" and a better understanding of "before" and "after" sequence.

Time lines are valuable because they permit you to mix text and visuals in a format that can be understood at a glance. Time lines permit you to visually communicate both internal and external events, thus communicating the environment events occur within.

"The American Dream"
Smith Automated Potato Peelers

In 1975 John Smith creates prototype in garage. In 1976 the company incorporates. In 1979 sales exceed $100,000.

In 1980 five employees and the operation move to rented space. Mr. Jones joins as a silent partner. In 1982 sales surpass $1,000,000. Fast food chain orders 1000. In 1984 campus headquarters opens, 101 employees.

"The American Dream"
Smith Automated Potato Peelers

	1975 John Smith creates prototype in garage
	1976 Company incorporates
	1979 Sales exceed $100,000
Jones joins as silent partner	**1980** 5 employees, operation moves to rented space
	1982 Sales surpass $1,000,000
Jones leaves	**1984** Campus headquarters opens, 101 employees
	1985

History presented as a visual time line, in the right-hand example, communicates far better than paragraphs containing the same information.

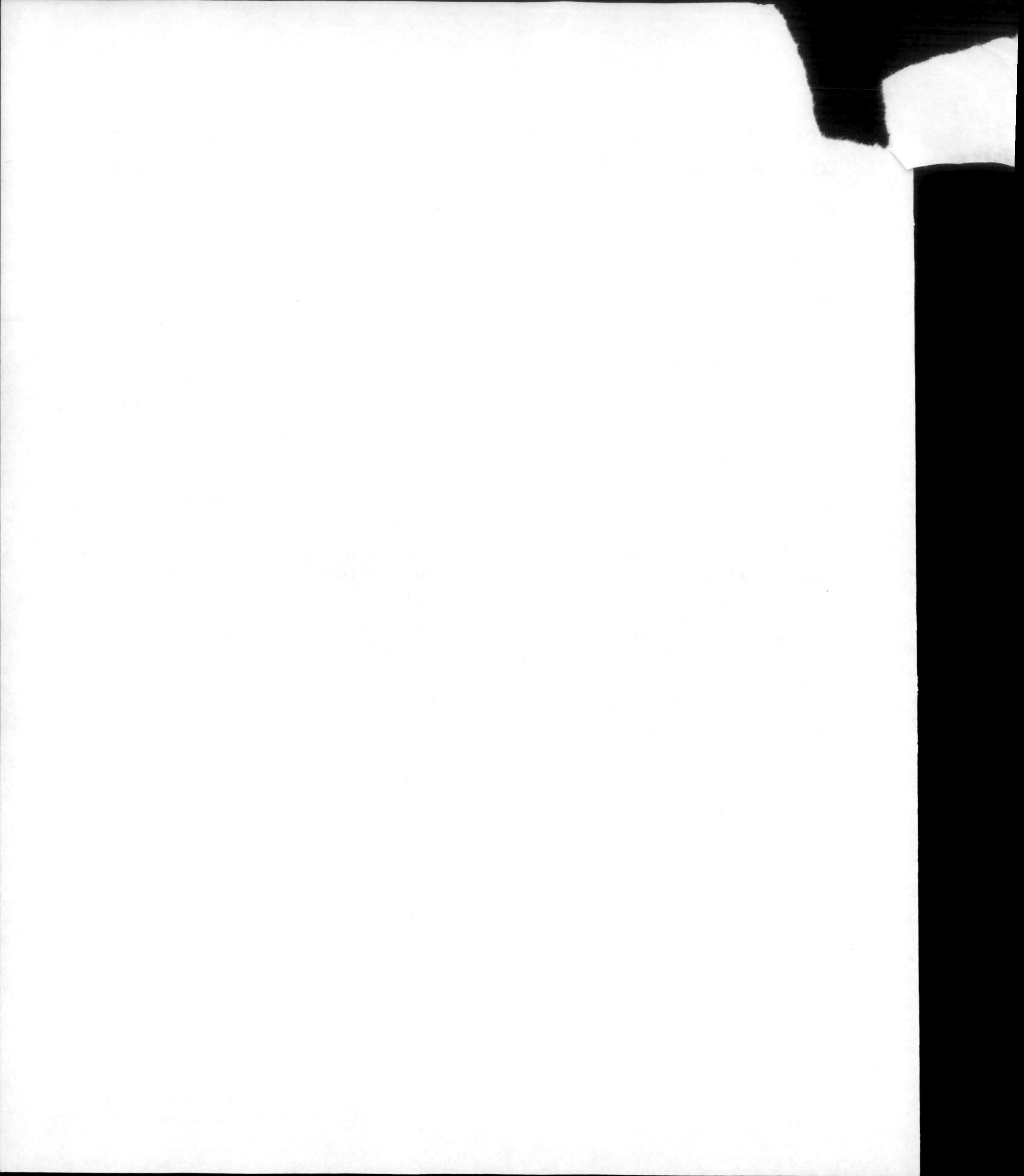

Tables

Tables, *information organized in row and column format, make it easy for readers to quickly get an overview of a topic, as well as analyze details and how they relate to each other.*

Replace detailed text with tables.

133

Tables present information in a format that encourages comparison and retention. Information presented in row-and-column format can be read and understood at a glance. Tables communicate faster and are more concise because you can omit verbs and transitional phrases, permitting readers to focus on important information.

Notice, below, how the table simplifies and visually displays information that must be carefully read and extracted from the text. Notice how the table makes it easy to relate times to events.

A typical week at Morningside Academy begins with morning prayers from 6:00 a.m. until 6:30. Breakfast is served between 6:45 and 7:15, followed by calisthenics from 7:30 to 8:15.

During the week, the first period begins at 8:30 and extends until 9:20. Second period begins at 9:30 and extends until 10:20. A half-hour coffee break extends until 10:50.

Third period begins at 11:00 a.m. and extends until 11:50. Lunch is served beginning at 12:00 noon.

On Saturdays, students are free after a first period lab or discussion group. On Sundays, students enjoy free time after breakfast until services begin at 11:00.

Which example would you prefer reading?

Which makes comparisons easier?

Compare the grayness of the top paragraph with the openness of the same information reformatted into rows and columns.

Morning Activities

Time	Weekday	Saturdays	Sundays
6:00 - 6:30	Prayer	Prayer	Prayer
6:45 - 7:15	Breakfast	Breakfast	Breakfast
7:30 - 8:15	Calisthenics	Calisthenics	
8:30 - 9:20	First period	Lab/Discussion	
9:30 - 10:20	Second period		
10:20 - 10:50	Coffee break		
11:00 - 11:50	Third period		Services
12:00	Lunch	Lunch	Lunch

134 Bottom align column headings.

Avoid trapped white space that emphasizes the differences in height between long and short column headings. Use hard returns to force the first line of short headers down so that the bottoms all of the headers align with each other.

In the example on the top, the shorter headings in the first and second columns create an "unfinished" look and separate the header from the column information.

In the example on the bottom, the headings are bottom aligned and the white space has been pushed above the heading, where it looks purposeful and adds emphasis.

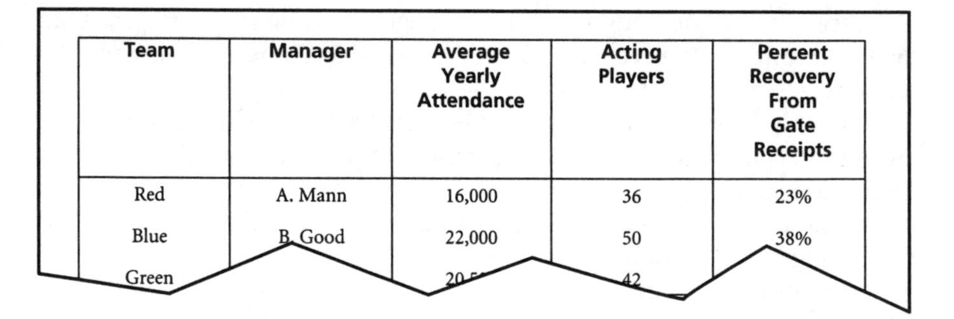

Team	Manager	Average Yearly Attendance	Acting Players	Percent Recovery From Gate Receipts
Red	A. Mann	16,000	36	23%
Blue	B. Good	22,000	50	38%
Green		20,5	42	

Top alignment of headers often traps white space within tables.

Team	Manager	Average Yearly Attendance	Acting Players	Percent Recovery From Gate Receipts
Red	A. Mann	16,000	36	23%
Blue	B. Good	22,000	50	38%
Green		20,5	42	

Bottom alignment unifies the tables.

135

Choose the proper alignment for text.

You can often simplify the appearance of tables by using the proper text alignment. For example, flush-right alignment of the descriptions in the left-hand column "locks" the information to the rest of the table.

Use decimal alignment for cells containing numbers so that the numbers are always aligned with each other, no matter how much the numbers differ.

Notice that centered column headers often don't appear to align with the flush-left material they introduce. When this occurs, reposition the header relative to the information that follows.

Although these alignment differences may appear subtle, their cumulative effect is major, as the examples below illustrate.

Average Achievement

	First String	Second String	Reserves
Metropolitan	1800.250	900.000	250.500
Rural	66.000	180.750	9.1250
Suburban	250.500	1650.500	1000.000
County	14.950	1366.666	875.500
Regional	750.250	480.000	645.140

The top example contains white space trapped between the left-hand row headers and the information they introduce. In addition, the numbers in the following rows do not line up.

Average Achievement

	First String	Second String	Reserves
Metropolitan	1800.250	900.000	250.500
Rural	66.000	180.750	9.125
Suburban	250.500	1650.500	1000.000
County	14.950	1366.666	875.500
Regional	750.250	480.000	645.140

In the bottom example, the row headers are closely aligned to the information they introduce. The table also presents a neater appearance because the numbers are decimal aligned.

136 Reduce the number of rules in and around tables.

Use the minimum number of lines necessary to separate tables from adjacent text and organize the information inside. Often, white space alone is sufficient to separate adjacent categories of information.

Your software program's defaults usually create horizontal and vertical rules of equal weight that surround the table, as well as separate the cells. The clutter caused by these rules often competes with the information contained in the table.

Simplify your tables by removing all but the most important rules. In many cases, a single pair of top and bottom rules are sufficient.

In the top example, the information inside the table is dwarfed by the rules around the table and between the cells.

First & Second Quarter Quotas

	Jan.	Feb.	Mar.	Apr.	May	Jun.
East	135	160	180	175	140	120
West	225	265	260	240	255	232
Midwest	316	390	400	402	425	375
South	85	110	125	180	202	225

The bottom example is both easier to read and presents a more contemporary image.

First & Second Quarter Quotas

	Jan.	Feb.	Mar.	Apr.	May	Jun.
East	135	160	180	175	140	120
West	225	265	260	240	255	232
Midwest	316	390	400	402	425	375
South	85	110	125	180	202	225

Charts and Graphs

Charts and graphs help readers quickly interpret the importance of numbers. A paragraph of numbers, no matter how well written, can rarely communicate relationships, sequences, or trends as effectively as a good chart or graph.

Choose the proper type of chart or graph.

137

Choosing the proper type of visual to illustrate your points is crucial to the success of your visuals. Each type of visual excels at highlighting a different type of information.

Bar and column charts make comparisons easy.

Pie charts dramatize part/whole relationships.

Line charts communicate trends at a glance.

Scatter charts display distribution.

High-low charts communicate ranges.

All the charts and graphs communicate with more impact and fewer words than paragraphs of text containing the same information.

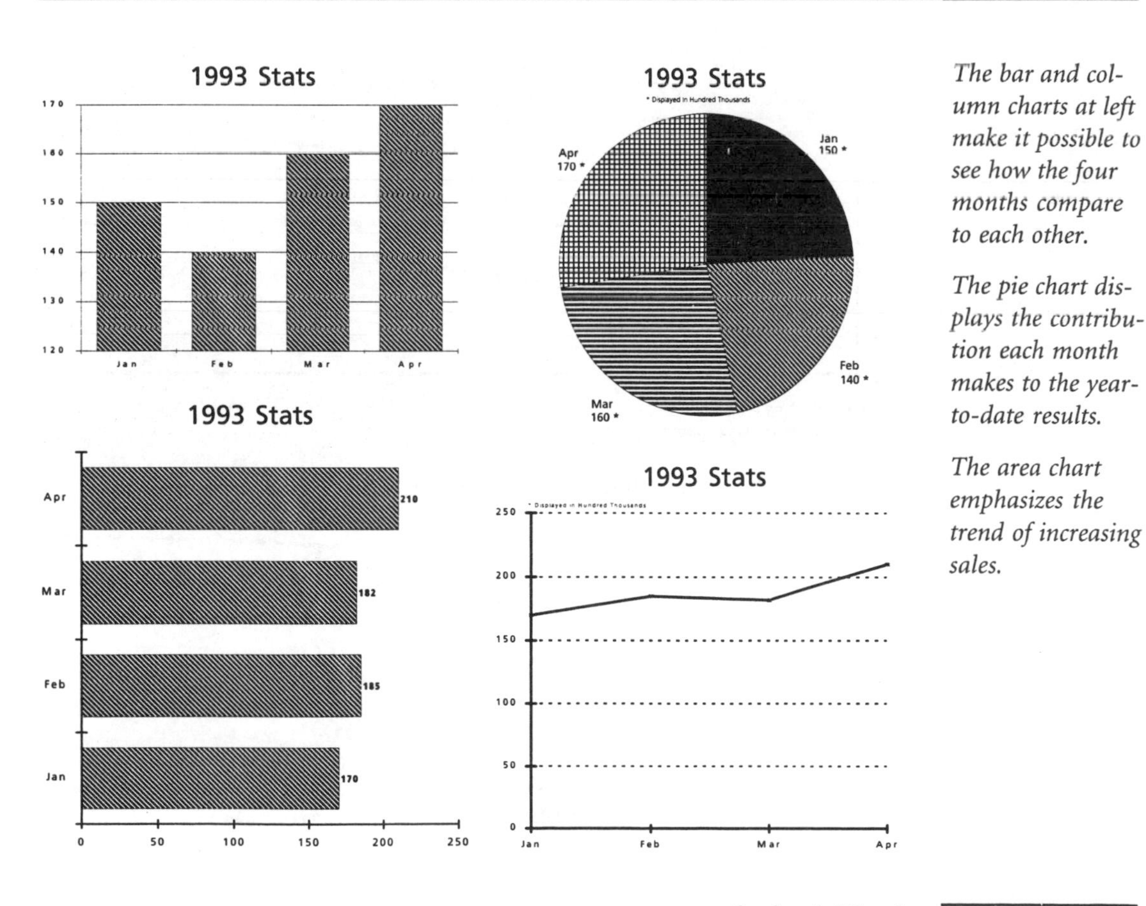

The bar and column charts at left make it possible to see how the four months compare to each other.

The pie chart displays the contribution each month makes to the year-to-date results.

The area chart emphasizes the trend of increasing sales.

138 Use the scale that communicates objectively.

The wrong scale can lead readers to erroneous conclusions. In the top example, sales appear to be increasing dramatically. Yet, this is an illusion caused by the scale used, which begins at 125,000 units.

When total sales are compared, however, as in the bottom example, the actual sales increases are far more modest.

Another way charts and graphs can lead to confusion is when logarithmic scales are used. These amplify differences.

Objectivity requires that you pay as much attention to choosing the scale as you do to entering or importing data into your software.

In the top example, based on truncated charts, sales appear to be growing at a rapid rate.

Yet, when one views sales increases in the context of total sales, as in the bottom example, the sales increases appear far more modest.

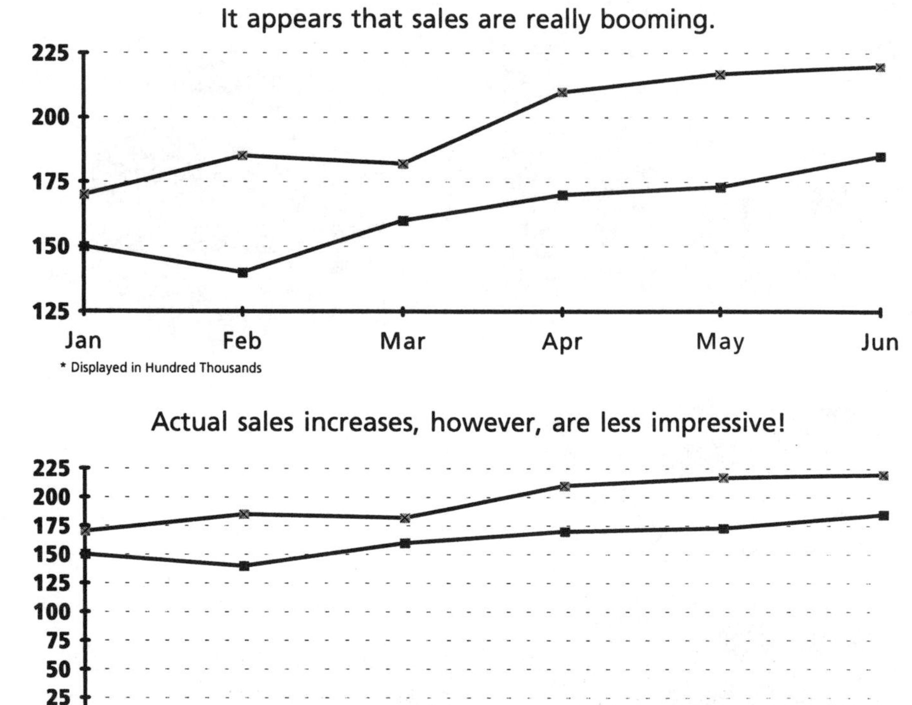

Eliminate unnecessary detail from charts and graphs.

Use only those accents that enhance, or are necessary for communicating, the information or interpretation you want to stress. You can often improve the appearance of charts, for example, by eliminating unnecessary grid lines or tick marks. Often, your software program's defaults add unnecessary background vertical and horizontal lines.

Scale and exact numeric amounts and relations are less important when your point is to emphasize trends, for instance.

Use only those rules absolutely necessary to organize the categories of material.

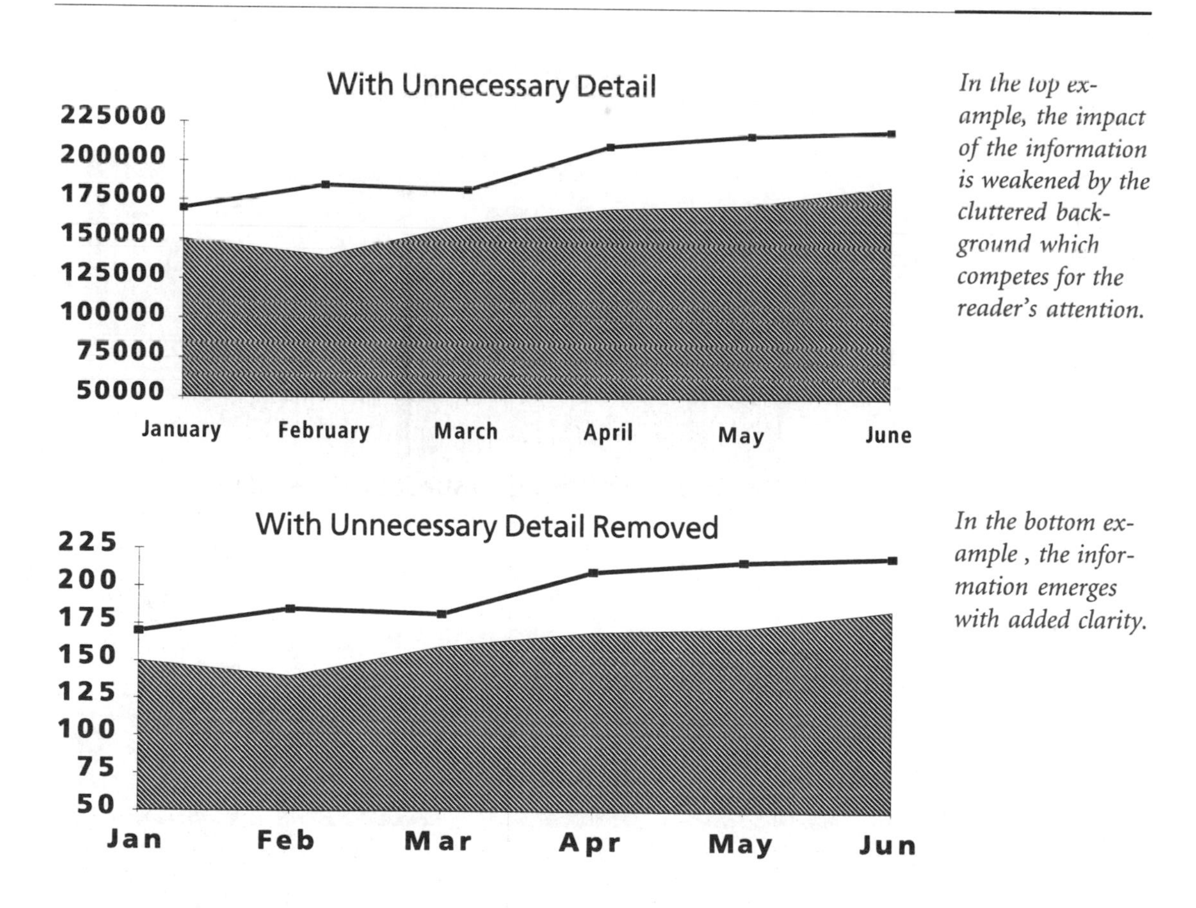

In the top example, the impact of the information is weakened by the cluttered background which competes for the reader's attention.

In the bottom example , the information emerges with added clarity.

140 Provide titles that interpret visuals rather than restate the obvious.

Titles are as important as headlines in encouraging readers to pay attention to the material that follows. Meaningful titles encourage readers to pay attention to your visuals. In addition, titles present you with an opportunity to interpret and reinforce the information contained in the visual, preselling readers on the conclusion you're presenting.

Notice how much less impact the top example has than the bottom example, which contains an interpretive title set in a subject-verb-noun sentence format.

The top example lacks impact because the title only identifies the obvious.

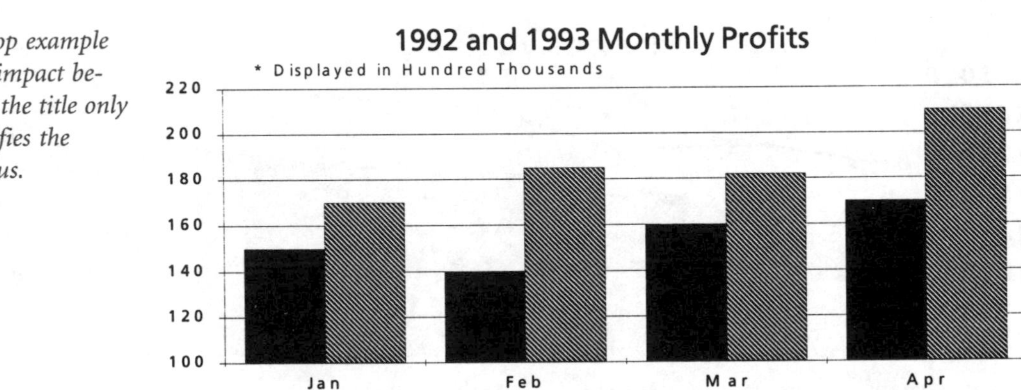

In the bottom example, your attention is directed to the sales increases.

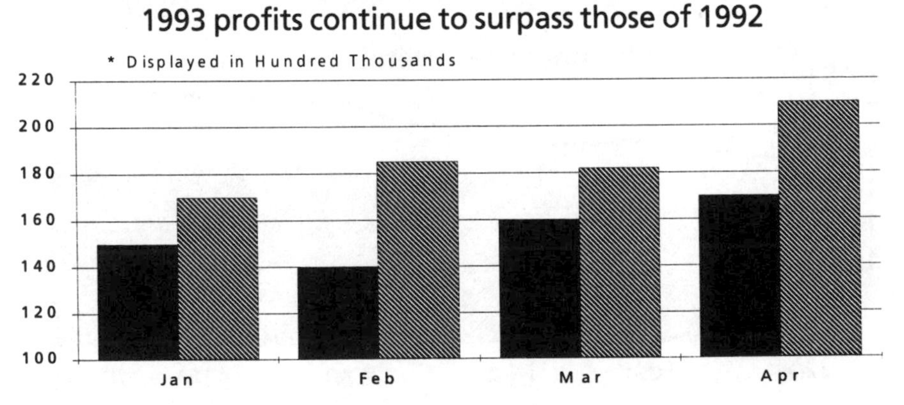

Simplify x-y axis information.

141

Use a minimum number of words and the shortest possible numbers. You can simplify your charts and graphs by rounding off numbers and abbreviating words.

In the top example, the x-axis is cluttered by unnecessarily long numbers. The numbers in the bottom example are shortened by having each number represent 10,000 units.

Likewise, the y-axis is unnecessarily cluttered because the months are spelled out. You can simplify the chart and increase its readability by abbreviating the names of the months and placing them in a larger type size.

Remember to include labels that clearly identify the scale used.

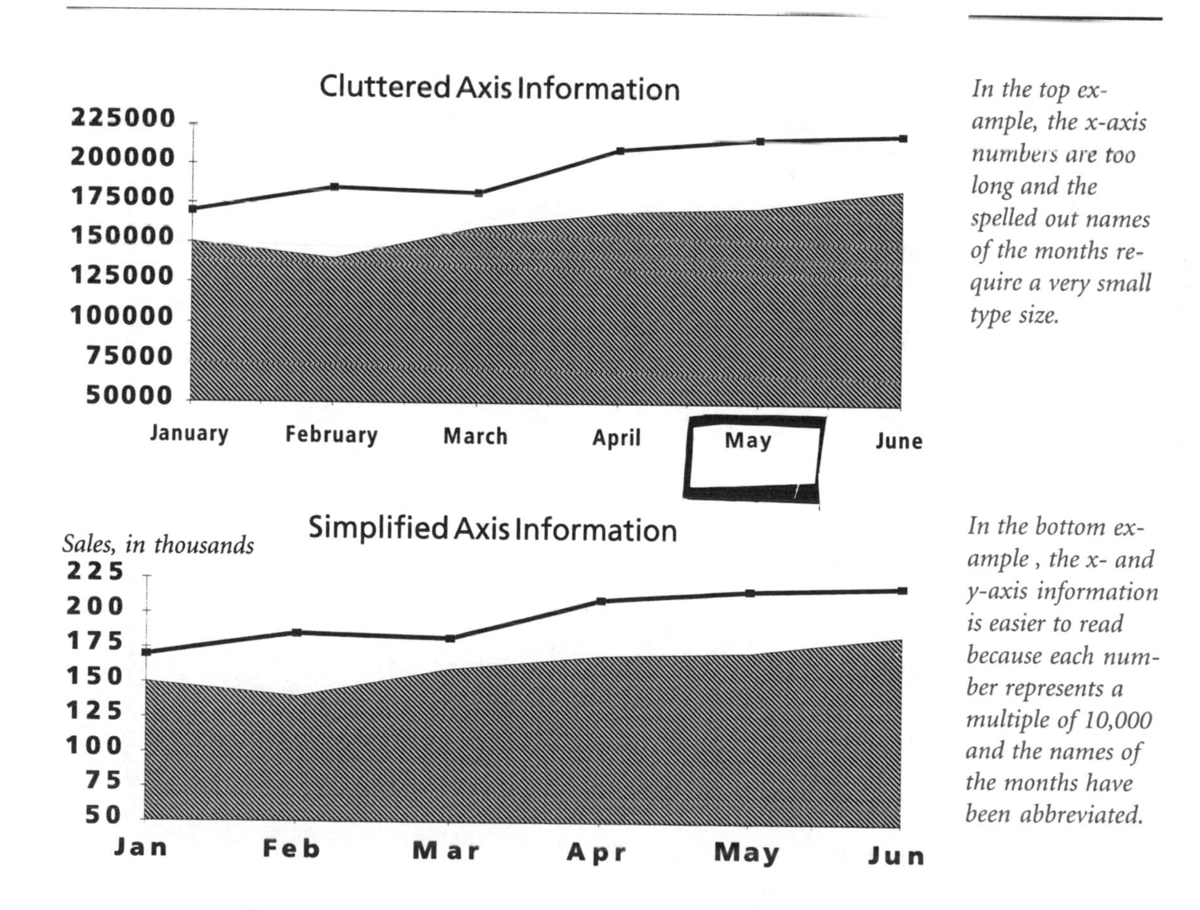

In the top example, the x-axis numbers are too long and the spelled out names of the months require a very small type size.

In the bottom example , the x- and y-axis information is easier to read because each number represents a multiple of 10,000 and the names of the months have been abbreviated.

142 Use area charts to emphasize trends.

Area charts dramatize trends by the visual weight of the filled-in area. Both the line, or "fever" chart and the area chart below communicate the same information. Yet the area chart communicates with far more impact because the trend in the line chart is obscured by the weakness of the line and the competition with the background grid.

In the lower example, things are obviously looking up! The information is communicated with far more impact.

You can enhance the impact of area charts by replacing fill patterns with colors (when two-color printing is available).

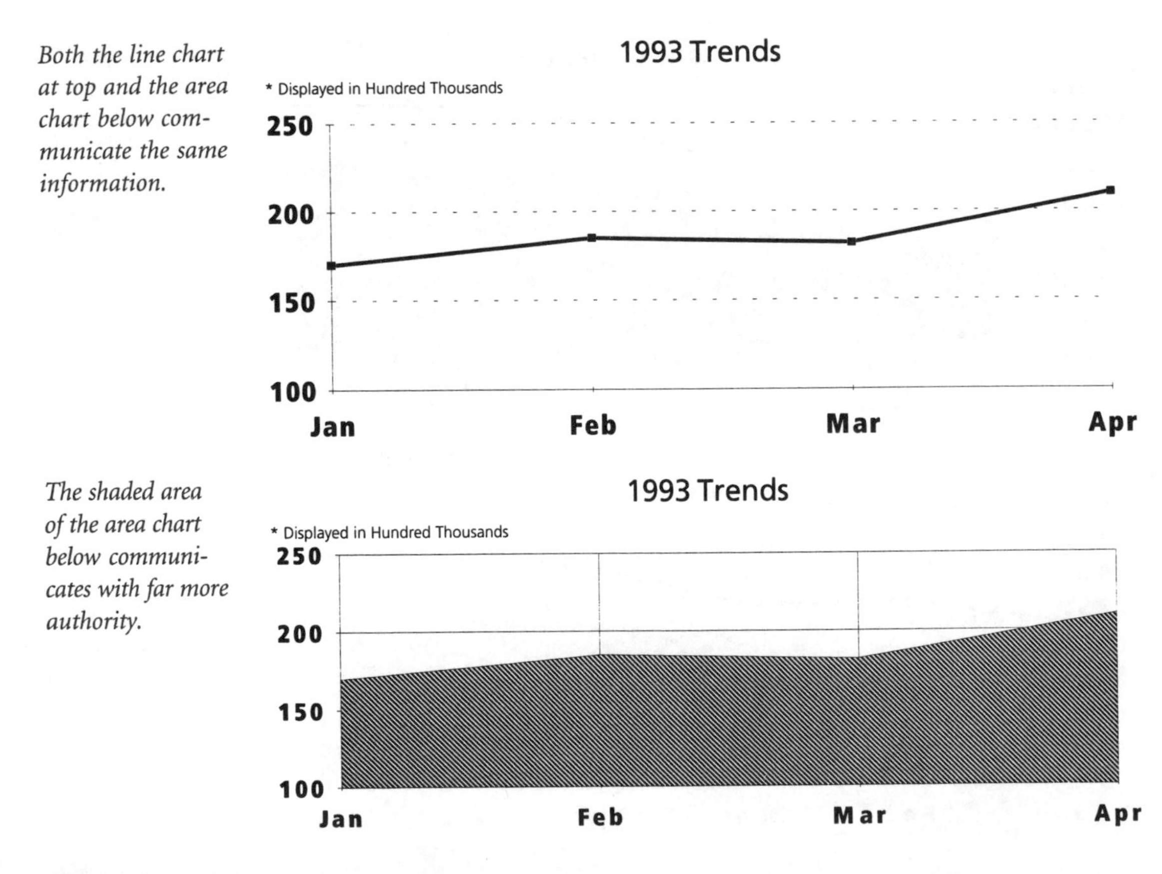

Both the line chart at top and the area chart below communicate the same information.

The shaded area of the area chart below communicates with far more authority.

143

Avoid scattered, small clip art.

A single large illustration is often more effective than several small illustrations randomly placed on a page. Choose the most important illustration and reproduce it large enough to become the dominant visual element, rather than scatter smaller illustrations throughout the page.

Several small illustrations clutter a page rather than create an atmosphere, especially if the smaller illustrations create numerous text wraps. In addition, the resolution, or sharpness, of small illustrations suffers compared to the same illustrations reproduced at a larger size, further detracting from the professional image you want your publication to project.

Christmas Fair

St. Joseph's Church
Saturday, December 1
9:00 AM to 5:00 PM

Come and enjoy crafts,
goodies, and more!

The small illustrations in the example at left clutter the page. The single large illustration in the right-hand example provides a focal point that organizes the page.

Section 6

Graphic Accents

Graphic accents permit you to add selective emphasis to text or visual. Graphic accents play an important role in establishing the unique "look" of your documents.

Use reverses and shaded backgrounds to organize information.

Reverses and shaded backgrounds permit you to add impact to information graphics and tables. Reverses and shaded backgrounds can work together to visually communicate hierarchies of importance.

You can use reverses to emphasize the top levels of an organization chart or crucial decision points in a flow chart. You can use lighter, shaded backgrounds to indicate secondary levels requiring selective emphasis.

Reverses and shaded backgrounds should be used with restraint and with large, simple words set in a bold typeface.

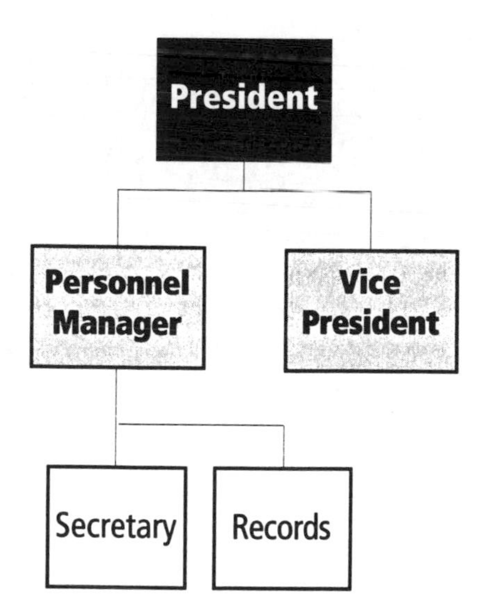

Widgets	5.0	685	49.56	29
Pipes	6.7	544	68.20	51
Nails	4.8	655	89.23	58
Slats	5.2	689	99.29	42
Hoops	3.8	321	62.80	75
Jacks	9.2	848	78.56	59
Caps	9.6	685	79.56	29
Hoists	6.7	544	68.20	51
Chisels	4.8	655	29.30	28
Slats	5.2	389	99.26	42
Meters	3.8	821	72.80	75
Bulbs	9.2	848	88.56	65
Blues	9.2	848	78.56	59
Chems	9.6	685	79.56	29
Violas	6.7	544	68.20	51

Reversed and shaded backgrounds indicate points of primary and secondary emphasis in the organization chart at left.

The alternating shaded backgrounds help organize spreadsheet information without the distraction and barriers that horizontal rules would introduce.

145 Use reversed text with restraint.

Avoid white type against a black background that calls inappropriate or unwanted attention to a relatively unimportant text element. Reverses can be very effective, but can also create visual distractions.

One or two small reversed elements on a page, for example, often draw far more attention than is warranted.

Use reverses strategically to emphasize important information, rather than to emphasize unimportant or obvious information.

Save your reverses for headlines or titles that you want to make the *single dominant element* on a page!

In the left-hand example, the small reversed "Inside" and "Editorial" department heads attract the reader's eye at the expense of the adjacent headline.

In the right-hand example, large reversed text both adds impact to the publication title and separates it from the headline.

Community Investment

Planning Board Begins Hearings

Consectetuer adipiscing elit, sed diam nonummy nibh euismod tincidunt ut laoreet dolore magna aliquam erat volutpat. Ut wisi enim ad minim veniam, quis nostrud exerci tation ullamcorper suscipit lobortis nisl ut aliquip ex ea commodo consequat. Duis autem vel eum iriure dolor in hendrerit tincidunt ut laoreet dolore Nonummy nibh euismod orem ipsum dolor sit amet,

Inside [reversed]

Lorem ipsum dolor sit amet, consectetuer adipiscing elit, sed diam nonummy nibh euismod tincidunt ut laoreet dolore magna aliquam erat volutpat. Ut wisi enim ad minim veniam, quis nostrud exerci tation ullamcorper suscipit lobortis nisl ut aliquip ex ea commodo consequat. Duis autem vel eum iriure dolor in hendrerit

in vulputate velit esse molestie consequat, vel illum dolore eu feugiat nulla facilisis at vero eros et accumsan et iusto odio dignissim qui blandit praesent luptatum

Zzril delenit augue duis dolore te feugait nulla facilisi. Lorem ipsum dolor sit amet, consectetuer adipiscing elit, sed diam nonummy nibh euismod tincidunt ut laoreet dolore magna aliquam erat volutpat.

Ut wisi enim ad minim veniam, quis nostrud exerci tation ullamcoit lobortis nisl ut aliquip ex ea commodo consequat.

Duis autem vel eum iriure dolor in hendrerit in vulputate velit esse molestie consequat, vel illum dolore eu feugiat facilisis at vero

Reros et accumsan et iusto odio dignissim qui blandit praesent luptatum zzril delenit augue duis dolore te Nonummy nibh euismod orem ipsum dolor sit amet,

Editorial [reversed]

Consectetuer adipiscing elit, sed diam nonummy nibh euismod tincidunt ut laoreet dolore magna aliquam erat volutpat. Ut wisi enim ad minim veniam, quis nostrud exerci tation ullamcorper suscipit lobortis nisl ut aliquip ex ea commodo consequat. Duis autem vel eum iriure dolor in hendrerit tincidunt ut laoreet dolore magna aliquam erat volutpat. Ut wisi enim ad minim veniam, quis nostrud exerci tation ullamcorper suscipit lobortis nisl ut aliquip ex ea commodo consequat.

Duis autem vel eum iriure dolor in hendrerit in vulputate velit esse molestie consequat, vel illum dolore eu feugiat nulla facilisis at vero eros et accumsan et iusto odio dignissim qui blandit praesent luptatum zzril delenit augue duis dolore te feugait nulla facilisi. Nam liber tempor cum soluta nihil imperdiet

Community Investment [reversed]

Planning Board Begins Hearings

Consectetuer adipiscing elit, sed diam nonummy nibh euismod tincidunt ut laoreet dolore magna aliquam erat volutpat. Ut wisi enim ad minim veniam, quis nostrud exerci tation ullamcorper suscipit lobortis nisl ut aliquip ex ea commodo consequat. Duis autem vel eum iriure dolor in hendrerit tincidunt ut laoreet dolore Nonummy nibh euismod orem ipsum dolor sit amet,

Inside

Lorem ipsum dolor sit amet, consectetuer adipiscing elit, sed diam nonummy nibh euismod tincidunt ut laoreet dolore magna aliquam erat volutpat. Ut wisi enim ad minim veniam, quis nostrud exerci tation ullamcorper suscipit lobortis nisl ut aliquip ex ea commodo consequat. Duis autem vel eum iriure dolor in hendrerit

in vulputate velit esse molestie consequat, vel illum dolore eu feugiat nulla facilisis at vero eros et accumsan et iusto odio dignissim qui blandit praesent luptatum

Zzril delenit augue duis dolore te feugait nulla facilisi. Lorem ipsum dolor sit amet, consectetuer adipiscing elit, sed diam nonummy nibh euismod tincidunt ut laoreet dolore magna aliquam erat volutpat.

Ut wisi enim ad minim veniam, quis nostrud exerci tation ullamcoit lobortis nisl ut aliquip ex ea commodo consequat.

Duis autem vel eum iriure dolor in hendrerit in vulputate velit esse molestie consequat, vel illum dolore eu feugiat facilisis at vero

Reros et accumsan et iusto odio dignissim qui blandit praesent luptatum zzril delenit augue duis dolore te Nonummy nibh euismod orem ipsum dolor sit amet,

Editorial

Consectetuer adipiscing elit, sed diam nonummy nibh euismod tincidunt ut laoreet dolore magna aliquam erat volutpat. Ut wisi enim ad minim veniam, quis nostrud exerci tation ullamcorper suscipit lobortis nisl ut aliquip ex ea commodo consequat. Duis autem vel eum iriure dolor in hendrerit tincidunt ut laoreet dolore magna aliquam erat volutpat. Ut wisi enim ad minim veniam, quis nostrud exerci tation ullamcorper suscipit lobortis nisl ut aliquip ex ea commodo consequat.

Duis autem vel eum iriure dolor in hendrerit in vulputate velit esse molestie consequat, vel illum dolore eu feugiat nulla facilisis at vero eros et accumsan et iusto odio dignissim qui blandit praesent luptatum zzril delenit augue duis dolore te feugait nulla facilisi. Nam liber tempor cum soluta nihil imperdiet doming id quod mazim placerat facer possim assum.

Replace reversed small serif type with large, bold sans serif type and extra spacing.

Use large, bold sans serif text for reverses. Reversed text is more difficult to read than black letters against a white background, especially small reversed serif text. The serifs tend to get lost in the background, and counters – open spaces within the letters – often fill in.

Whenever possible, use a sans serif typeface when reversing text, especially at small sizes.

Other ways to increase the legibility of reversed text is to use bold type and add additional letterspacing. (You can also set the type a little larger than normal to compensate for the inevitable loss of detail.)

Note: All examples below are set the same size.

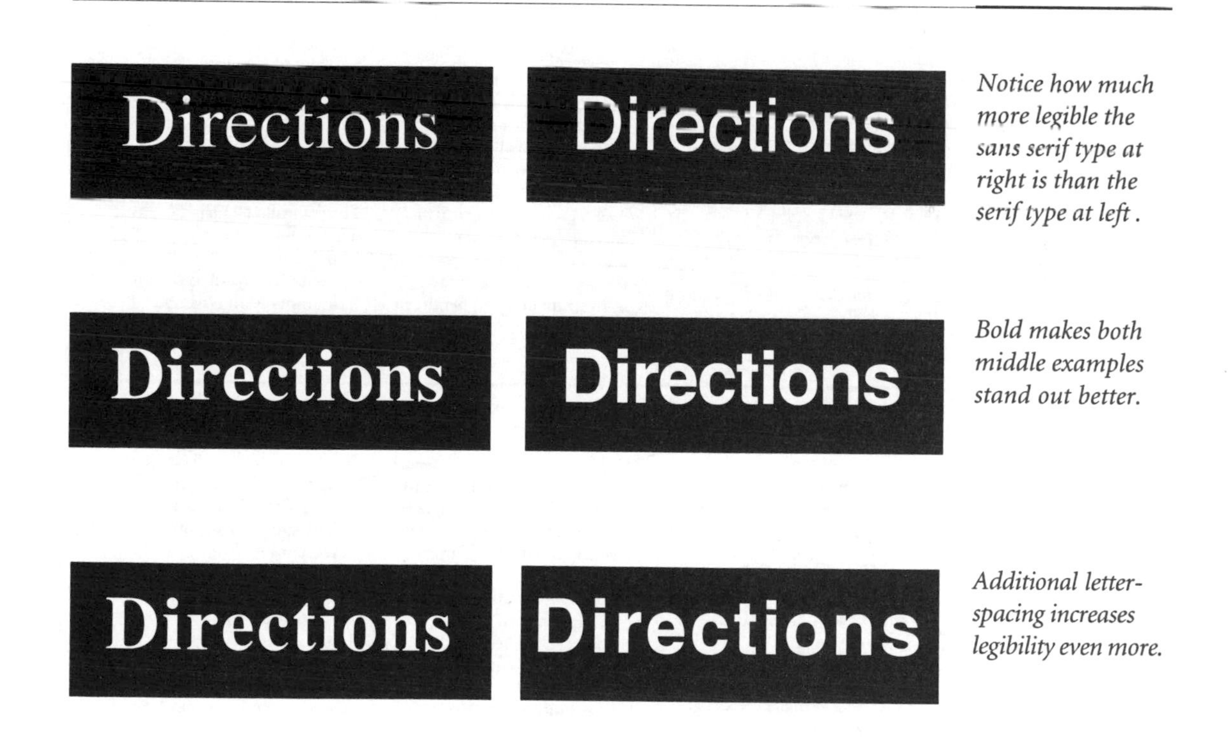

Notice how much more legible the sans serif type at right is than the serif type at left.

Bold makes both middle examples stand out better.

Additional letter-spacing increases legibility even more.

147 Avoid overusing screened or tinted backgrounds.

Legibility and readability depend on maximum foreground/background contrast. Anything that reduces text/background contrast also reduces your reader's ability to decipher letters and words.

Thus, screened backgrounds should be used with restraint. Be especially careful when running type across gray backgrounds. Although the screened background may attract the reader's eyes to a short text element, like a table of contents or sidebar (short article-within-an-article), it will be more difficult to read – exactly opposite the designer's intent!

One way you can compensate for reduced foreground/background contrast is to use a slightly larger type size or a heavier typeface when running type across screened backgrounds.

Reducing foreground/background contrast compromises legibility by making it harder for readers to identify letters, as the top example shows.

Table of Contents

President's Message 2
Secretary's Report 3
Outreach Report 4
Special Report 5
Membership Report 6
Calendar of Events 7

elit, se... nummy nibh euismod tincidunt ut laoreet dolore magna aliquam erat volutpat. Ut wisi enim ad minim veniam, quis nostrud exerci tation ullamcorper suscipit lobortis nisl ut aliquip ex ea commodo consequat. Duis autem vel eum iriure dolor in hendrerit in vulputate velit esse

...nulla ...o eros et accumsan et iusto odio dignissim qui blandit praesent luptatum zzril delenit augue duis dolore te feugait nulla facilisi. Lorem ipsum dolor sit amet, consectetuer.

Adipiscing elit, sed diam nonummy nibh euismod tincidunt ut laoreet dolore

As the bottom example shows, black against white is far easier to read than black type against a gray background.

Table of Contents

President's Message 2
Secretary's Report 3
Outreach Report 4
Special Report 5
Membership Report 6
Calendar of Events 7

elit, se... nummy nibh euismod tincidunt ut laoreet dolore magna aliquam erat volutpat. Ut wisi enim ad minim veniam, quis nostrud exerci tation ullamcorper suscipit lobortis nisl ut aliquip ex ea commodo consequat. Duis autem vel eum iriure dolor in hendrerit in vulputate velit esse

...nulla ...o eros et accumsan et iusto odio dignissim qui blandit praesent luptatum zzril delenit augue duis dolore te feugait nulla facilisi. Lorem ipsum dolor sit amet, consectetuer.

Adipiscing elit, sed diam nonummy nibh euismod tincidunt ut laoreet dolore

Relate the width of graphic accents to adjacent text.

148

Use rules of the same weight as the text they're enhancing when using horizontal rules to amplify a headline or the title of a publication. Rules that reflect the stroke width of adjacent text can help unify the elements, creating added impact on the page.

Conversely, thicker or thinner rules often add clutter rather than the desired emphasis.

The need to match stroke weight to rule weight is especially important with sans serif typefaces, which tend to lack stress, or the thick-to-thin variations typical of serif typefaces.

The top example lacks unity, because the thinner rules appear to be decorative afterthoughts, unconnected to the headline.

Satisfaction guaranteed
or your money back

In the bottom example, rules of the same weight as the type do a better job of reinforcing the headline.

149 Avoid unnecessary boxes and rules.

When reviewing your use of boxes and rules, always ask yourself: "Is this absolutely necessary?" Graphic accents are often added out of habit rather than necessity. Often, better use of white space or stronger typographic contrast does a better job of adding emphasis than do boxes, rules, and screens.

Notice the clutter created by the numerous graphic accents in the left-hand example. Notice how the right-hand example, which uses stronger typographic contrast, projects a simpler, less cluttered image, and yet makes a more professional impression.

Note how white space and typographic contrast used in the right-hand illustration project a more professional image than the cluttered graphic accents in the left-hand illustration.

The clutter created by the many unnecessary rules and boxes in the left-hand example is at odds with a luxury image.

By replacing graphic accents with white space and typographic contrast, the example at right presents a far more upscale image.

LUXURY AUTOMOBILE

Published by the Guild of European Automobile Enthusiasts

NEW MODELS INTRODUCED

Lorem ipsum dolor sit amet, consectetuer adipiscing elit, sed diam nonummy nibh euismod tincidunt ut laoreet dolore magna aliquam erat volutpat. Ut wisi enim ad minim veniam, quis nostrud exerci tation ullamcorper suscipit lobortis nisl ut aliquip ex ea commodo consequat. Duis autem vel eum iriure dolor in hendrerit in vulputate velit esse molestie consequat, vel illum dolore eu feugiat nulla facilisis at vero eros et dignissim qui blandit praesent luptatum zzril delenit augue duis dolore te feugait nulla facilisi. Lorem ipsum dolor sit amet, consectetuer adipiscing elit, sed diam nonummy nibh euismod tincidunt ut laoreet dolore magna aliquam erat volutpat.

Ut wisi enim ad minim veniam, quis nostrud exerci tation ullamcoit lobortis nisl ut aliquip ex ea commodo consequat.

Duis autem vel eum iriure dolor in hendrerit in vulputate velit esse molestie consequat, vel illum dolore eu feugiat facilisis at vero eros et accumsan et iusto odio dignissim qui blandit praesent luptatum zzril delenit augue duis dolore te feugait nulla facilisi.

Nam liber tempor cum soluta nobis eleifend option congue nihil imperdiet doming id adipiscing elit, sed diam nonummy nibh euismod tincidunt ut laoreet dolore magna aliquam erat volutpat. Ut wisi enim ad minim veniam, quis nostrud exerci tation ullamcorper suscipit lobortis nisl ut aliquip ex ea commodo consequat.

Duis autem vel eum iriure dolor in hendrerit in voole.

TO LEASE OR BUY?

Consequat vel illum dolore eu feugiat nulla facilisis at vero eros et accumsan et iusto odio dignissim qui blandit praesent luptatum zzril delenit augue duis dolore te feugait nulla facilisi.

Nam liber tempor cum soluta nobis eleifend option congue nihil imperdiet doming id quod mazim placerat facer possim assum.

INSIDE

Fall Rally Program Announced	2
Engineering Changes In England	4
New Generation German Cars Announced	5
Swedes Build Ultimate Safety Car	8
Foreign Investment - Pros and Cons	9

Volume 3, Number 4 July, 1994

LUXURY AUTOMOBILE

Published by the Guild of European Automobile Enthusiasts

NEW MODELS INTRODUCED

Lorem ipsum dolor sit amet, consectetuer adipiscing elit, sed diam nonummy nibh euismod tincidunt ut laoreet dolore magna aliquam erat volutpat. Ut wisi enim ad minim veniam, quis nostrud exerci tation ullamcorper suscipit lobortis nisl ut aliquip ex ea commodo consequat. Duis autem vel eum iriure dolor in hendrerit in vulputate velit esse molestie consequat, vel illum dolore eu feugiat nulla facilisis at vero eros et dignissim qui blandit praesent luptatum zzril delenit augue duis dolore te feugait nulla facilisi. Lorem ipsum dolor sit amet, consectetuer adipiscing elit, sed diam nonummy nibh euismod tincidunt ut laoreet dolore magna aliquam erat volutpat.

Ut wisi enim ad minim veniam, quis nostrud exerci tation ullamcoit lobortis nisl ut aliquip ex ea commodo consequat.

Duis autem vel eum iriure dolor in hendrerit in vulputate velit esse molestie consequat, vel illum dolore eu feugiat facilisis at vero eros et accumsan et iusto odio dignissim qui blandit praesent luptatum zzril delenit augue duis dolore te feugait nulla facilisi.

Nam liber tempor cum soluta nobis eleifend option congue nihil imperdiet doming id adipiscing elit, sed diam nonummy nibh euismod tincidunt ut laoreet dolore magna aliquam erat volutpat. Ut wisi enim ad minim veniam, quis nostrud exerci tation ullamcorper suscipit lobortis nisl ut aliquip ex ea commodo consequat.

Duis autem vel eum iriure dolor in hendrerit in voole. ☆

TO LEASE OR BUY?

Consequat vel illum dolore eu feugiat nulla facilisis at vero eros et accumsan et iusto odio dignissim qui blandit praesent luptatum zzril delenit augue duis dolore te feugait nulla facilisi.

Nam liber tempor cum soluta nobis eleifend option congue nihil doming id quod mazim placerat facer possim assum. ☆

INSIDE

Fall Rally Program Announced	2
Engineering Changes In England	4
New Generation German Cars Announced	5
Swedes Build Ultimate Safety Car	8
Foreign Investment - Pros and Cons	9

Volume 3, Number 4 July, 1994

Use bleeds to avoid unwanted borders. 150

Bleeds refer to text or graphic elements that extend to the physical borders, or trim size, of a page. Although they increase printing costs, bleeds add impact and character to your pages. Here are three reasons to consider adding bleeds to your pages:

Photographs that bleed to the edges of a page appear larger than adjacent text or graphics.

Horizontal rules that extend to the edges of a page often make the page appear wider than it actually is.

A bleed behind a *newsletter nameplate* eliminates an unwanted white border around the nameplate.

Although they increase printing costs, bleeds are often well worth the additional expense.

Community Investment

Planning Board Begins Hearings

Consectetuer adipiscing elit, sed diam nonummy nibh euismod tincidunt ut laoreet dolore magna aliquam erat volutpat. Ut wisi enim ad minim veniam, quis nostrud exerci tation ullamcorper suscipit lobortis nisl ut aliquip ex ea commodo consequat. Duis autem vel eum iriure dolor in hendrerit tincidunt ut laoreet dolore Nonummy nibh euismod orem ipsum dolor sit amet,

Inside

Lorem ipsum dolor sit amet, consectetuer adipiscing elit, sed diam nonummy nibh euismod tincidunt ut laoreet dolore magna aliquam erat volutpat. Ut wisi enim ad minim veniam, quis nostrud exerci tation ullamcorper suscipit lobortis nisl ut aliquip ex ea commodo consequat. Duis autem vel eum iriure dolor in hendrerit

in vulputate velit esse molestie consequat, vel illum dolore eu feugiat nulla facilisis at vero eros et accumsan et iusto odio dignissim qui blandit praesent luptatum

Zzril delenit augue duis dolore te feugait nulla facilisi. Lorem ipsum dolor sit amet, consectetuer adipiscing elit, sed diam nonummy nibh euismod tincidunt ut laoreet dolore magna aliquam erat volutpat.

Ut wisi enim ad minim veniam, quis nostrud exerci tation ullamcoit lobortis nisl ut aliquip ex ea commodo consequat.

Duis autem vel eum iriure dolor in hendrerit in vulputate velit esse molestie consequat, vel illum dolore eu feugiat facilisis at vero

Reros et accumsan et iusto odio dignissim qui blandit praesent luptatum zzril delenit augue duis dolore te Nonummy nibh euismod orem ipsum dolor sit amet,

Editorial

Consectetuer adipiscing elit, sed diam nonummy nibh euismod tincidunt ut laoreet dolore magna aliquam erat volutpat. Ut wisi enim ad minim veniam, quis nostrud exerci tation ullamcorper suscipit lobortis nisl ut aliquip ex ea commodo consequat. Duis autem vel eum iriure dolor in hendrerit tincidunt ut laoreet dolore magna aliquam erat volutpat. Ut wisi enim ad minim veniam, quis nostrud exerci tation ullamcorper suscipit lobortis nisl ut aliquip ex ea commodo consequat.

Duis autem vel eum iriure dolor in hendrerit in vulputate velit esse molestie consequat, vel illum dolore eu feugiat nulla facilisis at vero eros et accumsan et iusto odio dignissim qui blandit praesent luptatum zzril delenit augue duis dolore te feugait nulla facilisi. Nam liber tempor cum soluta nihil imperdiet doming id quod mazim placerat facer possim assum.

Community Investment

Planning Board Begins Hearings

Consectetuer adipiscing elit, sed diam nonummy nibh euismod tincidunt ut laoreet dolore magna aliquam erat volutpat. Ut wisi enim ad minim veniam, quis nostrud exerci tation ullamcorper suscipit lobortis nisl ut aliquip ex ea commodo consequat. Duis autem vel eum iriure dolor in hendrerit tincidunt ut laoreet dolore Nonummy nibh euismod orem ipsum dolor sit amet,

Inside

Lorem ipsum dolor sit amet, consectetuer adipiscing elit, sed diam nonummy nibh euismod tincidunt ut laoreet dolore magna aliquam erat volutpat. Ut wisi enim ad minim veniam, quis nostrud exerci tation ullamcorper suscipit lobortis nisl ut aliquip ex ea commodo consequat. Duis autem vel eum iriure dolor in hendrerit

in vulputate velit esse molestie consequat, vel illum dolore eu feugiat nulla facilisis at vero eros et accumsan et iusto odio dignissim qui blandit praesent luptatum

Zzril delenit augue duis dolore te feugait nulla facilisi. Lorem ipsum dolor sit amet, consectetuer adipiscing elit, sed diam nonummy nibh euismod tincidunt ut laoreet dolore magna aliquam erat volutpat.

Ut wisi enim ad minim veniam, quis nostrud exerci tation ullamcoit lobortis nisl ut aliquip ex ea commodo consequat.

Duis autem vel eum iriure dolor in hendrerit in vulputate velit esse molestie consequat, vel illum dolore eu feugiat facilisis at vero

Reros et accumsan et iusto odio dignissim qui blandit praesent luptatum zzril delenit augue duis dolore te Nonummy nibh euismod orem ipsum dolor sit amet,

Editorial

Consectetuer adipiscing elit, sed diam nonummy nibh euismod tincidunt ut laoreet dolore magna aliquam erat volutpat. Ut wisi enim ad minim veniam, quis nostrud exerci tation ullamcorper suscipit lobortis nisl ut aliquip ex ea commodo consequat. Duis autem vel eum iriure dolor in hendrerit tincidunt ut laoreet dolore magna aliquam erat volutpat. Ut wisi enim ad minim veniam, quis nostrud exerci tation ullamcorper suscipit lobortis nisl ut aliquip ex ea commodo consequat.

Duis autem vel eum iriure dolor in hendrerit in vulputate velit esse molestie consequat, vel illum dolore eu feugiat nulla facilisis at vero eros et accumsan et iusto odio dignissim qui blandit praesent luptatum zzril delenit augue duis dolore te feugait nulla facilisi. Nam liber tempor cum soluta nihil imperdiet doming id quod mazim placerat facer possim assum.

In the example at left, the white frame around the nameplate diminishes the impact of the title.

The lack of the distracting white border in the right-hand example adds impact to the title.

Section 7
Color

Color permits you to add a new dimension of communicating power to your documents. Color refers to your choice of both ink and paper, and it operates on several levels. Your readers will immediately and subconsciously react to your color choices.

Replace scattered color with concentrated color.

151

To be effective, color must be concentrated in a few large areas. Small isolated areas set in color – like isolated text or subheads – actually become harder to read and have less impact than when they are not set in color, exactly the opposite effect as desired.

Likewise, when set in color, thin lines – like vertical rules between columns – and graphic accents – like end-of-story symbols – become visual distractions rather than strong design statements.

Color, like white space, is effective to the extent that it is concentrated, not scattered over a page. Large white letters reversed against a red background stand out far better than small red letters against a white background.

Compare the effective reversed nameplate in the example on the left with the "lost" color in the vertical rules and subheads to the right.

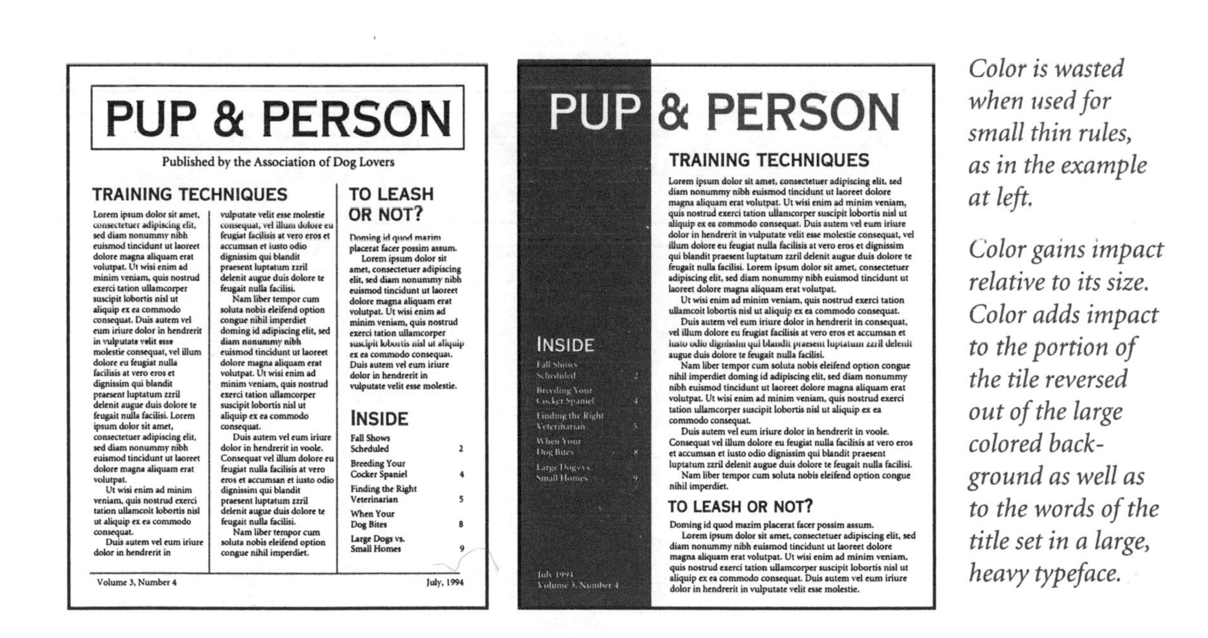

Color is wasted when used for small thin rules, as in the example at left.

Color gains impact relative to its size. Color adds impact to the portion of the tile reversed out of the large colored background as well as to the words of the title set in a large, heavy typeface.

152 Use two-color printing to emphasize the most important word in a headline or title.

Use color to emphasize the most important word in a headline or title. There are three ways you can do this:

You can run the most important word in a second color. This is especially true if you are using a large, bold, or heavy sans serif typeface. This technique is especially strong if the word is short, or you are using an acronym for a title.

You can also reverse the most important word out of a colored background. Again, this works best if you are using a bold sans serif typeface, or a short serif typeface at a large size.

A final option is to use an outline typeface, either a special typeface design or one you create using a drawing program. You can color the outline of the words and run the words against a black (reversed) or gray (screened) background.

When both words are set in red, as in the top example, neither emerges with impact.

But, in the lower example, when red is contrasted with black, the red gains far more impact.

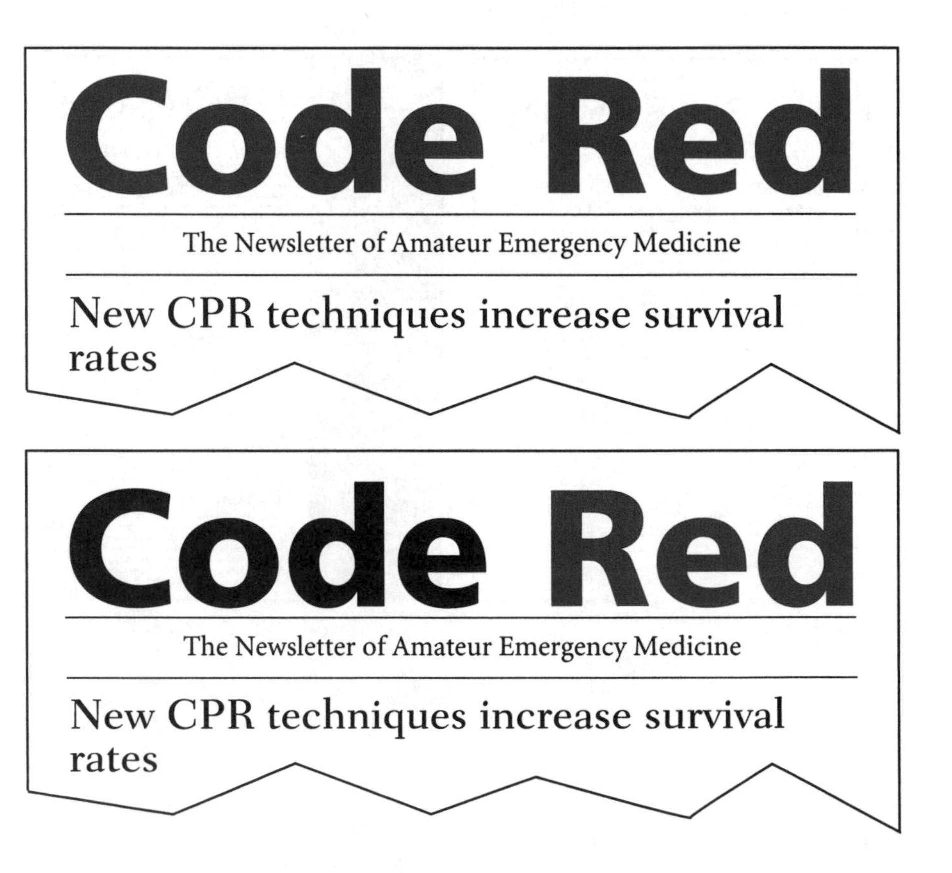

Use color to identify and unify publication segments.

153

Color makes it easy for readers to locate desired sections of long publications. When preparing long documents like training materials, you can make it easy for readers to locate a particular section by running the second color as a vertical bleed along the outside border of each page in that part.

Then, just as color makes it easy to locate the Yellow Pages of your telephone book, readers can quickly identify categories of information, like pre- or post-installation recommendations and troubleshooting.

To work, however, the colors must appear on a significant number of pages.

Set-up

Lorem ipsum dolor sit amet, consectetuer adipiscing elit, sed diam nonummy nibh euismod tincidunt ut laoreet dolore magna aliquam erat volutpat. Ut wisi enim ad minim veniam, quis nostrud exerci tation ullamcorper suscipit lobortis nisl ut aliquip ex ea commodo consequat.

Duis autem vel eum iriure dolor in hendrerit

In vulputate velit esse molestie consequat, vel illum dolore eu feugiat nulla facilisis at vero eros et accumsan et iusto odio dignissim qui blandit praesent luptatum zzril delenit augue duis dolore te feugait nulla facilisi. Lorem ipsum dolor sit amet, consectetuer adipiscing elit, sed diam nonummy nibh euismod tincidunt ut laoreet dolore magna aliquam erat volutpat. Ut wisi enim ad minim veniam, quis nostrud exerci tation ullamcorper suscipit lobortis nisl ut aliquip ex ea commodo consequat.

Duis autem vel eum iriure eros et accumsan

Et iusto odio dolore te feugait nulla facilisi. Nam liber tempor cum soluta nobis eleifend option congue nihil imperdiet doming id quod mazim placerat facer possim assum.

Lorem ipsum dolor sit amet

Lorem ipsum dolor sit amet, consectetuer adipiscing elit, sed diam nonummy nibh euismod tincidunt ut laoreet dolore magna aliquam erat volutpat. Ut wisi enim ad minim veniam, quis nostrud exerci tation ullamcorper suscipit lobortis nisl ut aliquip ex ea commodo consequat.

59

Set up

Operation

Lorem ipsum dolor sit amet, consectetuer adipiscing elit, sed diam nonummy nibh euismod tincidunt ut laoreet dolore magna aliquam erat volutpat. Ut wisi enim ad minim veniam, quis nostrud exerci tation velit esse molestie consequat, vel illum.

Vel eum iriure dolor in hendrerit zzril delenit augue duis

Vel illum dolore eu feugiat nulla facilisis at vero eros et accumsan et iusto odio dignissim qui blandit praesent luptatum zzril delenit augue duis dolore te feugait nulla facilisi. Lorem ipsum dolor sit amet, consectetuer adipiscing elit, sed diam nonummy nibh euismod tincidunt ut laoreet dolore magna aliquam erat volutpat.

Iriure eros et accumsan

Et iusto odio dolore te feugait nulla facilisi. Nam liber tempor cum soluta nobis eleifend option congue nihil imperdiet doming id quod mazim placerat facer possim assum.

Ipsum dolor sit amet augue duis

Lorem ipsum dolor sit amet, consectetuer adipiscing elit, sed diam nonummy nibh euismod tincidunt ut laoreet dolore magna aliquam erat volutpat. Ut wisi enim ad minim veniam, quis nostrud exerci tation ullamcorper suscipit lobortis nisl ut aliquip ex ea commodo consequat. Duis autem vel eum iriure dolor in hendrerit in vulputate

97

Operation

Maintenance

Lorem ipsum dolor sit amet, consectetuer adipiscing elit, sed diam nonummy nibh euismod tincidunt ut laoreet dolore magna aliquam erat volutpat. Ut wisi enim ad minim veniam, quis nostrud exerci tation.

Vel eum iriure dolor in hendrerit

In vulputate velit esse molestie consequat, vel illum dolore eu feugiat nulla facilisis at vero eros et accumsan et iusto odio dignissim qui blandit praesent luptatum zzril delenit augue duis dolore te feugait nulla facilisi. Lorem ipsum dolor sit amet, consectetuer adipiscing elit, sed diam nonummy nibh euismod tincidunt ut laoreet dolore magna aliquam erat volutpat.

Autem vel eum iriure eros et accumsan

Et iusto odio dolore te feugait nulla facilisi. Nam liber tempor cum soluta nobis eleifend option congue nihil imperdiet doming id quod mazim placerat facer possim assum.

Ipsum dolor sit amet

Lorem ipsum dolor sit amet, consectetuer adipiscing elit, sed diam nonummy nibh euismod tincidunt ut laoreet dolore magna aliquam erat volutpat. Ut wisi enim ad minim veniam, quis nostrud exerci tation ullamcorper suscipit lobortis nisl ut aliquip ex ea commodo consequat. Duis autem vel eum iriure dolor in hendrerit in vulputate velit esse molestie consequat, vel illum dolore eu feugiat

133

Maintenance

Options

Lorem ipsum dolor sit amet, consectetuer adipiscing elit, sed diam nonummy nibh euismod tincidunt ut laoreet dolore magna aliquam erat volutpat. Ut wisi enim ad minim veniam, quis nostrud exerci tation.

Dolor in hendrerit vel eum iriure

In vulputate velit esse molestie consequat, vel illum dolore eu feugiat nulla facilisis at vero eros et accumsan et iusto odio dignissim qui blandit praesent luptatum zzril delenit augue duis dolore te feugait nulla facilisi. Lorem ipsum dolor sit amet, consectetuer adipiscing elit, sed diam.

Vel autem eum iriure eros

Et iusto odio dolore te feugait nulla facilisi. Nam liber tempor cum soluta nobis eleifend option congue nihil imperdiet doming id quod mazim placerat facer possim assum.

Ipsum dolor sit amet vel ipsum consect

Lorem ipsum dolor sit amet, consectetuer adipiscing elit, sed diam nonummy nibh euismod tincidunt ut laoreet dolore magna aliquam erat volutpat. Ut wisi enim ad minim veniam, quis nostrud exerci tation ullamcorper suscipit lobortis nisl ut aliquip ex ea commodo consequat. Duis autem vel eum iriure dolor in hendrerit in vulputate velit esse molestie consequat, vel illum dolore eu feugiat nulla facilisis at vero eros et accumsan et iusto odio dignissim qui blandit praesent luptatum zzril delenit

155

Options

Thick vertical bars along the edge of each page help readers quickly locate desired sections of the publication.

154 Use color to highlight important information.

Color draws attention to important information, such as recommendations, warnings, or conclusions. Here are five ways you can use color to highlight important information:

When using a bold sans serif typeface, set important text in a colored background. When using a serif typeface, place the text below thick colored accents – like horizontal rules.

Reproduce symbols in color to draw attention to adjacent important information.

Use a background tint behind every other entry, or every five entries, to help readers keep their place in long tables.

Draw your reader's attention to the "totals" section of spreadsheets by reversing the text out of a colored background.

Use color to emphasize the most important segment of a chart or graph.

It's impossible to overlook the most important days of the month when the dates are reversed out of a colored background.

September

Monday	Tuesday	Wednesday	Thursday	Friday	Saturday	Sunday
		1	2	3	4 **Glee Club Recital**	5
Founder's Day	7 **Faculty Tea for Honor Students**	8	9	10 **Fraternity Open Houses**	11	12
13	14 **European Exchange Tea**	15	16	17	**Parents'**	**Weekend**
Parents' Weekend	21 **Pep rally and bonfire**	**Football Game**	23	24	25 **Theatre Showcase opens**	26
27	28 **Faculty retreat**	29	**Alumni Brunch**			

Use color to "code" each issue of your publication.

You can make every issue of your newsletter visually distinctive by using a different second color for the nameplate, as well as for graphic accents such as borders and end-of-story symbols. Inside the newsletter, you can repeat this second color to reinforce further the unique identity of each issue.

You can use the second color to highlight end-of-story symbols, the nameplate or title if it is repeated at reduced size on each page. You can also use the second color to highlight photographs, charts, graphs, or rules used in tables.

Color coding is especially important if your publication is likely to be saved or referred back to in the future.

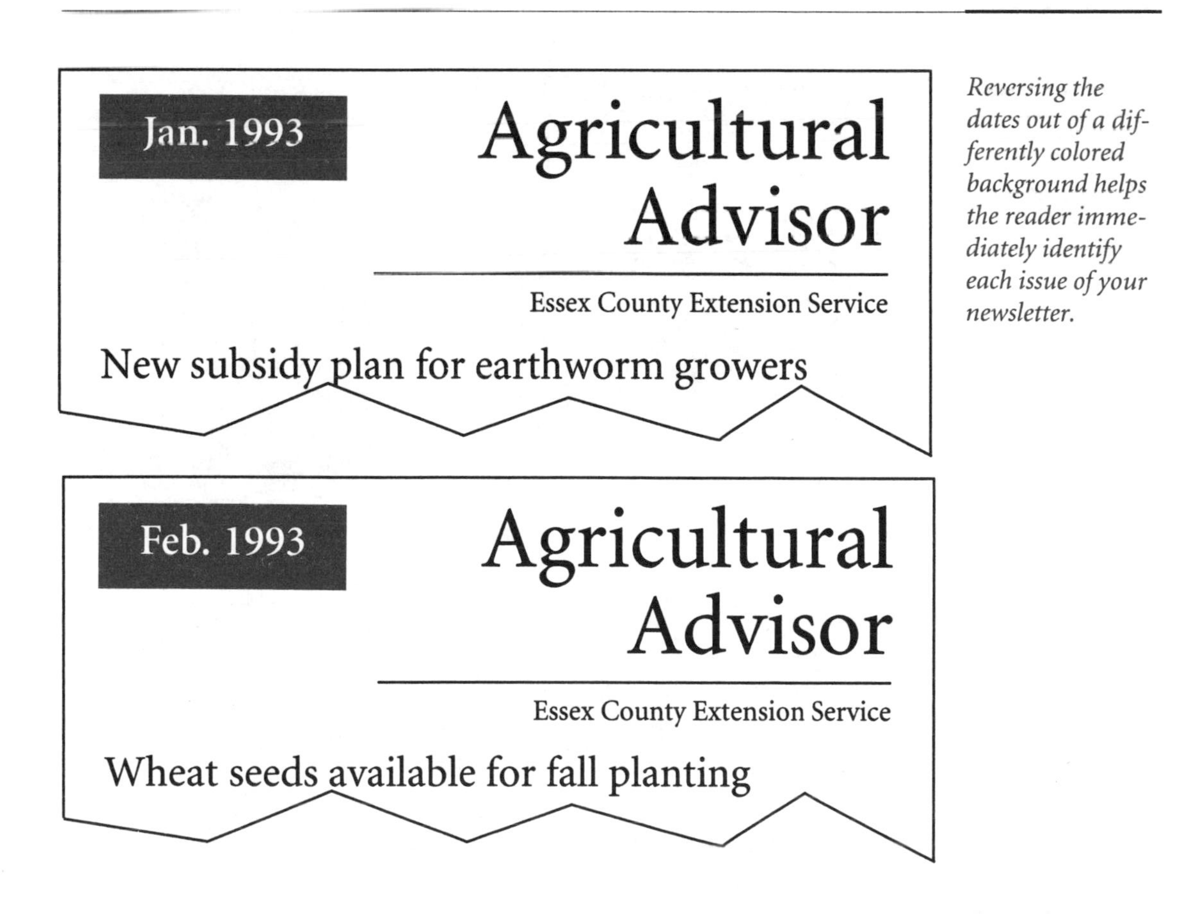

Reversing the dates out of a differently colored background helps the reader immediately identify each issue of your newsletter.

156 Choose colors with the desired visual impact and appropriate emotional messages.

You can use colors to communicate with readers on an overt visual level and on a subliminal level. Light colors, like yellow, advance or move forward (become more noticeable), while cooler colors, like blues and greens, recede (attract less attention). Thus, the same visual element can have more or less visual impact depending on its color.

Color also operates on a psychological level. Each color carries its own associations. Browns and greens have "outdoor" or "natural" connotations; reds have negative associations for accountants and bankers.

Always choose color with an eye to its impact on the page, as well as its desired emotional response.

Colors carry strong emotional messages. Don't end up like this poor art director!

Set colored text bolder and larger than black text.

Always compensate for the reduced foreground/background contrast of text set in color. Text set in color is characterized by reduced legibility. Italicized text – frequently used as in subheads – is especially difficult to read when run in color and set in the same size as adjacent text.

If you do decide to set text in color, either increase the type size or use bold type. The added stroke thickness compensates for the weakened contrast caused by the color.

If you want to use color to emphasize subheads, as an alternative to running subhead text in color, consider running black subheads under horizontal rules set in a second color. Or set the subheads in a larger, bold sans serif typeface reversed out of a colored background.

Lorem ipsum dolor

Sit amet, consectetuer adipiscing elit, sed diam nonummy nibh euismod tincidunt ut laoreet dolore magna aliquam erat.

Lorem ipsum dolor

Sit amet, consectetuer adipiscing elit, sed diam nonummy nibh euismod tincidunt ut laoreet dolore magna aliquam erat.

Lorem ipsum dolor

Sit amet, consectetuer adipiscing elit, sed diam nonummy nibh euismod tincidunt ut laoreet dolore magna aliquam erat.

Lorem ipsum dolor

Sit amet, consectetuer adipiscing elit, sed diam nonummy nibh euismod tincidunt ut laoreet dolore magna aliquam erat.

Subheads set in color are often less prominent than when set in black, as the first and second examples show.

You can compensate by using a bolder or heavier typeface or switching to a sans serif typeface (bottom two examples).

158 Use care when screening or tinting color.

Color quickly loses its impact when screened or run at less than full strength. Bright colors – like red –that are strong and vibrant when run at full strength, become much weaker when screened. Likewise, screened blues, yellows, and greens quickly disappear, or become weak and lose their impact.

Although screened colors can be attractive when deliberately employed, screened colors can cause your document to project an "undecided" – or even physically unsettling – image.

Be especially careful when adding tints to colors behind newsletter mastheads, pull-quotes, or sidebars – short article segments isolated and run parallel to the main article.

A great deal of trial-and-error testing may be needed to arrive at a background screen strong enough to attract attention yet not interfere with the foreground/background contrast needed for easy reading.

Colors rapidly lose their impact when screened, as the sign to the right illustrates. Instead of strength, it represents weakness. The reversed word is also more difficult to read.

Avoid inadvertantly printing photographs in a second color.

159

Avoid running black-and-white photographs in a second color unless you're absolutely sure of the results. This is especially important when the resulting photograph shows food or people in red, blue, or green. Red or blue people appear unnatural, and green food simply isn't very appetizing!

If your publication is printed on quality paper and you are working with high-quality photographs, however, consider printing the photographs as duotones. Duotones are photographs using black, plus gray or a dark second color.

Duotones add depth to black-and-white photographs by restoring shadow and highlight detail that would otherwise be lost.

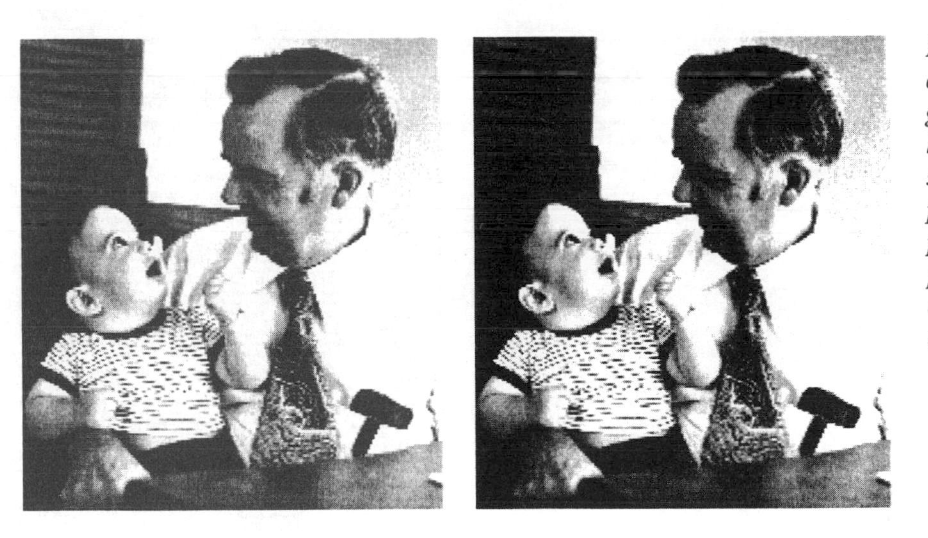

Restrict your use of color to backgrounds and large, heavy text. You should rarely print photographs of people in your publication's second, or accent color.

160 Investigate preprinting second-color accents.

You can save money by restricting your use of a second color to elements like publication title and borders repeated in each issue and printing the second color accents for several issues in advance. After the second color for several issues has been printed, each of the following issues becomes a single color print job. By preprinting several issues worth of your newsletter's second color, you can save significant amounts of money over the cost of two-color printing for each issue.

This approach also forces you to use color as a major design element of publication continuity, rather than dissipate the power of color by using it for subheads, downrules, or other small text of visual elements that change from issue to issue.

The example at left shows the "empty" preprinted second-color module that will be used as the basis for future newsletters.

The example at right shows a finished newsletter, with issue-specific text and graphics printed in a single color.

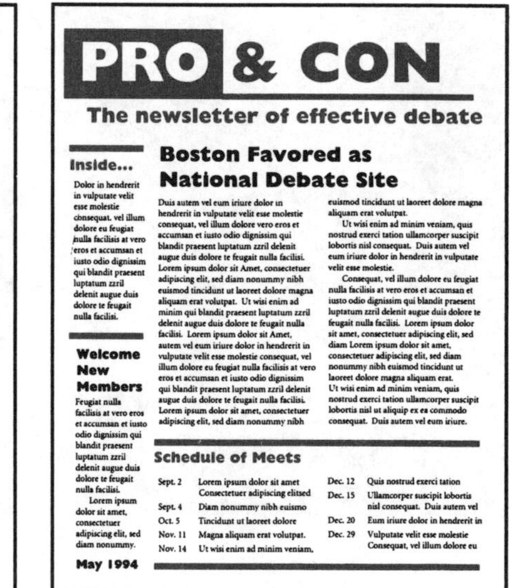

Section 8

Project-Specific Hints

The purpose of this section is to show how you can apply many of the ideas presented in the preceding sections to specific categories of projects.

We start with advertisements and flyers because of their near-universal use by associations and businesses of all sizes. Ads and flyers run the gamut from small ads in the classified sections of daily newspapers and yard sale announcements hung on telephone poles to formal ads placed in trade or consumer publications. Regardless of size, the same basic principles apply.

161

Use a deep indent to add impact to small ads.

A deep left-hand indent helps small advertisements, such as those appearing in the newspaper classified section, appear larger and more noticeable. The vertical band of white space created by a deep indent applied to both headline and text allows a relatively small advertisement to emerge from the clutter of adjacent advertisements.

Headlines and subheads can be "hung" in the white space to the left.

You can enhance the impact of the indent with one or more horizontal rules, or a logo, running the full width of the ad. These help define the white space, preventing the white space from looking "accidental."

Acquisition Manager

Lorem ipsum dolor sit amet, consectetuer adipiscing elit, sed diam nonummy nibh euismod tincidunt ut laoreet dolore magna aliquam erat volutpat. Ut wisi enim ad minim veniam, quis nostrud exerci tation ullamcorper suscipit lobortis nisl ut aliquip ex ea commodo consequat.
Duis autem vel eum iriure dolor in hendrerit in vulputate velit esse molestie consequat, vel illum dolore.

BVM Corporation
123 Fourth St., Dover, NH 56789

WANTED
Acquisition Manager

IF YOU lorem ipsum dolor sit amet, consect etuer adipiscing elit, sed diam nonummy nibh euismod tin cidunt ut laoreet dolore magna ali quam erat volu tpat.

THEN duis autem vel eum iriure dolor in hendrerit in vulputate velit esse molestie consequat, vel illum dolore. Ut wisi enim ad minim veniam, quis nos trud exer ci ta tion ulla.

BVM
Corporation
123 Fourth St.
Dover, NH 56789

Compare the "full width" ad on the left with the deeply indented ad to the right.

Notice how the vertical white space both separates the add from other ads as well as helps the headlines and subheads emerge with added clarity.

162 Avoid headlines that create distracting shapes.

When working with multiline headlines, strive to make the lines approximately equal in length. Unusually long or short headlines can be very distracting. Avoid headlines that create shapes like pyramids or steps.

When unequal line lengths are inevitable, place the longest line on the top of the headline rather than the bottom. Otherwise, the headline will appear to become harder with each passing line.

Editing may be necessary to avoid the creation of distracting shapes.

An easy way to avoid the "shape" problems characteristic of centered headlines is to left align them.

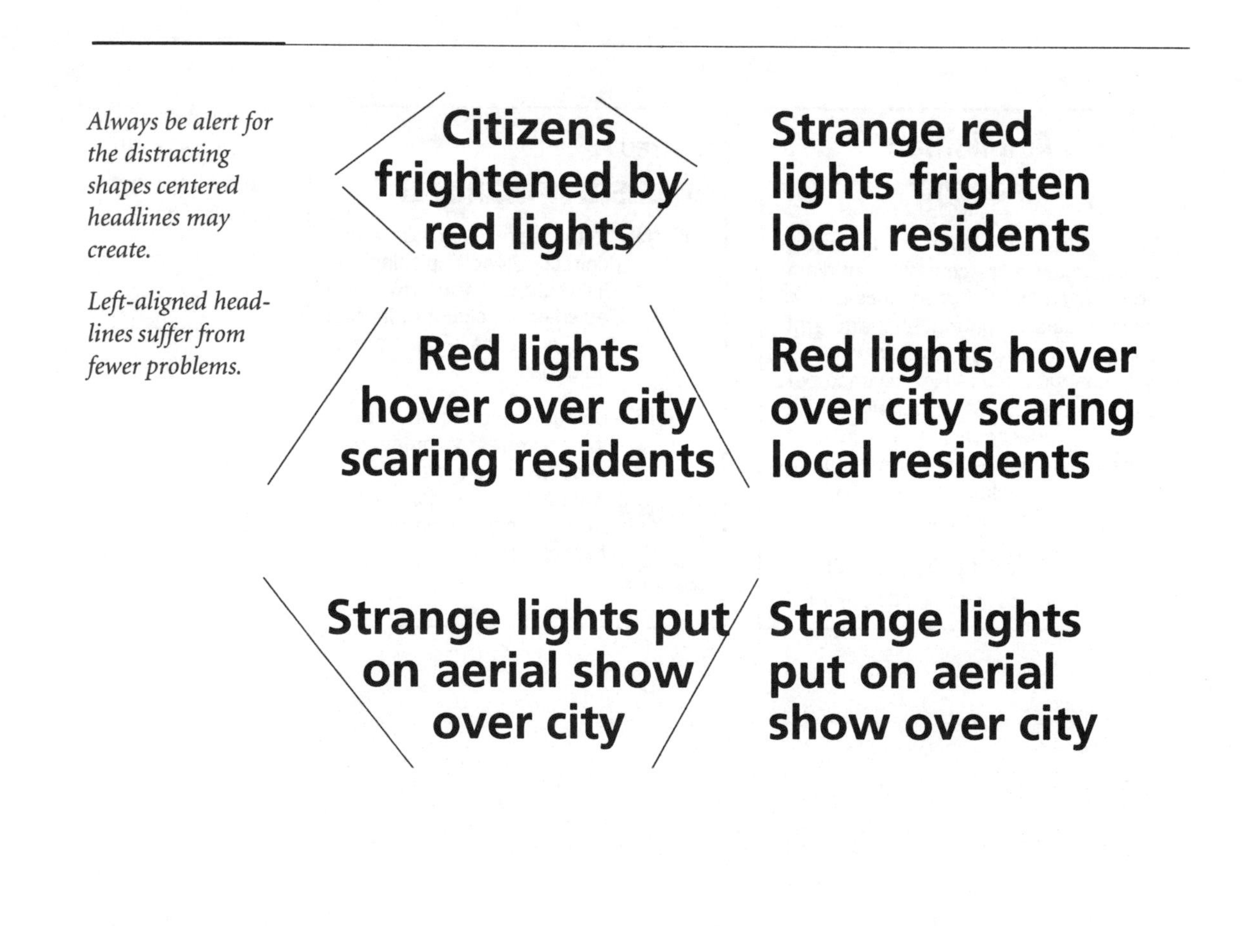

Always be alert for the distracting shapes centered headlines may create.

Left-aligned headlines suffer from fewer problems.

Anchor small advertisements with a reversed logo and address.

163

Use reversed text to "weight" the bottom of advertisements. One of the easiest and least expensive ways to add impact to small advertisements is to reverse your firm's name and address. This "weights" the bottom of the ad and forms a strong contrast with the white space surrounding your headline.

This technique is especially effective if you want to emphasize a phone number set in a large type. It also works well if your firm has a short name or a large, simple logo.

Make the reversed area as large as necessary to permit you to use a large type size for phone and address information without detracting from the rest of the ad.

Adding a thick bar at the top of the ad unites the ad.

Double Your Money!

New Overseas Investment Plan Now Available to U.S. Citizens

LOREM IPSUM dolor sit amet, consectetuer adipiscing elit, sed diam nonummy nibh euismod tincidunt ut laoreet dolore magna aliquam erat volutpat. Ut wisi enim ad minim veniam, quis nostrud exerci tation ullamcorper suscipit lobortis nisl ut aliquip ex ea commodo consequat.

Duis autem vel eum iriure dolor in hendrerit in vulputate velit esse molestie consequat, vel illum dolore eu feugiat nulla facilisis at vero eros et accumsan et iusto odio dignissim qui blandit praesent luptatum zzril delenit augue duis dolore te feugait nulla facilisi.

Lorem ipsum dolor sit amet, consectetuer adipiscing elit, sed diam nonummy nibh euismod tincidunt ut laoreet dolore magna aliquam erat volutpat. UT WISI ENIM AD MINIM VENIAM, QUIS NOSTRUD EXER.

Mutual Funds International
456 First Street
Anyplace, NY 01234
999-999-9999

Although this is a relatively small ad, the reversed address area at the bottom and the heavy bar at the top permit it to emerge from its surroundings.

164 Use extreme typography contrast in flyers.

Headlines of flyers have to be large to attract attention. This is especially true if flyers are going to be hung on bulletin boards or placed under windshield wipers. All will be lost if the headline isn't large enough to immediately attract the reader's attention from several feet away.

Once you have the reader's attention, however, you can use a significantly smaller typeface for the remaining "Who," "What," "Where," "When," and "Why" information in the remainder of the flyer. Once the headline has attracted the reader's attention, the reader will move closer or pick up the flyer, permitting easy reading of the smaller type.

Headlines in flyers have to be large so they can attract attention from a long distance away. Once the reader is interested, however, they will pick up the flyer and read the supporting text at a normal reading distance, permitting use of a smaller type size.

NEIGHBORHOOD GARAGE SALE!

Saturday, June 26

What	Where	Time
Lorem ipsum dolor sit amet, consectetuer adipiscing elit, sed diam nonummy nibh euismod tincidunt ut laoreet dolore magna aliquam erat volutpat. Ut wisi enim ad minim veniam, quis nostrud exerci tation.	Ullamcorper suscipit lobortis nisl ut aliquip ex ea commodo consequat. Duis autem vel eum iriure dolor in hendrerit in vulputate velit esse molestie consequat, vel illum dolore eu feugiat nulla facilisis at vero eros.	Etaccumsan et iusto odio dignissim qui blandit praesent luptatum zzril delenit augue duis dolore te feugait nulla facilisi. Lorem ipsum dolor sit amet, consectetuer adipiscing elit, sed

Books and Documentation

Training is an ongoing part of the work of most businesses and associations. Although few firms and associations publish books, most publish instruction books, procedural manuals, and training materials for their staffs. Such formal documents succeed to the extent that they incorporate the lessons used in formal book publishing. In all cases, the goal is to organize and present information in as accessible a format as possible.

Maintain consistent spacing between chapter titles and the text that follows.

165

Build multiline chapter titles from the bottom up. When titles on the opening pages of each chapter vary between one and two lines, build the titles from the bottom line up rather than from the top down.

It is more important to maintain consistent spacing between the bottom of the title and the first line of text than between the top of the page and the top of the title.

Readers are more apt to notice inconsistent spacing between the title and the text than inconsistent spacing between the top of the page and the first line of the title because small differences in spacing are more noticeable than large differences.

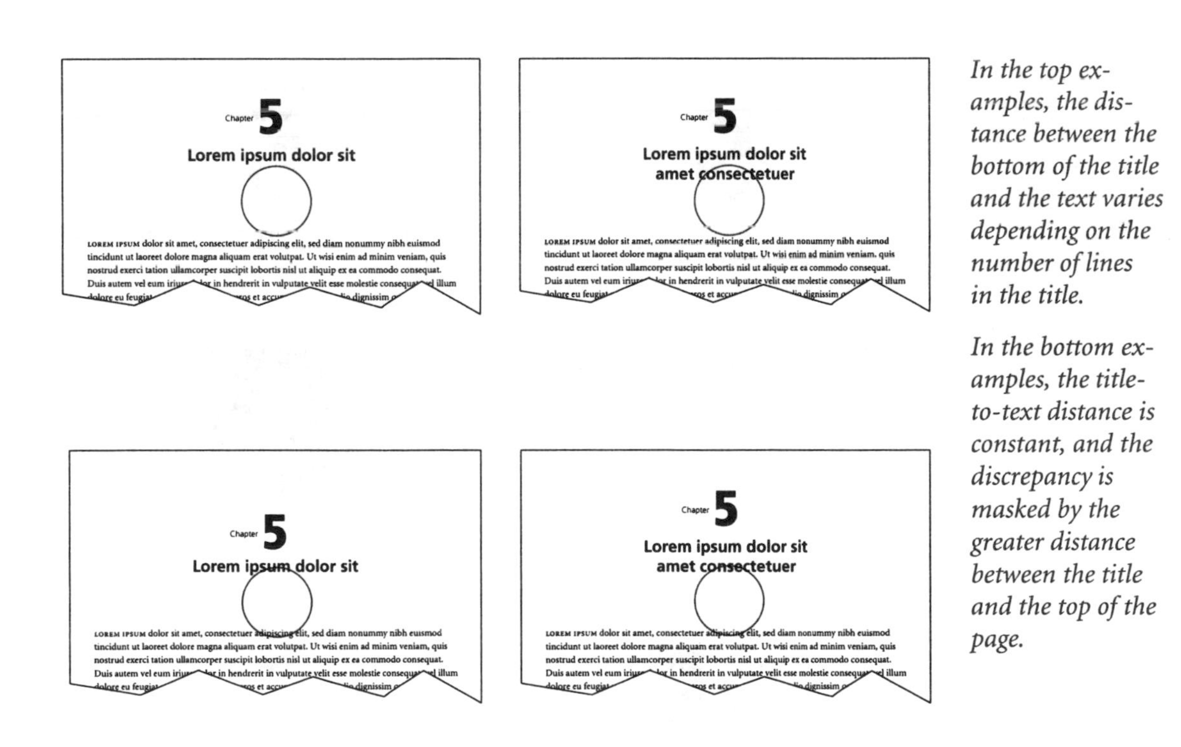

In the top examples, the distance between the bottom of the title and the text varies depending on the number of lines in the title.

In the bottom examples, the title-to-text distance is constant, and the discrepancy is masked by the greater distance between the title and the top of the page.

166 Use typographic contrast to add character to opening pages.

Avoid using the same typeface, type size, and type style for chapter number and chapter title. Often, you can achieve good-looking results by using the same typeface design in both the chapter number and the chapter title, but using a heavy weight for the chapter number and a light version of the same typeface design for the chapter title (or vice versa).

When chapters are untitled, as in fiction books, consider omitting the word "Chapter" at the start of each chapter and simply setting the chapter number extra large in a contrasting typeface. You can also replace "Chapter" with graphic accents, as "chapter" can be assumed.

These are just a few of the ways you can add visual interest to the pages introducing new chapters.

Such techniques are often one of the few ways you can add character to text-only books like novels or mysteries.

Chapter
5

5

C
h
a
p
t
e
r
5

5

Chapter **5**

5

Provide sufficient page margins for facing pages.

Use margins to frame the text and unify text on facing pages. In order of size, place the narrowest margins between the text columns on facing pages, use more white space between the top of the text columns and the top border of the page, and even more space between the text columns and the left and right borders of the page.

Place the greatest amount of white space between the bottom of the text columns and the bottoms of the pages.

By creating margins of increasing size, in the rough order of 2:3:4:6, you will create facing pages which approximate the Golden Mean, a height-to-width ratio found in nature as well as architecture and painting.

The classic way to create margins is by drawing diagonals, in the sequence below. The intersection of lines 2-3 and 4-5 determines the placement of 6-7, which, in turn, determines the inside margin created by line 7-8.

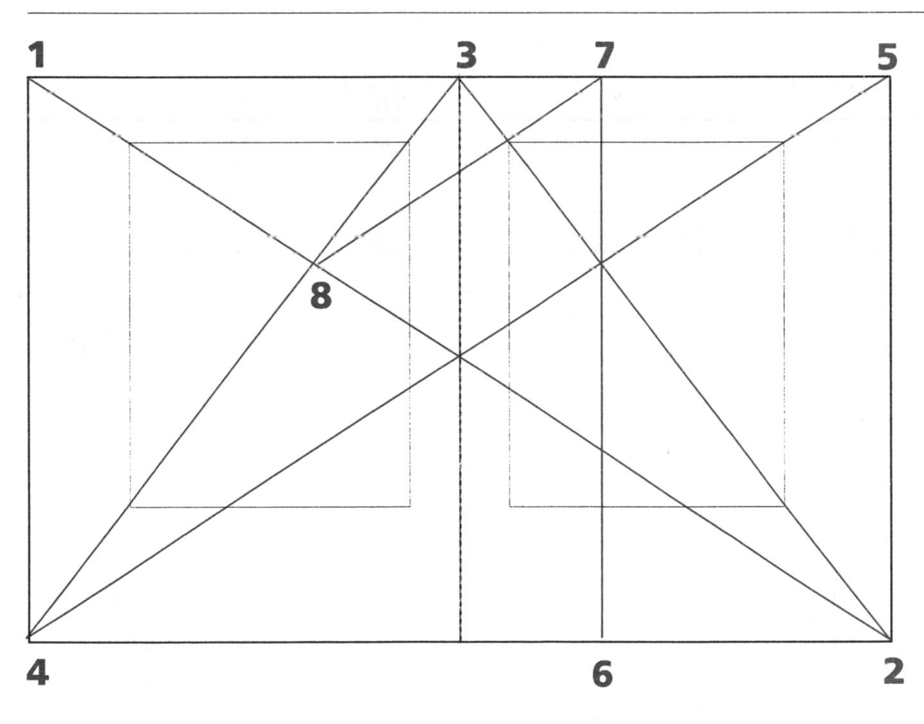

Notice the increasing amounts of white space between text and inside margins; text and page tops; text and outside margins; and the text and the bottoms of the pages.

You may have to adjust the distance between columns to make sure that the space between the two text columns will accommodate how your publication will be bound.

Check with your commercial printer before proceeding too far.

168 Use special display or titling typefaces when available.

When setting type at large sizes, use typeface designs especially designed for use at large sizes. Many typefaces look better set small than they do set large. This is because their proportions change when set at large sizes. Often, the horizontal and vertical strokes become undesirably thick.

To overcome this unwanted distortion, use the special Display or Titling Capitals that are available for many serif typefaces. These maintain the typeface designer's original desired proportions at large sizes.

Notice the differences between the two samples below. The serifs in the right-hand examples are more detailed and delicate than in the left-hand examples. The right-hand examples also show a greater thick-to-thin contrast.

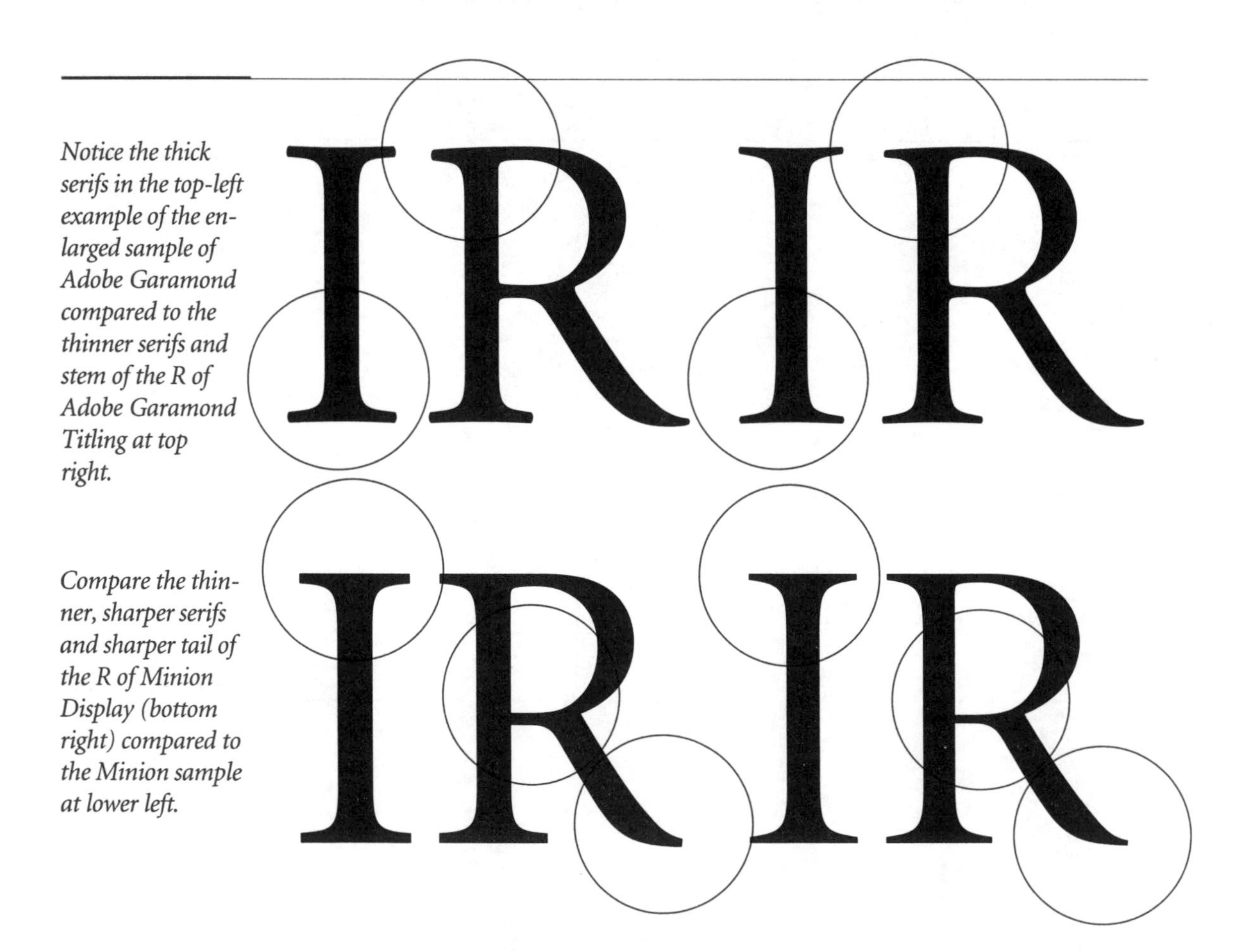

Notice the thick serifs in the top-left example of the enlarged sample of Adobe Garamond compared to the thinner serifs and stem of the R of Adobe Garamond Titling at top right.

Compare the thinner, sharper serifs and sharper tail of the R of Minion Display (bottom right) compared to the Minion sample at lower left.

Experiment with alternative header and footer placement.

Publication titles and chapter headings do not necessarily have to appear at the tops of each page. Alternative placement can add visual interest to your book and separate it from other books on the topic.

In the sample below, for example, notice how the book title is placed in the white space to the left of the text on the left-hand page and the chapter title is placed in the white space to the right of the text column on the right-hand page. Notice how the thin rules and the placement of the page numbers help define the white space so it doesn't appear "accidental."

In addition to creating a more "open" book, the added length of the text columns provides less interruption. This technique is best used for text-oriented books.

White Mountain Railroading

Lorem ipsum dolor sit amet, consectetuer adipiscing elit, sed diam nonummy nibh euismod tincidunt ut laoreet dolore magna aliquam erat volutpat. Ut wisi enim ad minim veniam, quis nostrud exerci tation ullamcorper suscipit lobortis nisl ut aliquip ex ea commodo consequat. Duis autem vel eum iriure dolor in hendrerit in vulputate velit esse molestie consequat, vel illum dolore eu feugiat nulla facilisis at vero eros et accumsan et iusto odio dignissim qui blandit praesent luptatum zzril delenit augue duis dolore te feugait nulla facilisi. Lorem ipsum dolor sit amet, consectetuer adipiscing elit, sed diam nonummy nibh euismod tincidunt ut laoreet dolore magna aliquam erat volutpat. Ut wisi enim ad minim veniam, quis nostrud exerci tation ullamcorper suscipit lobortis nisl ut aliquip ex ea commodo consequat.

Duis autem vel eum iriure dolor in hendrerit in vulputate velit esse molestie consequat, vel illum dolore eu feugiat nulla facilisis at vero eros et accumsan et iusto odio dignissim qui blandit praesent luptatum zzril delenit augue duis dolore te feugait nulla facilisi. Nam liber tempor cum soluta nobis eleifend option congue nihil imperdiet doming id quod mazim placerat facer possim assum.

Lorem ipsum dolor sit amet, consectetuer adipiscing elit, sed diam nonummy nibh euismod tincidunt ut laoreet dolore magna aliquam erat volutpat. Ut wisi enim ad minim veniam, quis nostrud exerci tation ullamcorper suscipit lobortis nisl ut

66

aliquip ex ea commodo consequat. Duis autem vel eum iriure dolor in hendrerit in vulputate velit esse molestie consequat, vel illum dolore eu feugiat nulla facilisis at vero eros et accumsan et iusto odio dignissim qui blandit praesent luptatum zzril delenit augue duis dolore te feugait nulla facilisi. Lorem ipsum dolor sit amet, consectetuer adipiscing elit, sed diam nonummy nibh euismod tincidunt ut laoreet dolore magna aliquam erat volutpat.

The Glory Years

Ut wisi enim ad minim veniam, quis nostrud exerci tation ullamcorper suscipit lobortis nisl ut aliquip ex ea commodo consequat. Duis autem vel eum iriure dolor in hendrerit in vulputate velit esse molestie consequat, vel illum dolore eu feugiat nulla facilisis at vero eros et accumsan et iusto odio dignissim qui blandit praesent luptatum zzril delenit augue duis dolore te feugait nulla facilisi. Lorem ipsum dolor sit amet, consectetuer adipiscing elit, sed diam nonummy nibh euismod tincidunt ut laoreet dolore magna aliquam erat volutpat.

Ut wisi enim ad minim veniam, quis nostrud exerci tation ullamcorper suscipit lobortis nisl ut aliquip ex ea commodo consequat. Duis autem vel eum iriure dolor in hendrerit in vulputate velit esse molestie consequat, vel illum dolore eu feugiat nulla facilisis at vero eros et accumsan et iusto odio dignissim qui blandit praesent luptatum zzril delenit augue duis dolore te feugait nulla facilisi.

Lorem ipsum dolor sit amet, consectetuer adipiscing elit, sed diam nonummy nibh euismod

67

Placing header and footer information adjacent to the text columns, instead of above and below the text columns, creates longer, easier-to-read columns plus builds white space into each two-page spread.

170 Align text and visuals on facing pages.

Unify pages by aligning text and visual elements along a common axis. Always view facing pages the way readers will encounter them – as a single unit.

By aligning text and visuals along well-defined horizons spanning both pages, you can unify the pages and create white space to frame the headline and force the reader's attention to the picture below.

The courage to simultaneously employ significant size contrast and align elements on facing pages is a characteristic of experienced designers. This technique can be used for all types of print communications.

Note the significant size contrast between the large and small photographs, as well as how they top-align with each other.

Note, also, the way the text columns top-align with each other, forming a pool of white space to emphasize the headline.

Coastal Villages

Lorem ipsum dolor sit amet, consectetuer adipiscing elit, sed diam nonummy nibh euismod tincidunt ut laoreet dolore magna aliquam erat volutpat.

Ut wisi enim ad minim veniam, quis

Ut wisi enim ad minim veniam, quis nostrud exerci tation ullamcorper suscipit lobortis nisl ut aliquip ex ea commodo consequat. Duis autem vel eum iriure dolor in

nostrud exerci tation ullamcorper suscipit lobortis nisl ut aliquip ex ea commodo consequat. Duis autem vel eum iriure dolor in hendrerit in vulputate velit esse molestie consequat, vel illum dolore eu feugiat nulla facilisis at vero eros et accumsan et iusto odio dignissim qui blandit praesent luptatum zzril delenit augue duis dolore te feugait nulla facilisi. Lorem ipsum dolor sit amet, consectetuer adipiscing elit, sed diam nonummy nibh euismod tincidunt ut laoreet dolore magna aliquam erat volutpat. Ut wisi enim ad minim veniam, quis nostrud exerci tation ullamcorper suscipit

lobortis nisl ut aliquip ex ea commodo consequat.

Duis autem vel eum iriure dolor in hendrerit in vulputate velit esse molestie consequat, vel illum dolore eu feugiat nulla facilisis at vero eros et accumsan et iusto odio dignissim qui blandit praesent luptatum zzril delenit augue duis dolore te feugait nulla facilisi. Nam liber tempor cum soluta nobis eleifend option congue nihil imperdiet doming id quod mazim placerat facer possim assum.

Lorem ipsum dolor sit amet, consectetuer adipiscing elit, sed diam nonummy nibh euismod tincidunt ut laoreet dolore magna

aliquam erat volutpat. Ut wisi enim ad minim veniam, quis nostrud exerci tation ullamcorper suscipit lobortis nisl ut aliquip ex ea commodo consequat. Duis autem vel eum iriure

dolor in hendrerit in vulputate velit esse molestie consequat, vel illum dolore eu feugiat nulla facilisis at vero eros et accumsan et iusto odio dignissim qui blandit praesent luptatum zzril delenit

augue duis dolore te feugait nulla facilisi. Lorem ipsum dolor sit amet, consectetuer adipiscing elit, sed diam nonummy nibh euismod tincidunt ut laoreet dolore magna aliquam erat volutpat.

Create tension between text and visuals on facing pages.

Use size and position contrasts to balance text and visuals on opposite pages. One of the effective ways to add interest to books where the emphasis is equally divided between text and visuals is to create dynamic left-right or top-bottom tension between the two pages.

One way you can achieve this is by viewing both the left- and right-hand pages as a single unit and contrasting text and visuals of unequal sizes and weights.

In the example, the left-aligned headline at the top of the left-hand page, set in a large, heavy typeface balances the large, right-aligned photograph at the bottom of the two pages.

Rails Across America

Lorem ipsum dolor sit amet, consectetuer adipiscing elit, sed diam nonummy nibh euismod tincidunt ut laoreet dolore magna aliquam erat volutpat.

Ut wisi enim ad minim veniam, quis nostrud exerci tation ullamcorper suscipit lobortis nisl ut aliquip ex ea commodo consequat. Duis autem vel eum iriure dolor in hendrerit in vulputate velit esse molestie consequat, vel illum dolore eu feugiat nulla facilisis at vero eros et accumsan et iusto odio dignissim qui blandit praesent luptatum zzril delenit augue duis dolore te feugait nulla facilisi. Lorem ipsum dolor sit amet, consectetuer adipiscing elit, sed diam nonummy nibh euismod tincidunt ut laoreet dolore magna aliquam erat volutpat. Ut wisi enim ad minim veniam, quis nostrud exerci tation ullamcorper suscipit lobortis nisl ut aliquip ex ea commodo consequat.

Duis autem vel eum iriure dolor in hendrerit in vulputate velit esse molestie consequat, vel illum dolore eu feugiat nulla facilisis at vero eros et accumsan et iusto odio dignissim qui blandit praesent luptatum zzril delenit augue duis dolore te feugait nulla facilisi. Nam liber tempor cum soluta nobis eleifend option congue nihil imperdiet doming id quod mazim placerat facer possim assum.

Lorem ipsum dolor sit amet, consectetuer adipiscing elit, sed diam nonummy nibh euismod tincidunt ut laoreet dolore magna aliquam erat volutpat. Ut wisi enim ad minim veniam, quis nostrud exerci tation ullamcorper suscipit lobortis nisl ut aliquip ex ea commodo consequat. Duis autem vel eum iriure dolor in hendrerit in vulputate velit

The headline at the top of the left-hand page balances the photograph at the bottom of the two-page spread.

172 Present information in layers.

Use visual layering to separate different categories of information on a page. Rarely are all the words on a page of equal importance. Unless you are formatting a linear book designed to be read from cover to cover like a novel, most books contain an ongoing narrative with numerous digressions (or paragraphs of related information).

Layering permits you to visually signal digressions, annotations, or opposing points of view, so readers can choose the level of information they want to read. Readers can read just the narrative, for example, or they can go back and read just the digressions or amplifications, or they can jump back and forth between them.

Typeface, type size, and weight contrast are typically used to visually separate the ongoing narrative from the digressions and amplifications.

The left-hand example is visually boring and lacks the cues readers need to quickly identify the digressons and annotations.

The right-hand example, by using serif and sans serif typefaces, immediately directs the reader's attention to the different layers of information.

Duis autem vel eum iriure dolor in hendrerit in vulputate velit esse molestie consequat, vel illum dolore eu feugiat.

"Ut wisi enim ad minim veniam, quis nostru exerci tation."
- Jane Smith

Imperdiet doming id quod mazim placerat facer.

Lorem ipsum dolor sit amet, consectetuer adipiscing elit, sed diam nonummy nibh euismod tincidunt ut laoreet dolore magna aliquam erat volutpat. Ut wisi enim ad minim veniam, quis nostrud exerci tation ullamcorper suscipit lobortis nisl ut aliquip ex ea commodo consequat. Duis autem vel eum iriure dolor in hendrerit in vulputate velit esse molestie consequat, vel illum dolore eu feugiat nulla facilisis at vero eros et accumsan et iusto odio dignissim qui blandit praesent luptatum zzril delenit augue duis dolore te feugait nulla facilisi. Lorem ipsum dolor sit amet, consectetuer adipiscing elit, sed diam nonummy nibh euismod tincidunt ut laoreet dolore magna aliquam erat volutpat. Ut wisi enim ad minim veniam, quis nostrud exerci tation ullamcorper suscipit lobortis nisl ut aliquip ex ea commodo consequat.

Duis autem vel eum iriure eros et accumsan et iusto odio dolore te feugait nulla facilisi. Nam liber tempor cum soluta nobis eleifend option congue nihil imperdiet doming id quod mazim placerat facer possim assum.

Lorem ipsum dolor sit amet, consectetuer adipiscing elit, sed diam nonummy nibh euismod tincidunt ut laoreet dolore magna aliquam erat volutpat. Ut wisi enim ad minim veniam, quis nostrud exerci tation ullamcorper suscipit lobortis nisl ut aliquip ex ea commodo consequat. Duis autem vel eum iriure dolor in hendrerit in vulputate velit esse molestie

9

Duis autem vel eum iriure dolor in hendrerit in vulputate velit esse molestie consequat, vel illum dolore eu feugiat.

"Ut wisi enim ad minim veniam, quis nostru exerci tation."
- Jane Smith

Imperdiet doming id quod mazim placerat facer.

Lorem ipsum dolor sit amet, consectetuer adipiscing elit, sed diam nonummy nibh euismod tincidunt ut laoreet dolore magna aliquam erat volutpat. Ut wisi enim ad minim veniam, quis nostrud exerci tation ullamcorper suscipit lobortis nisl ut aliquip ex ea commodo consequat. Duis autem vel eum iriure dolor in hendrerit in vulputate velit esse molestie consequat, vel illum dolore eu feugiat nulla facilisis at vero eros et accumsan et iusto odio dignissim qui blandit praesent luptatum zzril delenit augue duis dolore te feugait nulla facilisi. Lorem ipsum dolor sit amet, consectetuer adipiscing elit, sed diam nonummy nibh euismod tincidunt ut laoreet dolore magna aliquam erat volutpat. Ut wisi enim ad minim veniam, quis nostrud exerci tation ullamcorper suscipit lobortis nisl ut aliquip ex ea commodo consequat.

Duis autem vel eum iriure eros et accumsan et iusto odio dolore te feugait nulla facilisi. Nam liber tempor cum soluta nobis eleifend option congue nihil imperdiet doming id quod mazim placerat facer possim assum.

Lorem ipsum dolor sit amet, consectetuer adipiscing elit, sed diam nonummy nibh euismod tincidunt ut laoreet dolore magna aliquam erat volutpat. Ut wisi enim ad minim veniam, quis nostrud exerci tation ullamcorper suscipit lobortis nisl ut aliquip ex ea commodo consequat. Duis autem vel eum iriure dolor in hendrerit in vulputate velit esse molestie

9

Use typographic contrast and graphic accents to clearly indicate each level of information.

173

Avoid ambiguity. Introduce each level of information with subheads differentiated by visually distinctive typography. Choose between the following typographic tools of contrast: typeface, type size, type style, case, weight, and style.

You can enhance these contrast tools by combining them with hanging indents of various depths, graphic accents, side heads, and run-ins to add further distinctness to each level of information.

Subhead levels could be further differentiated by setting level one subheads in uppercase type or by adding horizontal rules above the level one subheads.

Automatic Reactor Safety

Low water related

Lorem ipsum dolor sit amet, consectetuer adipiscing elit, sed diam nonummy nibh euismod tincidunt ut laoreet dolore magna aliquam erat volutpat. Ut wisi enim ad minim veniam, quis nostrud exerci tation ullamcorper suscipit lobortis nisl ut aliquip ex ea commodo consequat. Duis autem vel eum iriure dolor in hendrerit in vulputate velit esse molestie consequat, vel illum dolore eu feugiat nulla facilisis at vero eros et accumsan et iusto odio dignissim qui blandit praesent luptatum zzril delenit augue duis dolore te feugait nulla facilisi. Lorem ipsum dolor sit amet, consectetuer adipiscing elit, sed diam nonummy nibh euismod tincidunt ut laoreet dolore magna aliquam erat volutpat. Ut wisi enim ad minim veniam, quis nostrud exerci tation ullamcorper suscipit lobortis nisl ut aliquip ex ea commodo consequat.

Duis autem vel eum iriure eros et accumsan et iusto odio dolore te feugait nulla facilisi. Nam liber tempor cum soluta nobis eleifend option congue nihil imperdiet doming id quod mazim placerat facer possim assum.

Employee vacation related

Lorem ipsum dolor sit amet, consectetuer adipiscing elit, sed diam nonummy nibh euismod tincidunt ut laoreet dolore magna aliquam erat volutpat. Ut wisi enim ad minim veniam, quis nostrud exerci tation ullamcorper suscipit lobortis nisl ut aliquip ex ea commodo consequat. Duis autem vel eum iriure dolor in hendrerit in vulputate velit esse molestie consequat, vel illum dolore eu feugiat nulla facilisis at vero eros et accumsan et iusto odio dignissim qui blandit praesent luptatum zzril delenit augue duis dolore te feugait nulla facilisi. Lorem ipsum dolor sit amet, consectetuer adipiscing elit, sed diam nonummy nibh euismod tincidunt ut laoreet dolore magna aliquam erat volutpat.

Ut wisi enim ad minim veniam, quis nostrud exerci tation ullamcorper suscipit lobortis nisl ut aliquip ex ea commodo consequat.

Automatic Reactor Safety

Low water related

Lorem ipsum dolor sit amet, consectetuer adipiscing elit, sed diam nonummy nibh euismod tincidunt ut laoreet dolore magna aliquam erat volutpat. Ut wisi enim ad minim veniam, quis nostrud exerci tation ullamcorper suscipit lobortis nisl ut aliquip ex ea commodo consequat. Duis autem vel eum iriure dolor in hendrerit in vulputate velit esse molestie consequat, vel illum dolore eu feugiat nulla facilisis at vero eros et accumsan et iusto odio dignissim qui blandit praesent luptatum zzril delenit augue duis dolore te feugait nulla facilisi.

Lorem ipsum dolor sit amet, consectetuer adipiscing elit, sed diam nonummy nibh euismod tincidunt ut laoreet dolore magna aliquam erat volutpat. Ut wisi enim ad minim veniam, quis nostrud exerci tation ullamcorper suscipit lobortis nisl ut aliquip ex ea commodo consequat.
Duis autem vel eum iriure eros et accumsan et iusto odio dolore te feugait nulla facilisi. Nam liber tempor cum soluta nobis eleifend option congue nihil imperdiet doming id quod mazim placerat facer possim assum.

Employee vacation related

Lorem ipsum dolor sit amet, consectetuer adipiscing elit, sed diam nonummy nibh euismod tincidunt ut laoreet dolore magna aliquam erat volutpat. Ut wisi enim ad minim veniam, quis nostrud exerci tation ullamcorper suscipit lobortis nisl ut aliquip ex ea commodo consequat.

Duis autem vel sim qui blandit praesent luptatum zzril delenit augue duis dolore te feugait nulla facilisi. Lorem ipsumd lor seum iriure dolor in hendrerivel illum dolore eu feugiat nulla

The example at left is both visually boring and ambiguous. Subheads lack significant contrast with the text.

Ambiguity is removed at right by employing typeface and type size contrast as well as hanging indents. As a result,each level becomes visually distinct.

174 Use icons to draw attention to different categories of information.

Use icons to draw your readers' attention to various levels of information in documentation. Icons make it easy for readers to quickly locate desired information and skip information they can return to at a later date. Icons allow readers to concentrate on just the level of information they're interested in at any given time.

Icons are typically used in documentation design to indicate warnings, troubleshooting tips, and areas to avoid.

Just as the meaning of a "stop" sign along the side of the road is immediately obvious to drivers without being read, icons offer immediate visual communication.

Hint: Familiarize your readers with your icon system by explaining what each one means in the introduction of your documentation.

The left-hand example, without icons, is both visually boring and lacks the reader cues necessary to identify the purpose of the text blocks.

The right-hand example immediately directs the reader's attention to different levels of information.

Bright Idea No. 1

Lorem ipsum dolor sit amet, consectetuer adipiscing elit, sed diam nonummy nibh euismod tincidunt ut laoreet.

Lorem ipsum dolor sit amet, consectetuer adipiscing elit, sed diam nonummy nibh euismod tincidunt ut laoreet dolore magna aliquam erat volutpat. Ut wisi enim ad minim veniam, quis nostrud exerci tation ullamcorper suscipit lobortis nisl ut aliquip ex ea commodo consequat.

Duis autem vel eum iriure dolor in hendrerit in vulputate velit esse molestie consequat, vel illum dolore eu feugiat nulla facilisis at vero eros et accumsan et iusto odio dignissim qui blandit praesent luptatum zzril delenit augue duis dolore te feugait nulla facilisi.

Telephone Marketing Strategies

Consec tuer quis nostrud orem ipsum dolor sit amet, adipis cing elit, sed diam nonummy.

Lorem ipsum dolor sit amet, consectetuer adipiscing elit, sed diam nonummy nibh euismod tincidunt ut laoreet dolore magna aliquam erat volutpat. Ut wisi enim ad minim veniam, quis nostrud exerci tation ullamcorper suscipit lobortis nisl ut aliquip ex ea commodo consequat.

Duis autem vel eum iriure eros et accumsan et iusto odio dolore te feugait nulla facilisi. Nam liber tempor cum soluta nobis eleifend option congue nihil imperdiet doming id quod mazim placerat facer possim assum.

Mass Mailing Strategies

Duis atem iriure dolor in vul velit esse molestie consequat, dignissim qui blandit.

Lorem ipsum dolor sit amet, consectetuer adipiscing elit, sed diam nonummy nibh euismod tincidunt ut laoreet dolore magna aliquam erat volutpat. Ut wisi enim ad minim veniam, quis nostrud exerci tation ullamcorper suscipit lobortis nisl ut aliquip ex ea commodo consequat.

Duis autem vel eum iriure dolor in hendrerit in vulputate velit esse molestie consequat, vel illum dolore eu feugiat nulla facilisis at vero eros et accumsan et iusto odio dignissim qui blandit praesent luptatum zzril delenit augue duis dolore te feugait nulla facilisi. Lorem ipsum dolor sit amet, consectetuer adipiscing elit, sed diam nonummy nibh euismod tincidunt ut laoreet dolore magna aliquam erat volutpat.

9

Bright Idea No. 1

Lorem ipsum dolor sit amet, consectetuer adipiscing elit, sed diam nonummy nibh euismod tincidunt ut laoreet.

Lorem ipsum dolor sit amet, consectetuer adipiscing elit, sed diam nonummy nibh euismod tincidunt ut laoreet dolore magna aliquam erat volutpat. Ut wisi enim ad minim veniam, quis nostrud exerci tation ullamcorper suscipit lobortis nisl ut aliquip ex ea commodo consequat.

Duis autem vel eum iriure dolor in hendrerit in vulputate velit esse molestie consequat, vel illum dolore eu feugiat nulla facilisis at vero eros et accumsan et iusto odio dignissim qui blandit praesent luptatum zzril delenit augue duis dolore te feugait nulla facilisi.

Telephone Marketing Strategies

Consec tuer quis nostrud orem ipsum dolor sit amet, adipis cing elit, sed diam nonummy.

Lorem ipsum dolor sit amet, consectetuer adipiscing elit, sed diam nonummy nibh euismod tincidunt ut laoreet dolore magna aliquam erat volutpat. Ut wisi enim ad minim veniam, quis nostrud exerci tation ullamcorper suscipit lobortis nisl ut aliquip ex ea commodo consequat.

Duis autem vel eum iriure eros et accumsan et iusto odio dolore te feugait nulla facilisi. Nam liber tempor cum soluta nobis eleifend option congue nihil imperdiet doming id quod mazim placerat facer possim assum.

Mass Mailing Strategies

Duis atem iriure dolor in vul velit esse molestie consequat, dignissim qui blandit.

Lorem ipsum dolor sit amet, consectetuer adipiscing elit, sed diam nonummy nibh euismod tincidunt ut laoreet dolore magna aliquam erat volutpat. Ut wisi enim ad minim veniam, quis nostrud exerci tation ullamcorper suscipit lobortis nisl ut aliquip ex ea commodo consequat.

Duis autem vel eum iriure dolor in hendrerit in vulputate velit esse molestie consequat, vel illum dolore eu feugiat nulla facilisis at vero eros et accumsan et iusto odio dignissim qui blandit praesent luptatum zzril delenit augue duis dolore te feugait nulla facilisi. Lorem ipsum dolor sit amet, consectetuer adipiscing elit, sed diam nonummy nibh euismod tincidunt ut laoreet dolore magna aliquam erat volutpat.

9

Provide a visual table of contents.

175

Tables of contents don't have to be dull! Consider replacing an all-text table of contents with one containing a mixture of different-sized text and graphic elements.

In addition to the chapter title, consider adding a sentence or phrase that summarizes the contents of each chapter. Include reduced-size copies of some of the important visuals found within each chapter. You can also include annotations describing your goals for the chapter or a summary of the topics included in it.

A visual table of contents spanning several pages not only makes information easier to locate, it also can establish the desired atmosphere for your publication, resulting in increased utilization of your documentation and increased bookstore sales. (Notice how the ONE-MINUTE DESIGNER includes an information map as well as a traditional table of contents.)

Chapter 1 Lorem ipsum dolor sit amet, consectetuer adipiscing elit, sed diam nonummy nibh 3

Chapter 2 Ut wisi enim ad minim veniam, quis nostrud exerci tation ullamcorper suscipit lobortis nisl ut aliquip ex ea commodo consequat 19

Chapter 3 Duis autem vel eum iriure dolor in hendrerit in vulputate velit esse molestie consequat 33

Chapter 4 Vel illum dolore eu feugiat nulla facilisis at vero eros et accumsan et iusto odio dignissim qui blandit 49

Chapter 5 Praesent luptatum zzril delenit augue duis dolore te feugait nulla facilisi. 61

Chapter 6 Lorem ipsum dolor sit amet, consectetuer adipiscing elit, sed diam nonummy nibh euismod tincidunt ut laoreet dolore magna aliquam erat volutpat 83

Chapter 5

Japan's natural resources

Nibh euismod tini cidunt ut laoreet dolor, mangna ali quam erat voutpat. Praesent luptatum zzril delenit augue duis dolore te feugait nulla facilisi.

61

Chapter 6

Japan's spiritual traditions

Ullam corper susc, ipit lobortis nisl ut. Aliquiep ex ea copmodo duis fish lorem ipsum dolor sit amet. Cons ectetuer adipiscing elit, sed diam non ummy nibh euis mod tincidunt ut laoreet dolore magna ali quam rat volutpat.

83

The traditional text-only table of contents in the example at left requires reading. Several chapters are shown on a single page.

The visual table of contents at right communicates at a glance. Because fewer chapters are described on a page, more detail can be included.

176 Avoid clutter.

Exercise restraint when layering information. Clutter can result if you include too many levels of information, use excessive typographic contrast, or incorporate too many graphic accents. Under such circumstances, guidance quickly turns into clutter.

You can avoid clutter by employing the minimum number of typographic and graphic accents necessary to separate levels of information on a page, which are scrupulously consistent from page to page; and by using different forms of contrast for primary and secondary information.

Secondary information should complement, but not visually compete with primary information. Readers should be able to easily read your ongoing narrative without being distracted by the typography and graphic accents used to indicate secondary, or supporting, information.

The left-hand example, employing too many graphic accents, is cluttered and results in visual competition between the primary and secondary text.

In the right-hand example, the secondary text complements the primary text, instead of competing with it.

Duis autem vel eum iriure dolor in hendrerit in vulputate velit esse molestie consequat, vel illum dolore eu feugiat. Velit esse molestie consequat, vel illum dolore eu feugiat.

"Ut wisi enim ad minim veniam, quis nostru exerci tation."
- Jane Smith

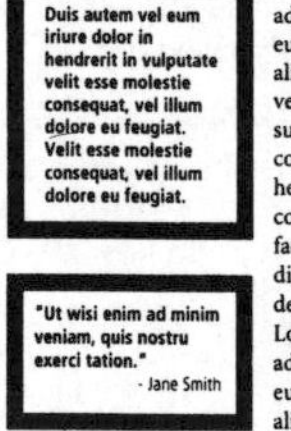

Imperdiet doming id quod mazim placerat facer. Ut wisi enim ad minim veniam, quis notrud exerci.

Lorem ipsum dolor sit amet, consectetuer adipiscing elit, sed diam nonummy nibh euismod tincidunt ut laoreet dolore magna aliquam erat volutpat. Ut wisi enim ad minim veniam, quis nostrud exerci tation ullamcorper suscipit lobortis nisl ut aliquip ex ea commodo consequat. Duis autem vel eum iriure dolor in hendrerit in vulputate velit esse molestie consequat, vel illum dolore eu feugiat nulla facilisis at vero eros et accumsan et iusto odio dignissim qui blandit praesent luptatum zzril delenit augue duis dolore te feugait nulla facilisi. Lorem ipsum dolor sit amet, consectetuer adipiscing elit, sed diam nonummy nibh euismod tincidunt ut laoreet dolore magna aliquam erat volutpat. Ut wisi enim ad minim veniam, quis nostrud exerci tation ullamcorper suscipit lobortis nisl ut aliquip ex ea commodo consequat.

Duis autem vel eum iriure eros et accumsan et iusto odio dolore te feugait nulla

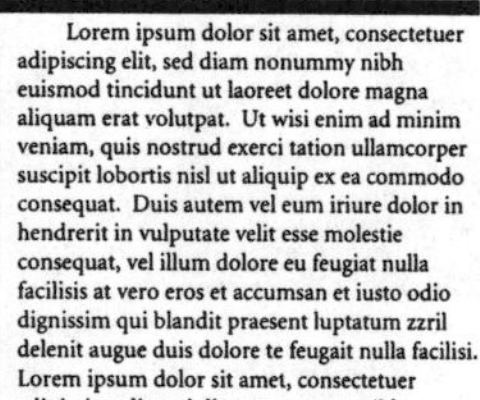

Lorem Ipsum				
Lorem	Ipsum	Dolor	Sit	Amet
Ut Wis	4	68.2	45%	G
Dolor Sit	1	73.5	10%	B
Te Geugait	6	88.2	25%	Y
Enim Ad	2	99.2	20%	Y
Velit Esse	2	44.8	11%	G

9

Duis autem vel eum iriure dolor in hendrerit in vulputate velit esse molestie consequat.

"Ut wisi enim ad minim veniam, quis nostru exerci tation."
- Jane Smith

Imperdiet doming id quod mazim placerat facer.

Lorem ipsum dolor sit amet, consectetuer adipiscing elit, sed diam nonummy nibh euismod tincidunt ut laoreet dolore magna aliquam erat volutpat. Ut wisi enim ad minim veniam, quis nostrud exerci tation ullamcorper suscipit lobortis nisl ut aliquip ex ea commodo consequat. Duis autem vel eum iriure dolor in hendrerit in vulputate velit esse molestie consequat, vel illum dolore eu feugiat nulla facilisis at vero eros et accumsan et iusto odio dignissim qui blandit praesent luptatum zzril delenit augue duis dolore te feugait nulla facilisi. Lorem ipsum dolor sit amet, consectetuer adipiscing elit, sed diam nonummy nibh euismod tincidunt ut laoreet dolore magna aliquam erat volutpat. Ut wisi enim ad minim veniam, quis nostrud exerci tation ullamcorper suscipit lobortis nisl ut aliquip ex ea commodo consequat.

Duis autem vel eum iriure eros et accumsan et iusto odio dolore te feugait nulla

Lorem Ipsum				
Lorem	Ipsum	Dolor	Sit	Amet
Ut Wis	4	68.2	45%	G
Dolor Sit	1	73.5	10%	B
Te Geugait	6	88.2	25%	Y
Enim Ad	2	99.2	20%	Y
Velit Esse	2	44.8	11%	G

9

Brochures

Brochures are "silent salespeople" that permit you to re-sell prospective supporters and customers before your initial face-to-face sales. Brochures can be as simple or elaborate as required to tell the whole story in as convincing a manner as possible. An effective brochure keeps on selling long after your first face-to-face contact. Brochures also permit long-distance selling.

Center the title one-third of the way down from the top of the first panel.

Avoid "floating" the title equidistant from the top and bottom of the front panel of the brochure. Floating titles are often difficult to read at a glance. Consider reducing the title size and line spacing and then centering the title one-third of the way down from the top of the page.

This approach permits you to position the title as a distinct visual unit at the reader's center of attention, rather than dissipate the words throughout the front panel, as in the left-hand example.

More importantly, placement one-third of the way down from the top of the panel creates a contrasting pool of white space below the title, which you can use to emphasize the brochure's subtitle or motto, or your firm's name, address, and phone numbers.

The
Sebago Lakes
Region:

Your 4 Season
Getaway

The
Sebago Lakes
Region:

Your 4 Season
Getaway

The vertically centered title in the left-hand example lacks impact because equal amounts of white space are above and below it.

Centering the title one-third of the way down presents a more positive impression and allows subsidiary information to emerge more clearly.

178 Use photographs to unify your brochure.

Grouped photographs can provide panel-to-panel unity. Several photographs of the same size and shape placed together can provide horizontal unity between panels. This technique is especially useful when the amount of text that must be accommodated doesn't permit you to add a lot of white space at the tops of each panel. Photographs cropped to horizontal rectangles work especially well. Often, a series of small photographs can provide alternate views and more visual variety than possible by using fewer, larger photographs.

A series of horizontal photographs carries the reader's eyes from panel to panel, unifying the panels of the brochure.

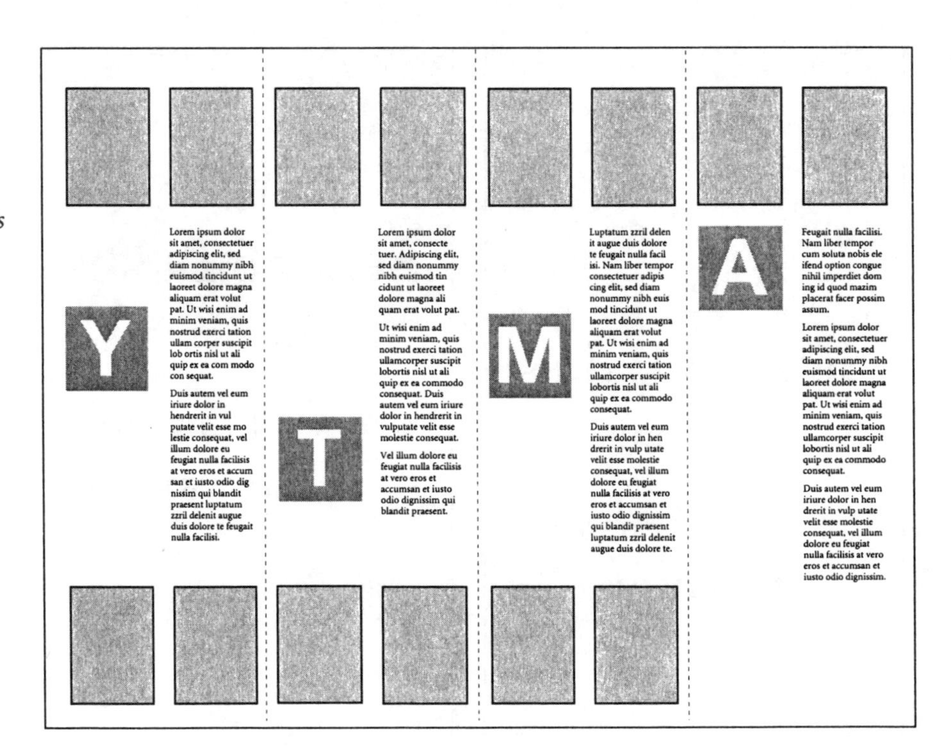

Use multicolumn formats for even simple brochures.

Even the simplest three-fold brochure can benefit from a multicolumn layout. A multicolumn format builds white space into each panel and provides an easy way to emphasize subheads placed flush right, next to the text they introduce.

In addition to framing text columns with white space, a multicolumn format provides a pool of white space to emphasize photographs. If you have access to a variety of text weights, you can add pull-quotes in a light or italicized typeface.

Notice the impact of the headline on the front panel, set flush left in a condensed, heavy typeface. This headline benefits from white space above and to its left. Notice how the type on the front page, set large with additional leading, provides a smooth transition between the headline and the body copy on the inside pages.

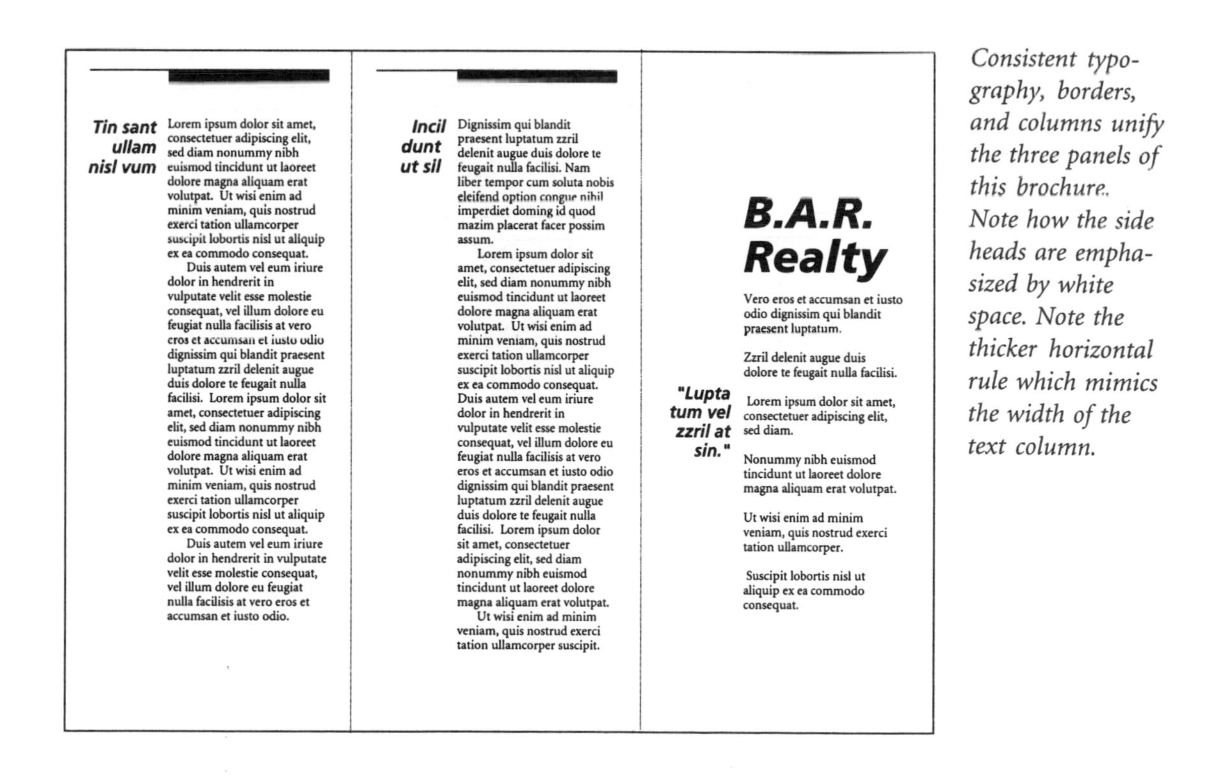

Tin sant ullam nisl vum

Lorem ipsum dolor sit amet, consectetuer adipiscing elit, sed diam nonummy nibh euismod tincidunt ut laoreet dolore magna aliquam erat volutpat. Ut wisi enim ad minim veniam, quis nostrud exerci tation ullamcorper suscipit lobortis nisl ut aliquip ex ea commodo consequat.

Duis autem vel eum iriure dolor in hendrerit in vulputate velit esse molestie consequat, vel illum dolore eu feugiat nulla facilisis at vero eros et accumsan et iusto odio dignissim qui blandit praesent luptatum zzril delenit augue duis dolore te feugait nulla facilisi. Lorem ipsum dolor sit amet, consectetuer adipiscing elit, sed diam nonummy nibh euismod tincidunt ut laoreet dolore magna aliquam erat volutpat. Ut wisi enim ad minim veniam, quis nostrud exerci tation ullamcorper suscipit lobortis nisl ut aliquip ex ea commodo consequat.

Duis autem vel eum iriure dolor in hendrerit in vulputate velit esse molestie consequat, vel illum dolore eu feugiat nulla facilisis at vero eros et accumsan et iusto odio.

Incil dunt ut sil

Dignissim qui blandit praesent luptatum zzril delenit augue duis dolore te feugait nulla facilisi. Nam liber tempor cum soluta nobis eleifend option congue nihil imperdiet doming id quod mazim placerat facer possim assum.

Lorem ipsum dolor sit amet, consectetuer adipiscing elit, sed diam nonummy nibh euismod tincidunt ut laoreet dolore magna aliquam erat volutpat. Ut wisi enim ad minim veniam, quis nostrud exerci tation ullamcorper suscipit lobortis nisl ut aliquip ex ea commodo consequat. Duis autem vel eum iriure dolor in hendrerit in vulputate velit esse molestie consequat, vel illum dolore eu feugiat nulla facilisis at vero eros et accumsan et iusto odio dignissim qui blandit praesent luptatum zzril delenit augue duis dolore te feugait nulla facilisi. Lorem ipsum dolor sit amet, consectetuer adipiscing elit, sed diam nonummy nibh euismod tincidunt ut laoreet dolore magna aliquam erat volutpat.

Ut wisi enim ad minim veniam, quis nostrud exerci tation ullamcorper suscipit.

B.A.R. Realty

Vero eros et accumsan et iusto odio dignissim qui blandit praesent luptatum.

Zzril delenit augue duis dolore te feugait nulla facilisi.

"Lupta tum vel zzril at sin."

Lorem ipsum dolor sit amet, consectetuer adipiscing elit, sed diam.

Nonummy nibh euismod tincidunt ut laoreet dolore magna aliquam erat volutpat.

Ut wisi enim ad minim veniam, quis nostrud exerci tation ullamcorper.

Suscipit lobortis nisl ut aliquip ex ea commodo consequat.

Consistent typography, borders, and columns unify the three panels of this brochure. Note how the side heads are emphasized by white space. Note the thicker horizontal rule which mimics the width of the text column.

Business Communications

Your correspondence tells a lot about you and the firm or association your print communications represent. Your letterheads and fax cover sheets can communicate either your willingness to pay attention to detail or a clichéd, half-hearted attitude.

Use consistent multicolumn grids and typography to unify your print communications. 180

Avoid the temptation to center every element. Centering vertically crowds the information and wastes valuable white space to the left and right of each entry, as the top examples illustrate.

Instead, use a multicolumn grid with uneven column widths as a framework for print communications. Right-align the firm's logo, address, main switchboard phone number, and fax number in the left-hand column. Left align the individual's name, position, and voice mail number in the right-hand column.

This preserves a logical hierarchy of information, separates "firm" from "individual" information, and frames the print communication with white space, as shown in the bottom examples.

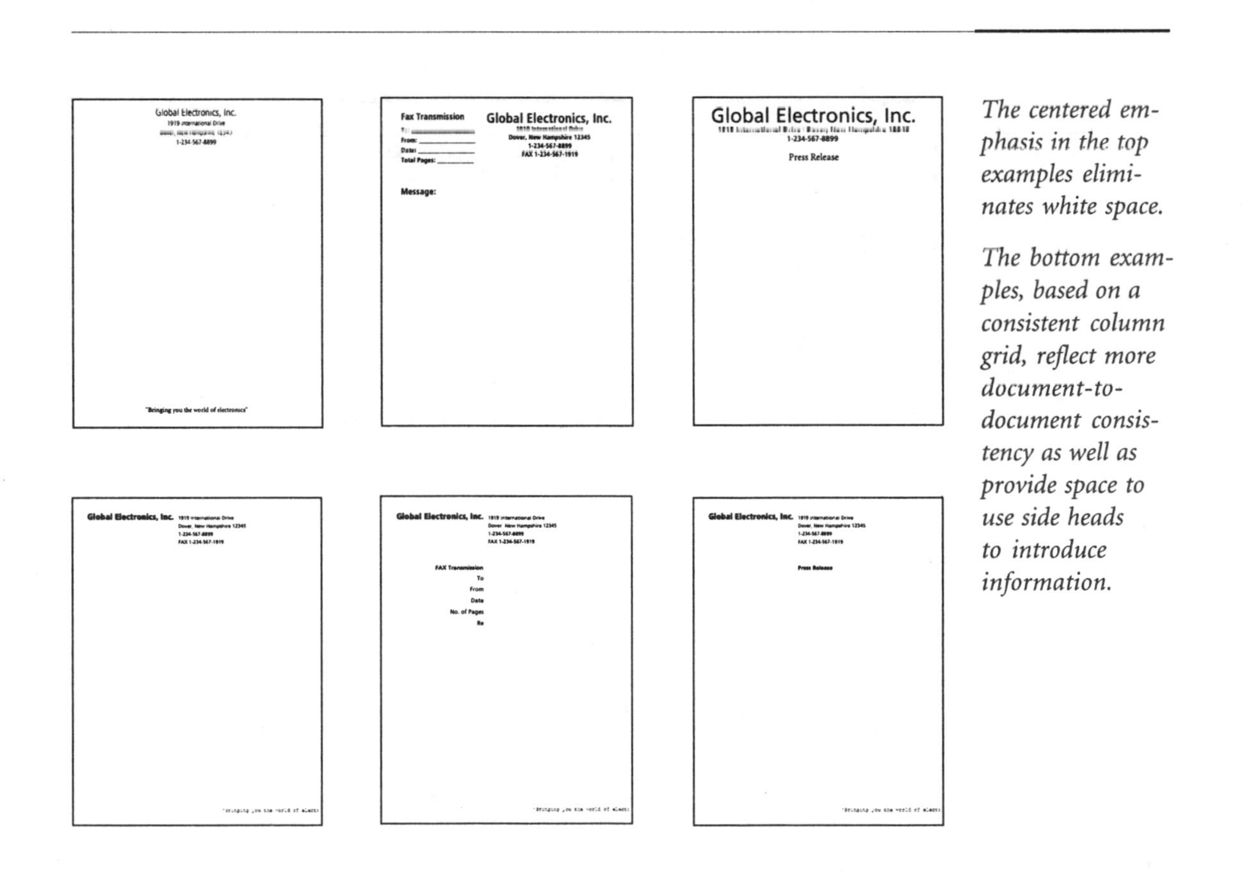

The centered emphasis in the top examples eliminates white space.

The bottom examples, based on a consistent column grid, reflect more document-to-document consistency as well as provide space to use side heads to introduce information.

181 Use white space and typographic contrast to separate "origin" and "destination" information.

Placing "to" and "from" information in your letters allows you to eliminate a separate fax cover sheet, saving both paper and long-distance transmission time. Here's a four-step way of creating a distinctive fax communication.

Step 1: Create a two-column format with a left-hand column wide enough to accommodate your logo.

Step 2: Add a fax identifier.

Step 3: Right align the "To," "From," and "Date" information in the left-hand column along the vertical spine of the page. Left align the information each field introduces.

Step 4: Left align the text of your letters in the right-hand column along the vertical spine that separates "To," "From," and "Date" information.

The trapped white space, unnecessary punctuation and whimsical, centered headline detract from the professionalism of the firm sending the fax shown in the top example.

The bottom example presents a more professional image. Note the alignment of the headline with the recipient information and date.

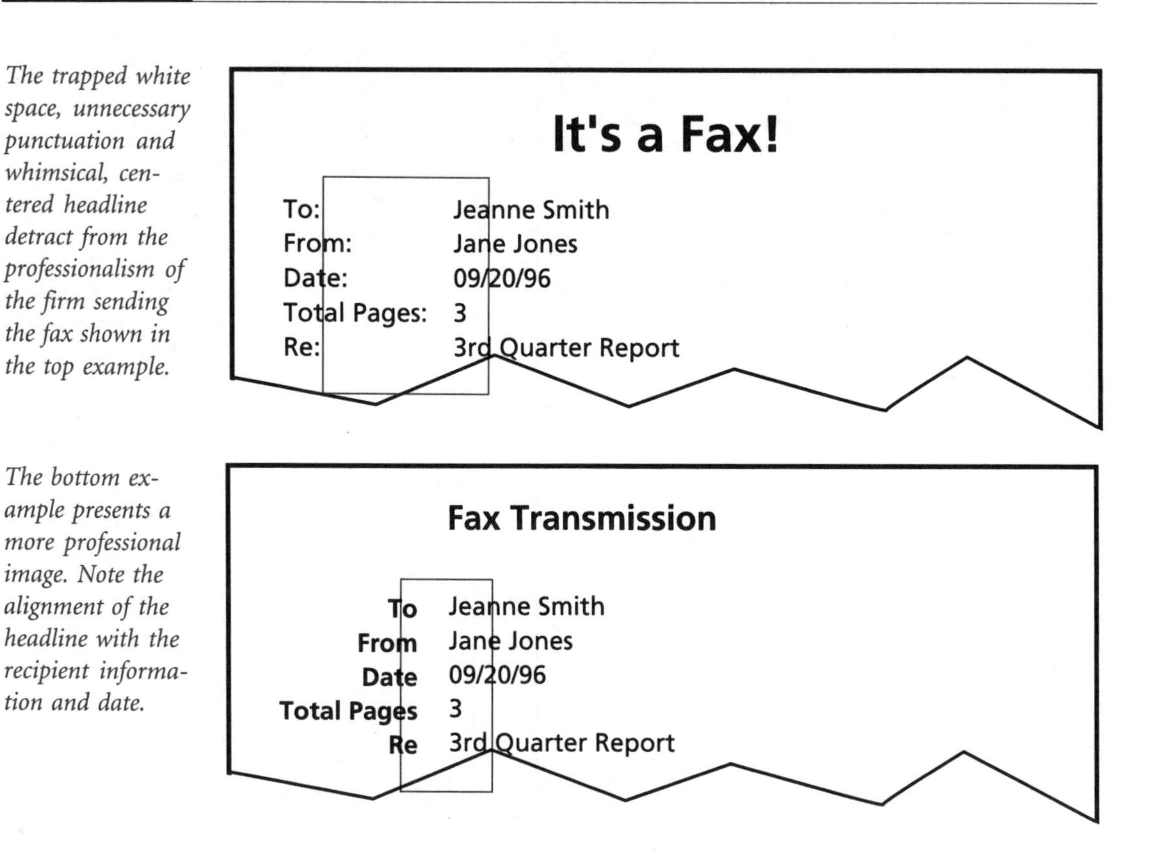

Plan your correspondence so type doesn't appear on fold lines.

Laser toner cracks and falls off on lines of type placed where the page is folded. Words that fall into the crack where you fold your letter are difficult to read. In addition, the folding may cause the laser toner to flake when the letter is unfolded.

To eliminate "toner peel" and illegible letters, align the top margin of the text so that lines of type do not appear where you fold your letter before placing it in an envelope.

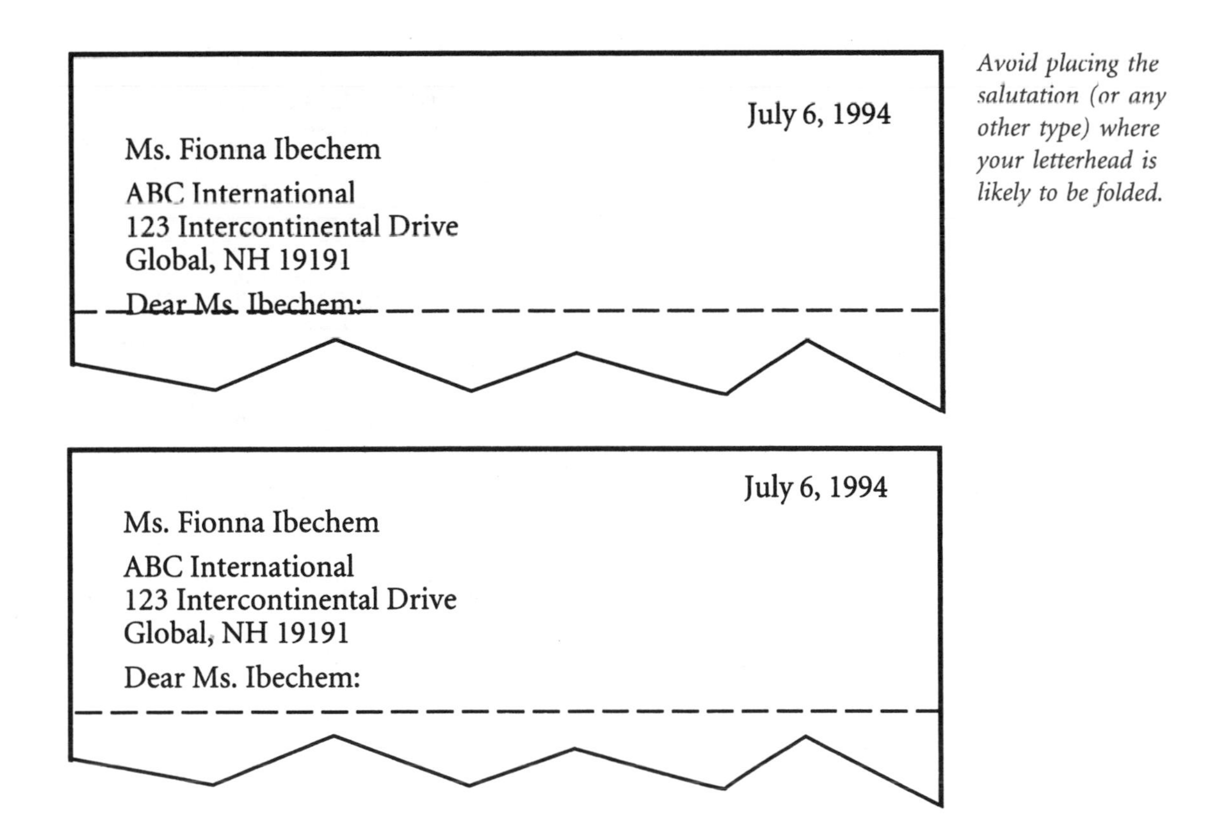

Avoid placing the salutation (or any other type) where your letterhead is likely to be folded.

183 Use typographic contrast and graphic accents to create a visual hierarchy of information.

Proposals, press releases, personnel background sheets, and department-level procedures and training materials are important parts of every association's and firm's print communications. You can pre-sell prospects on your professionalism and make your documents easier to read by using contrasting typography and graphic accents to clearly indicate each level of information.

Options include using a large, contrasting typeface set in uppercase type and accented by a strong horizontal rule to emphasize level one subheads, combined with lighter rules and level two subheads set in a smaller upper- and lowercase type. Level three subheads can be run-ins set in italics with the same typeface and type size used in the body copy.

Hanging indents can be used to further differentiate each subhead level.

Without typographic contrast, it is impossible to ascertain sequence or separate the important from the unimportant in the example at left.

In the right-hand example, typeface, type size, case, and varying indents make the different levels of information clearly obvious.

Handling Complaints

Listen without comment.

Lorem ipsum dolor sit amet, consectetuer adipiscing elit, sed diam nonummy nibh euismod tincidunt ut laoreet dolore magna aliquam erat volutpat. Ut wisi enim ad minim veniam, quis nostrud exerci tation ullamcorper suscipit lobortis nisl ut aliquip ex ea commodo consequat.

Purchase history.

Lorem ipsum dolor sit amet, consectetuer adipiscing elit, sed diam nonummy nibh euismod tincidunt ut laoreet dolore magna aliquam erat volutpat.

When purchased?

Et iusto odio dolore te feugait nulla facilisi. Nam liber tempor cum soluta nobis eleifend option congue nihil imperdiet doming id quod mazim placerat facer possim assum.

Where purchased?

Lorem ipsum dolor sit amet, consectetuer adipiscing elit, sed diam nonummy nibh euismod tincidunt ut laoreet dolore magna aliquam erat volutpat.

Reason for dissatisfaction.

Ut wisi enim ad minim veniam, quis nostrud exerci tation ullamcorper suscipit lobortis nisl ut aliquip ex ea commodo consequat. Duis autem vel eum iriure dolor in hendrerit in vulputate velit esse.

When did problem occur?

Molestie consequat, vel illum dolore eu feugiat nulla facilisis at vero eros et accumsan et iusto odio dignissim qui blandit praesent luptatum zzril delenit augue duis dolore te feugait nulla facilisi.

Lorem ipsum dolor sit amet, consectetuer adipiscing elit, sed diam nonummy nibh euismod tincidunt ut laoreet dolore magna aliquam erat

HANDLING COMPLAINTS

LISTEN WITHOUT COMMENT.

Lorem ipsum dolor sit amet, consectetuer adipiscing elit, sed diam nonummy nibh euismod tincidunt ut laoreet dolore magna aliquam erat volutpat. Ut wisi enim ad minim veniam, quis nostrud exerci tation ullamcorper suscipit lobortis nisl ut aliquip ex ea commodo consequat.

Purchase history.

Lorem ipsum dolor sit amet, consectetuer adipiscing elit, sed diam nonummy nibh euismod tincidunt ut laoreet dolore magna aliquam erat volutpat.

When purchased?

Et iusto odio dolore te feugait nulla facilisi. Nam liber tempor cum soluta nobis eleifend option congue nihil imperdiet doming id quod mazim placerat facer possim assum.

Where purchased?

Lorem ipsum dolor sit amet, consectetuer adipiscing elit, sed diam nonummy nibh euismod tincidunt ut laoreet dolore magna aliquam erat volutpat.

Reason for dissatisfaction.

Ut wisi enim ad minim veniam, quis nostrud exerci tation ullamcorper suscipit lobortis nisl ut aliquip ex ea commodo consequat. Duis autem vel eum iriure dolor in hendrerit in vulputate velit esse.

WHEN DID PROBLEM OCCUR?

Molestie consequat, vel illum dolore eu feugiat nulla facilisis at vero eros et accumsan et iusto odio dignissim qui blandit praesent luptatum zzril delenit augue duis dolore te feugait nulla facilisi.

Lorem ipsum dolor sit amet, consectetuer adipiscing elit, sed diam nonummy nibh euismod tincidunt ut laoreet dolore magna aliquam erat volutpat.

184

Align headers and footers with text.

Avoid centered headers with hanging indents and indented columns of text. The lack of alignment destroys publication unity. Instead, set header information flush left, aligned with the left edge of the text column. In addition, if you are using a horizontal rule to separate the header from the publication text, make sure the rule is only as wide as the text column.

Likewise, if you are placing the page numbers in the footers, align the page numbers with the left margin of the text column. To make the page numbers easier to find, you could emphasize them with a short horizontal rule.

Proposal To Ajax Chemicals
Re: Hazardous Waste Cleanup
Presented July 16, 1996

Lorem ipsum dolor sit amet, consectetuer adipiscing elit, sed diam nonummy nibh euismod tincidunt ut laoreet dolore magna aliquam erat volutpat. Ut wisi enim ad minim veniam, quis nostrud exerci tation ullamcorper suscipit lobortis nisl ut aliquip ex ea commodo consequat.

Duis autem vel eum iriure dolor in hendrerit

In vulputate velit esse molestie consequat, vel illum dolore eu feugiat nulla facilisis at vero eros et accumsan et iusto odio dignissim qui blandit praesent luptatum zzril delenit augue duis dolore te feugait nulla facilisi. Lorem ipsum dolor sit amet, consectetuer adipiscing elit, sed diam nonummy nibh euismod tincidunt ut laoreet dolore magna aliquam erat volutpat. Ut wisi enim ad minim veniam, quis nostrud exerci tation ullamcorper suscipit lobortis nisl ut aliquip ex ea commodo consequat.

Duis autem vel eum iriure eros et accumsan

Et iusto odio dolore te feugait nulla facilisi. Nam liber tempor cum soluta nobis eleifend option congue nihil imperdiet doming id quod mazim placerat facer possim assum.

Lorem ipsum dolor sit amet

Lorem ipsum dolor sit amet, consectetuer adipiscing elit, sed diam nonummy nibh euismod tincidunt ut laoreet dolore magna aliquam erat volutpat. Ut wisi enim ad minim veniam, quis nostrud exerci tation ullamcorper suscipit lobortis nisl ut aliquip ex ea commodo consequat. Duis autem vel eum iriure dolor in

Page 99

Proposal To Ajax Chemicals
Re: Hazardous Waste Cleanup
Presented July 16, 1996

Lorem ipsum dolor sit amet, consectetuer adipiscing elit, sed diam nonummy nibh euismod tincidunt ut laoreet dolore magna aliquam erat volutpat. Ut wisi enim ad minim veniam, quis nostrud exerci tation ullamcorper suscipit lobortis nisl ut aliquip ex ea commodo consequat.

Duis autem vel eum iriure dolor in hendrerit

In vulputate velit esse molestie consequat, vel illum dolore eu feugiat nulla facilisis at vero eros et accumsan et iusto odio dignissim qui blandit praesent luptatum zzril delenit augue duis dolore te feugait nulla facilisi. Lorem ipsum dolor sit amet, consectetuer adipiscing elit, sed diam nonummy nibh euismod tincidunt ut laoreet dolore magna aliquam erat volutpat. Ut wisi enim ad minim veniam, quis nostrud exerci tation ullamcorper suscipit lobortis nisl ut aliquip ex ea commodo consequat.

Duis autem vel eum iriure eros et accumsan

Et iusto odio dolore te feugait nulla facilisi. Nam liber tempor cum soluta nobis eleifend option congue nihil imperdiet doming id quod mazim placerat facer possim assum.

Lorem ipsum dolor sit amet

Lorem ipsum dolor sit amet, consectetuer adipiscing elit, sed diam nonummy nibh euismod tincidunt ut laoreet dolore magna aliquam erat volutpat. Ut wisi enim ad minim veniam, quis nostrud exerci tation ullamcorper suscipit lobortis nisl ut aliquip ex ea commodo consequat. Duis autem vel eum iriure dolor in

99

The centered header information and page number in the left-hand example detract from page unity and reduce the impact of the hanging indents.

Careful alignment of header information and page numbers in the right-hand example reinforces the text column and adds impact to the hanging indents.

185 Replace dot leaders with typographic contrast.

Dot leaders in price lists and menus can quickly become very distracting. The parallelism created by the dot leaders makes it difficult to read the adjacent text. As an alternative, set prices in a contrasting type face or type size, flush left with the text they describe.

For further emphasis and ease of reading, set prices flush left on their own line. This avoids the continuity problem encountered when prices are set flush right. When prices are set flush right, your readers' eyes are directed to the outer edges of the margin which makes it difficult for them to return to the next entry. When prices are set flush left on their own line, the prices are surrounded by white space and it is easier for readers to move on to the next entry.

The top example presents an uninteresting, gray appearance because of a lack of typographic contrast and the horizontal rows of dot leaders set at varying distances apart.

In the bottom example, a multi-column arrangement, employing typographic contrast and flush-left alignment presents a far more interesting arrangement.

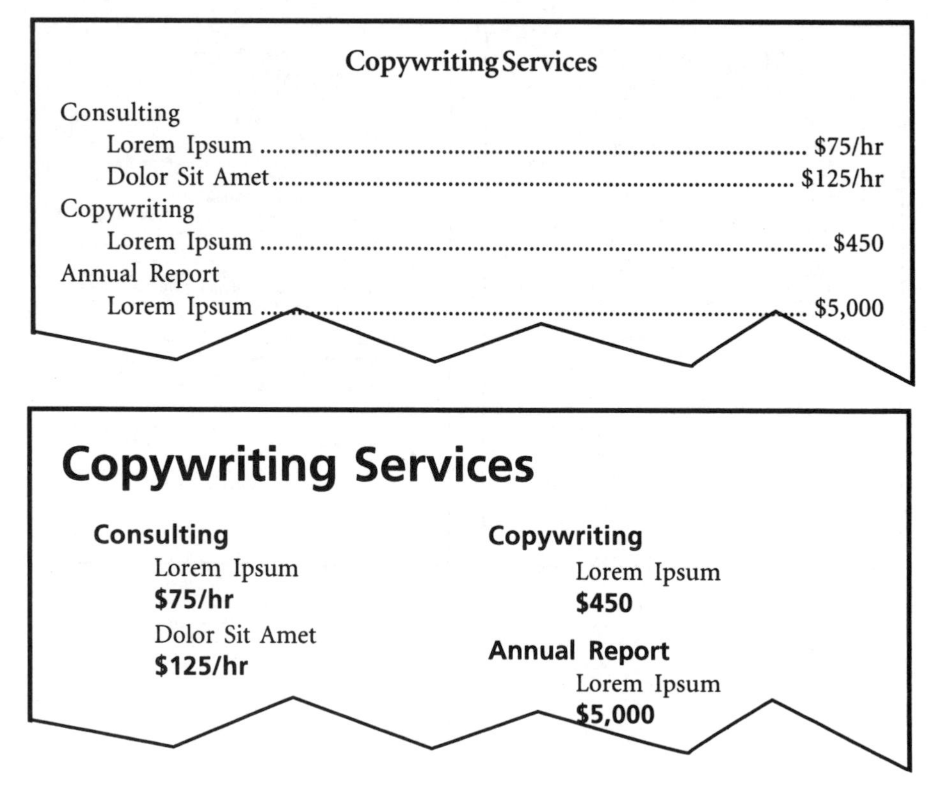

Newsletters

For many associations and firms, newsletters offer the most cost-effective way to keep in touch with employees, contributors, past customers, and prospective customers. Newsletters are economical to print and distribute since there is no "waste" circulation. You can target your message to those most likely to support you. In addition, newsletters permit you to present your message in a credible editorial framework.

Use undersize and oversize formats with discretion.

Traditional formats are easier to read and easier to save than innovative formats. Tabloid-sized newsletters are difficult to read because they are harder to hold and difficult to store on a shelf or in a file cabinet. In addition, the large size of a tabloid page often encourages you to use a type size too large to be comfortably read at arms length.

Likewise, half-sized newsletters are less likely to be saved because they can get easily "lost" in a filing cabinet and they offer less flexibility to accommodate graphics of varying size.

Properly used, the standard 8½-by-11-inch format offers the ideal compromise between flexibility, impact, and economy. The skillful use of typography, white space and color usually offer sufficient ways to differentiate your publication from your competitor's without compromising efficiency.

Issues like the age (and, in this case, size) of your audience and where your publication is likely to be read must play a role in publication planning. Tabloid-sized publications are especially difficult to read on airplanes!

187 Align the title and subtitle with the columns in the underlying grid.

Instead of centering your newsletter's title, set the title and subtitle flush left or flush right with one of the columns in the underlying grid. Centered nameplates often lack impact because white space is divided on both sides of the title, lessening the impact of the surrounding white space.

In addition, when the lines of a centered nameplate are almost, but not quite, the same length, the shorter line often looks accidentally indented.

You can add emphasis to the nameplate by aligning it with the underlying grid. This concentrates white space to the left of the title. The resulting asymmetry adds visual interest to the page. In addition, the page projects a more professional image because of the alignment between the nameplate and the text column below.

Right alignment of the subtitle also surrounds it with white space, instead of hiding it under the title.

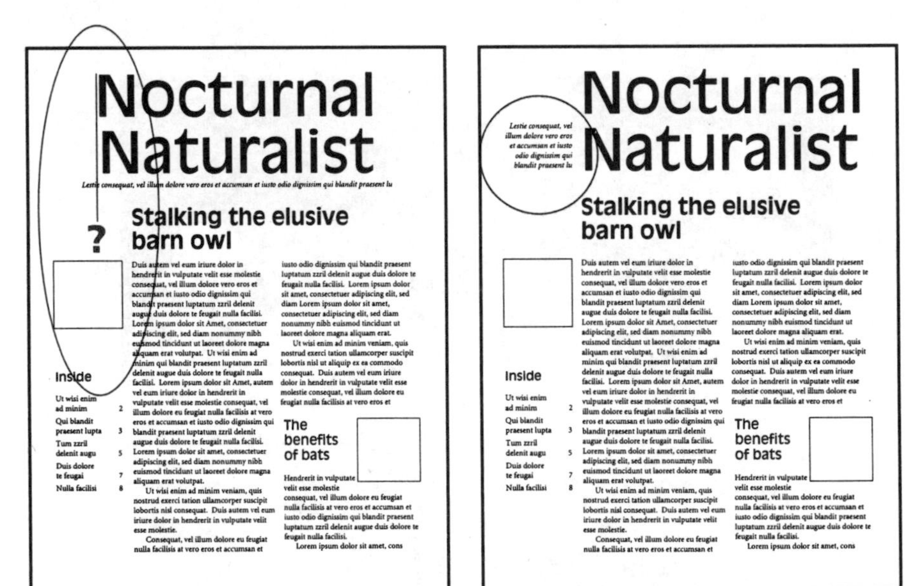

The second line of the centered nameplate at left looks accidentally indented because the words are of roughly the same length. In addition, the left-hand edge of the title does not align with the text or visuals on the page.

In the example on the right, left aligning the title with the text column creates a more professional appearance and provides space for the stacked flush-right subtitle.

Base the title of your newsletter on initials rather than words.

Instead of spelling out a long publication name, base the nameplate on a stylized interpretation of its initials and spell out the name in the subtitle. The nameplate in the top example lacks impact because it contains long words and has to be set in a relatively small type size.

The bottom example, however, based on the initials of the title amplified by spelled-out words, has far more impact. The result is a more visually compelling title.

This technique makes the title of your newsletter a friendly, easy-to-say acronym. After the first few issues the nameplate becomes less important. It becomes more a "graphic or icon to be recognized" than "text to be read." Readers will recognize its size and shape, and move on to the headlines that immediately follow.

It's hard to get excited over a newsletter title set in three words of equal size, as in the top example. Notice the lack of white space.

When the title is reduced to an acronym, the key letters can be set very large without detracting from surrounding white space.

189 Use typographic contrast to add impact to the most important word(s) in the nameplate.

Choose the most important word(s) in your title and make use of typographic contrast to make it stand out. Your options include the following contrast tools:

Typeface families, such as serif versus sans serif

Type size, i.e. large versus small

Type style, such as roman versus italic

Weight, i.e. light versus heavy

Letterspacing

Foreground/background (reverses or background screens)

Color

Any combination of the preceding tools can make the most important word(s) of your newsletter title emerge clearly.

The top example is lifeless because it consists of four words of roughly equal weight.

New Hampshire
Concerned Parent

How to begin a meaningful dialog with your teenager

dolore eu feugiat nulla facilisis at vero eros et accumsan et iusto odio dignissim qui blandit praesent l...tum zzril delenit a... ...lore

The bottom example emphasizes "Concerned Parent" and subordinates the "New Hampshire" modifier.

New Hampshire
Concerned Parent

How to begin a meaningful dialog with your teenager

dolore eu feugiat nulla facilisis at vero eros et accumsan et iusto odio dignissim qui blandit praesent l...tum zzril delenit a... ...lore

Avoid overemphasizing unimportant title information.

Reduce the size of publication information that is repeated from issue to issue. After readers encounter it once or twice, the words lose their value. Replace these "empty" words with larger headlines or more nameplate contrast.

Often, the date of publication and the volume/issue numbers are given far more prominence than needed. These words can create a barrier which slows down the reader's eye movement into the first headline.

Often, the volume and issue numbers can be omitted, unless the newsletter has long-term reference value or its many years of publication communicates credibility.

Reducing nameplate clutter enables you to use a larger, easier-to-use nameplate typography. It also permits you to increase the size of front page headlines and photographs.

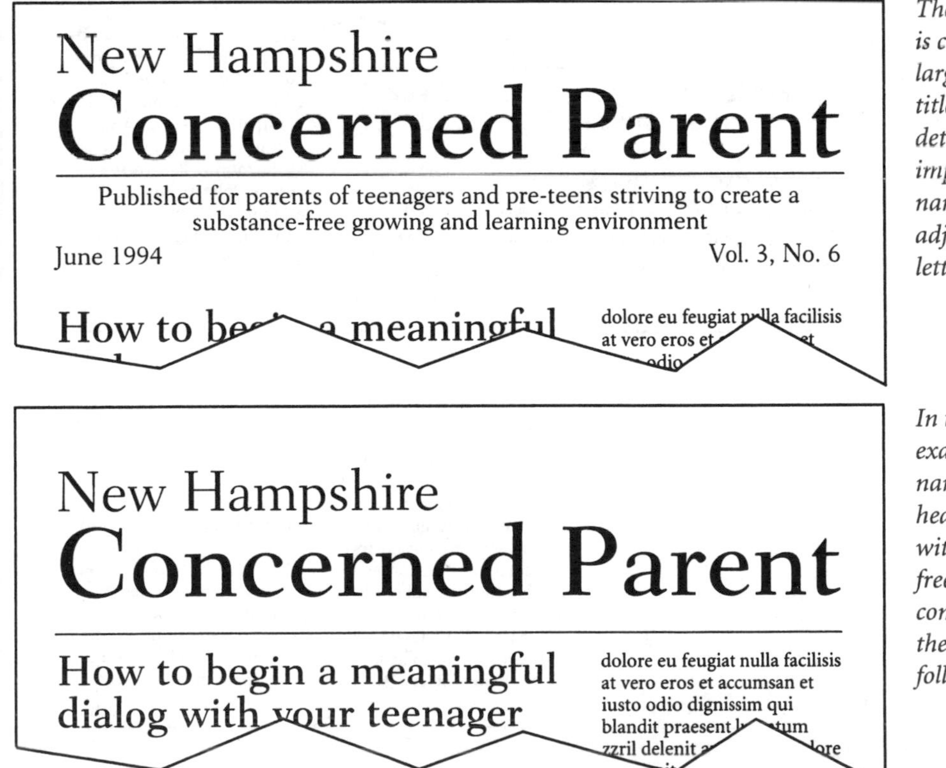

The top example is cluttered. The large folio and subtitle information detract from the impact of the nameplate and adjacent newsletter.

In the bottom example, the nameplate and headlines emerge with added impact, free from visual competition with the words that follow.

191 Include only relevant front-cover information.

Include a table of contents only when there is a chance that readers may miss important articles. Everything you omit from the front cover of your newsletter offers you an opportunity to include additional white space or increase typographic contrast by using a larger type size or heavier typeface design. Here are three things to watch for especially:

Add volume and issue number information only if your newsletter is likely to be saved or formally cataloged in a library.

If your newsletter contains only four pages, readers are likely to glance at every page, making a formal table of contents unnecessary.

Avoid listing front-page articles in a table of contents appearing on the front page. (If readers haven't noticed the article by the time they reach the table of contents, something is wrong with your headlines!)

There is rarely reason to list front-page articles in a front-page table of contents. Likewise, "Page" can be taken for granted, as the numbers certainly don't refer to hours, days, or months!

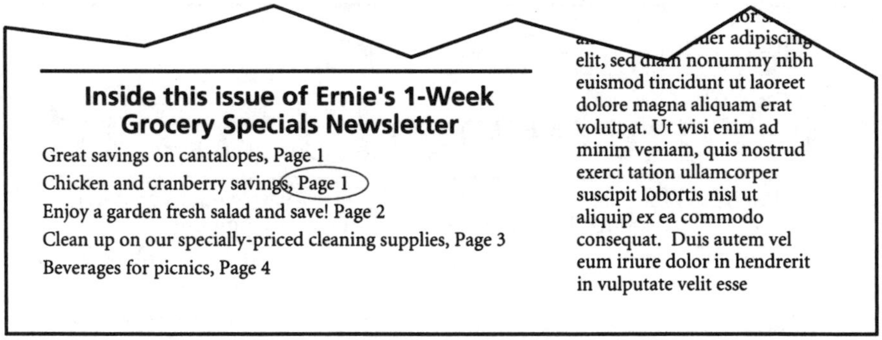

Inside this issue of Ernie's 1-Week Grocery Specials Newsletter

Great savings on cantalopes, Page 1
Chicken and cranberry savings, Page 1
Enjoy a garden fresh salad and save! Page 2
Clean up on our specially-priced cleaning supplies, Page 3
Beverages for picnics, Page 4

der adipiscing elit, sed diam nonummy nibh euismod tincidunt ut laoreet dolore magna aliquam erat volutpat. Ut wisi enim ad minim veniam, quis nostrud exerci tation ullamcorper suscipit lobortis nisl ut aliquip ex ea commodo consequat. Duis autem vel eum iriure dolor in hendrerit in vulputate velit esse

Eliminating unnecessary information in the bottom example simplifies the table of contents.

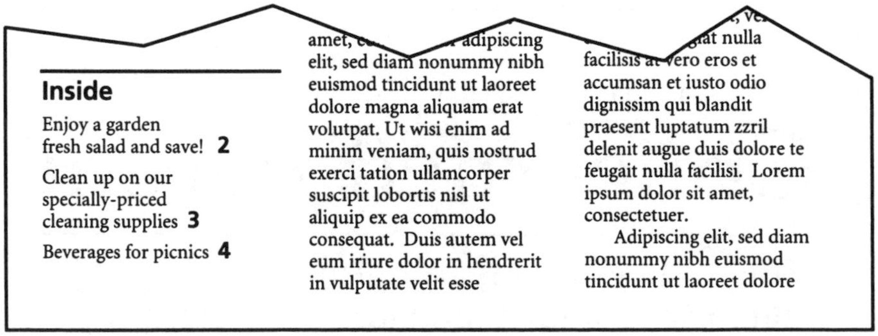

Inside

Enjoy a garden fresh salad and save! **2**
Clean up on our specially-priced cleaning supplies **3**
Beverages for picnics **4**

amet, adipiscing elit, sed diam nonummy nibh euismod tincidunt ut laoreet dolore magna aliquam erat volutpat. Ut wisi enim ad minim veniam, quis nostrud exerci tation ullamcorper suscipit lobortis nisl ut aliquip ex ea commodo consequat. Duis autem vel eum iriure dolor in hendrerit in vulputate velit esse

nulla facilisis at vero eros et accumsan et iusto odio dignissim qui blandit praesent luptatum zzril delenit augue duis dolore te feugait nulla facilisi. Lorem ipsum dolor sit amet, consectetuer.

Adipiscing elit, sed diam nonummy nibh euismod tincidunt ut laoreet dolore

Organize your newsletter with department heads that reflect nameplate typography.

192

Unify your newsletter by repeating the same typeface and type style choices in department heads throughout your newsletter. Department heads help your readers quickly locate desired categories of information. When created using the same typographic tools as employed in the nameplate, department heads reinforce the "look" established by the front page nameplate, emphasizing your newsletter's unique visual identity and providing page-to-page unity.

Effective department heads help readers immediately identify the category of information they introduce, as well as add character to the newsletter.

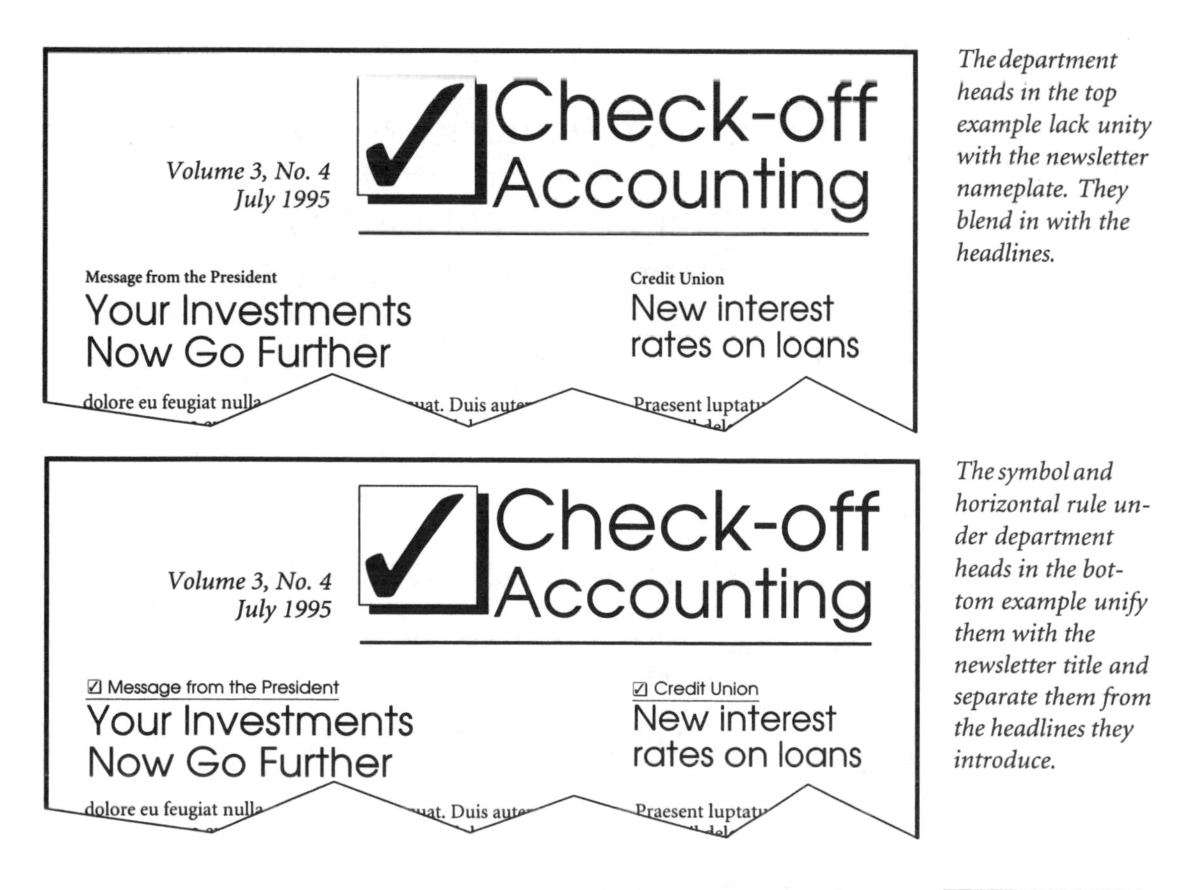

The department heads in the top example lack unity with the newsletter nameplate. They blend in with the headlines.

The symbol and horizontal rule under department heads in the bottom example unify them with the newsletter title and separate them from the headlines they introduce.

193 Avoid title/headline and department head/headline ambiguity.

The nameplate, or title, of your newsletter should not compete with front-page headlines. The nameplate should be prominent enough to identify your publication. Yet, the dominant visual elements on the front cover should be headlines and photographs.

Remember that, after the first issue, the title of your publication becomes an icon, or visual symbol, rather than a word or words to be consciously read.

Likewise, department heads should not be used as headlines. Words like "Editorial," "Message from the Editor," or "Letter from the Executive Director" are department heads, not headlines. Department heads should introduce headlines, not replace them.

In the top example, the title and headline, set in the same typeface and type size, compete with each other.

Journal of Pediatrics & Podiatrists

New Imaging Technology Promises Preventive Diagnostics

Duis autem vel eum iriure dolor in hendrerit in vulputate velit esse molestie consequat, vel illum dolore vero eros et
amet, consectetuer adipiscing elit, sed diam nonummy nibh euismod tincidunt ut laoreet dolore magna

In the lower example, typeface and type size contrasts separate the title and headline. In addition, flush-right placement is used to further separate title from headline.

Use a consistent grid throughout your newsletter.

194

Use the same column size and placement for each page of your newsletter. This unifies your newsletter, makes it easier to produce, and creates a pleasing page-to-page unity.

Disorganized pages result if column widths are adjusted to suit available photographs. Often, no two columns are the same width. In other cases, the columns are "almost, but not quite" equal in width, leading to ambiguity. Columns of different widths slow down readers because they have to constantly change their rhythmic left-to-right eye movements to suit lines of different length. Columns of irregular width often cause "shoehorned" text and trapped white space.

A consistent grid provides a repeating structure that unifies your newsletter.

Country Music Revival Hits New England!

The music that never left

All ages enjoy toe-tapping rhythms

More and more full-time musicians

New generation discovers its roots

Country Music Revival Hits New England!

The music that never left

All ages enjoy toe-tapping rhythms

More and more full-time musicians

New generation discovers its roots

The example at left, based on columns of irregular width, is hard to create and hard to read. The text above the photo appears to be "filler" material.

The example at right, utilizing two columns of equal width placed on a five-column grid, presents a more professional image, plus is easier to produce and easier to read.

195 Avoid "accidental" white space.

When using five- or seven-column grids, always include a text or visual element that provides purpose for the white space. White space must never appear "unfinished." Place a table of contents or a short feature in the white space, or perhaps allow a pull-quote, photograph, or chart from the adjacent text column to extend into the white space.

Narrow columns without any text or graphic elements look "unfinished." Readers may think a piece of artwork fell off on the way to the printer.

"Empty" white space columns are especially distracting when there is only a top border.

In the left-hand example, the white space adjacent to the text looks incomplete, like something was inadvertently omitted.

In the example at right, the white space is defined by photo and caption.

Experiment with horizontal page layouts.

196

Two parallel columns of text appear easier to read than a single long column. By organizing your articles in horizontal modules, using short, parallel columns, your articles will appear shorter. Horizontal newsletters are particularly effective for newsletters where the primary emphasis is on text and articles are of similar length.

Horizontal arrangements simplify production. Since they will appear in the same relative position, headlines can be of the same size and extend the full width of the columns. When the two columns are asymmetrically placed on the page, horizontal layouts reflect a contemporary appearance.

In horizontal arrangements, article placement should reflect the desired hierarchy of importance. Important articles should appear first.

POLITICAL
INSIGHTS

Election Reveals Widespread Discontent

Lorem ipsum dolor sit amet, consectetuer adipiscing elit, sed diam nonummy nibh euismod tincidunt ut laoreet dolore magna aliquam erat volutpat. Ut wisi enim ad minim veniam, quis nostrud exerci tation ullamcorper suscipit lobortis nisl ut aliquip ex ea commodo consequat. Duis autem vel eum iriure dolor in hendrerit in vulputate velit esse molestie consequat, vel illum dolore eu feugiat nulla facilisis at vero eros et accumsan et iusto odio dignissim qui blandit praesent luptatum zzril delenit augue duis dolore te feugait nulla facilisi. Lorem ipsum dolor sit amet, consectetuer adipiscing elit, sed diam nonummy nibh euismod tincidunt ut laoreet dolore magna aliquam erat volutpat.

Ut wisi enim ad minim veniam, quis nostrud exerci tation ullamcoit lobortis nisl ut aliquip ex ea commodo consequat.

Duis autem vel eum iriure dolor in hendrerit in vulputate velit esse molestie consequat, vel illum dolore eu feugiat facilisis at vero eros et accumsan et iusto odio dignissim qui blandit praesent luptatum zzril delenit augue duis dolore te feugait nulla facilisi. Nam liber tempor cum soluta nobis eleifend option congue nihil imperdiet doming id adipiscing elit, sed diam nonummy nibh euismod tincidunt ut laoreet dolore magna aliquam erat. Volutpat ut wisi enim ad minim.

Predictions Evaluated

Dignissim qui blandit praesent luptatum zzril delenit augue duis dolore te feugait nulla facilisi. Nam liber tempor cum soluta nobis eleifend option congue nihil imperdiet doming id quod mazim placerat facer possim assum.

Lorem ipsum dolor sit amet, consectetuer adipiscing elit, sed diam nonummy nibh euismod tincidunt ut laoreet veniam, quis nostrud exerci tation ullamcorper suscipit lobortis nisl ut aliquip ex ea commodo consequat.

Duis autem vel eum iriure dolor in hendrerit in vulputate velit esse molestie consequat, vel illum dolore eu feugiat nulla facilisis at vero eros et accumsan et iusto.

Fresh Start Next Time

Dolore magna aliquam erat volutpat. Ut wisi enim ad minim veniam, quis nostrud exerci tation ullamcorper suscipit lobortis nisl ut aliquip ex ea commodo consequat. Duis autem vel eum iriure dolor in hendrerit in vulputate velit esse molestie consequat, vel illum dolore eu feugiat nulla facilisis at vero eros et accumsan et iusto odio dignissim qui blandit praesent luptatum zzril delenit augue duis dolore te feugait nulla facilisi. Lorem ipsum dolor sit amet, consectetuer adipiscing elit.

POLITICAL
INSIGHTS

Election Reveals Widespread Discontent

Lorem ipsum dolor sit amet, consectetuer adipiscing elit, sed diam nonummy nibh euismod tincidunt ut laoreet dolore magna aliquam erat volutpat. Ut wisi enim ad minim veniam, quis nostrud exerci tation ullamcorper suscipit lobortis nisl ut aliquip ex ea commodo consequat. Duis autem vel eum iriure dolor in hendrerit in vulputate velit esse molestie consequat, vel illum dolore eu feugiat nulla facilisis at vero eros et accumsan et iusto odio dignissim qui blandit praesent luptatum zzril delenit augue duis dolore te feugait nulla facilisi. Lorem ipsum dolor sit amet. consectetuer adipiscing elit, sed diam nonummy nibh euismod tincidunt ut laoreet dolore magna aliquam erat volutpat.

Ut wisi enim ad minim veniam, quis nostrud exerci tation ullamcoit lobortis nisl ut aliquip ex ea commodo consequat.

Duis autem vel eum iriure dolor in hendrerit in vulputate velit esse molestie consequat, vel illum dolore eu feugiat facilisis at vero eros et accumsan et iusto odio dignissim qui blandit praesent luptatum zzril delenit augue duis dolore te feugait nulla facilisi. Nam liber tempor cum soluta nobis eleifend option congue nihil imperdiet doming id adipiscing elit, sed diam nonummy nibh euismod tincidunt ut laoreet dolore magna aliquam erat. Volutpat ut wisi enim ad minim.

Predictions Evaluated

Dignissim qui blandit praesent luptatum zzril delenit augue duis dolore te feugait nulla facilisi. Nam liber tempor cum soluta nobis eleifend option congue nihil imperdiet doming id quod mazim placerat facer possim assum.

Lorem ipsum dolor sit amet, consectetuer adipiscing elit, sed diam nonummy nibh euismod tincidunt ut laoreet veniam, quis nostrud exerci tation ullamcorper suscipit lobortis nisl ut aliquip ex ea commodo consequat.

Duis autem vel eum iriure dolor in hendrerit in vulputate velit esse molestie consequat, vel illum dolore eu feugiat nulla facilisis at vero eros et accumsan et iusto.

Fresh Start Next Time

Dolore magna aliquam erat volutpat. Ut wisi enim ad minim veniam, quis nostrud exerci tation ullamcorper suscipit lobortis nisl ut aliquip ex ea commodo consequat. Duis autem vel eum iriure dolor in hendrerit in vulputate velit esse molestie consequat, vel illum dolore eu feugiat nulla facilisis at vero eros et accumsan et iusto odio dignissim qui blandit praesent luptatum zzril delenit augue duis dolore te feugait nulla facilisi. Lorem ipsum dolor sit amet, consectetuer adipiscing elit.

In the left-hand example, the first article appears extremely long because it extends the full height of the page.

In the right-hand example, the articles appear shorter because they consist of shorter, side-by-side columns.

Presentation Visuals

At one time or another, just about everyone has to stand up in front of a group and present their opinion, recommendations, or sales arguments. The success of your presentation depends in great measure upon the quality of the presentation visuals you use to reinforce your words.

Avoid including too much information in each presentation visual.

197

Think of your overhead transparencies and 35mm slides as "shorthand" rather than "longhand." Visuals should provide a framework, not a word-for-word script. If you include too many words in each visual, you have to use a small typeface that is hard for your audience to read. In addition, when you include too many words, you are tempted to read your visuals word for word, rather than use them as an outline to interpret and expand upon. Use key words rather than complete sentences.

In addition, do not try to cover too many points in each visual. Divide long topics among several visuals.

A good rule of thumb: Each visual should cover no more than five or six points, each described by four to six words.

Demographic Trends Require New Approaches to Home Design

* Lorem ipsum dolor sit amet, consectetuer adipiscing elit, sed diam nonummy nibh euismod tincidunt ut laoreet dolore magna aliquam erat volutpat.
* Ut wisi enim ad minim veniam, quis nostrud exerci tation ullamcorper suscipit lobortis nisl ut aliquip ex ea commodo consequat.
* Duis autem vel eum iriure dolor in hendrerit in vulputate velit esse molestie consequat, vel illum dolore eu feugiat nulla facilisis at vero eros et accumsan et iusto odio dignissim qui blandit praesent luptatum zzril delenit augue duis dolore te feugait nulla facilisi.
* Lorem ipsum dolor sit amet, consectetuer adipiscing elit, sed diam nonummy nibh euismod tincidunt ut laoreet dolore magna aliquam erat volutpat. Ut wisi enim ad minim veniam, quis nostrud exerci tation ullamcorper suscipit lobortis nisl ut aliquip ex ea commodo consequat.
* Duis autem vel eum iriure dolor in hendrerit in vulputate velit esse molestie consequat, vel illum dolore eu feugiat nulla facilisis at vero eros et accumsan et iusto odio dignissim qui blandit praesent luptatum zzril delenit augue duis dolore te feugait nulla facilisi.Nam liber tempor cum soluta nobis eleifend option congue nihil imperdiet doming id quod mazim placerat facer possim assum.

Brooklyn/Seattle Planning Associates

Trends & Designs

- **Lorem ipsum dolor**
- **Ut wisi enim ad minim**
- **Duis autem vel eum**
- **Sit amet, consectetuer adipiscing**
- **Vel eum iriure dolor in hendrerit**

Brooklyn/Seattle Planning Associates

The example at left contains so much information that there is nothing left for the presenter to say. He might as well have stayed home and mailed copies of his overheads to the members of the audience!

The example at right, restricted to "shorthand," provides a framework for the presenter's discussion and elaboration.

198 Base presentation visuals on horizontal multicolumn grids.

Horizontal presentation visuals based on multicolumn grids force you to be concise and avoid the boring, centered look of most vertical overhead transparencies and 35mm slides. Horizontal orientation encourages you to use a *few lines of large type*, in contrast to vertical orientation which encourages a "typewritten" look, characterized by too many lines of small type in each visual.

In addition, those in the back of the audience invariably find it difficult to read text at the bottom of vertical overheads.

Multicolumn grids build in vertical white space and "hang" the title to the left of the topics contained in your overhead transparency or 35mm slide.

The vertical orientation of the left-hand example, encourages you to include too many lines of small type.

In the right-hand example, the title emerges clearly because it is shorter and begins to the left of the list it introduces.

Demographic Trends Require New Approaches to Home Design

* Lorem ipsum dolor sit amet, consectetuer adipiscing elit, sed diam nonummy nibh euismod tincidunt ut laoreet dolore magna aliquam erat volutpat.
* Ut wisi enim ad minim veniam, quis nostrud exerci tation ullamcorper suscipit lobortis nisl ut aliquip ex ea commodo consequat.
* Duis autem vel eum iriure dolor in hendrerit in vulputate velit esse molestie consequat, vel illum dolore eu feugiat nulla facilisis at vero eros et accumsan et iusto odio dignissim qui blandit praesent luptatum zzril delenit augue duis dolore te feugait nulla facilisi.
* Lorem ipsum dolor sit amet, consectetuer adipiscing elit, sed diam nonummy nibh euismod tincidunt ut laoreet dolore magna aliquam erat volutpat. Ut wisi enim ad minim veniam, quis nostrud exerci tation ullamcorper suscipit lobortis nisl ut aliquip ex ea commodo consequat.
* Duis autem vel eum iriure dolor in hendrerit in vulputate velit esse molestie consequat, vel illum dolore eu feugiat nulla facilisis at vero eros et accumsan et iusto odio dignissim qui blandit praesent luptatum zzril delenit augue duis dolore te feugait nulla facilisi.Nam liber tempor cum soluta nobis eleifend option congue nihil imperdiet doming id quod mazim placerat facer possim assum.
* Lorem ipsum dolor sit amet, consectetuer adipiscing elit, sed diam nonummy nibh euismod tincidunt ut laoreet dolore magna aliquam erat volutpat.

Brooklyn/Seattle Planning Associates

Trends & Designs

- **Lorem ipsum dolor**
- **Ut wisi enim ad minim**
- **Duis autem vel eum**
- **Sit amet, consectetuer adipiscing**
- **Vel eum iriure dolor in hendrerit**

Use sans serif typefaces for presentation visuals.

199

Unless you enjoy total control over your presentation environment, always design your presentation visuals for optimum viewing under the worst possible lighting conditions. "Worst-case-scenario" presentation designs force you to use the largest practical type size and keep the number of words to a minimum.

Large, bold sans serif typefaces with high x-heights offer the best possible "back-of-the-room" viewing under the widest variety of lighting conditions.

When projected, serif typefaces, with their detailed serifs and varying stroke width, often present a harder-to-read, "busier" appearance than simple sans serif typefaces.

TRENDS
Determine Design
- Lorem ipsum dolor
- Ut wisi enim ad minim
- Duis autem vel eum
- Sit amet, consectetuer adipiscing
- Vel eum iriure dolor in hendrerit
- Adipiscing elit, sed diam

TRENDS
Determine Design
- Lorem ipsum dolor
- Ut wisi enim ad minim
- Duis autem vel eum
- Sit amet, consectetuer adipiscing
- Vel eum iriure dolor in hendrerit
- Adipiscing elit, sed diam

As the example at left shows, the beauty of a serif typeface is often wasted when viewed from a distance. The details of the letters become lost at a distance.

Although less elegant, the sans serif typefaces in the example at right will be much easier to read when projected.

200 Number your presentation visuals.

Numbers help you organize your presentation and keep your audience informed of your progress. One of the easiest ways to create a presentation is to title it "25 Steps To Goal" (e.g. "Increased Sales"). Audiences appreciate numbered visuals because the numbers help them keep track of your presentation's progress.

In addition, you'll especially appreciate numbered visuals in case you accidentally drop your overhead transparencies or your 35mm slides get out of order.

Most presentation software programs automatically number your visuals. These numbers can be placed discretely along the bottom of each visual, or you can use the number to provide a dominant visual, especially useful if your visuals consist primarily of text.

The left-hand example, without a number, is an invitation to disaster in case the visuals get out of order.

The right-hand example not only makes it far easier to return the visuals to their proper order, but also keeps the audience informed of the presentation's progress.

TRENDS
Determine Design
Lorem ipsum dolor
Ut wisi enim ad minim
Duis autem vel eum
Sit amet, consectetuer adipiscing
Vel eum iriure dolor in hendrerit

32 TRENDS
Determine Design
Lorem ipsum dolor
Ut wisi enim ad minim
Duis autem vel eum
Sit amet, consectetuer adipiscing
Vel eum iriure dolor in hendrerit

Résumés

Your résumé is often the most important advertisement you ever write. Prospective employees often make "pass/fail" decisions on your qualifications by quickly glancing at your résumé. A good-looking résumé allows your past successes to emerge with clarity and impact, opening the door to an interview, so you can complete your selling job in person.

Use multicolumn formats and side heads to separate categories of information.

201

In order to fit as much information on a single page as possible, use a multicolumn format with side heads. Use flush-right side heads to organize information. Side heads avoid the wasted vertical space of subheads set between the paragraphs of text.

Flush-right alignment locks the side heads to the information they introduce.

By reducing line length, multicolumn formats permit a more comfortable relationship between type size and line length. Wide columns extending the width of a page force the use of a relatively large type size and line spacing.

Jeanne Q. Smith
123 Fourth St.
Dover, NH 56789

Position

Lorem ipsum dolor sit amet, consectetuer adipiscing elit, sed diam nonummy nibh euismod tincidunt ut laoreet dolore magna aliquam.

Employment History

1990 - Present. Lerat volutpat. Ut wisi enim ad minim veniam, quis nostrud exerci tation ullamcorper suscipit lobortis nisl ut aliquip ex ea commodo consequat. Duis autem vel eum iriure dolor in.

1987 - 1990. Hendrerit in vulputate. Velit esse molestie consequat, vel illum dolore eu feugiat nulla facilisis at vero eros et accumsan et iusto odio dignissim qui blandit praesent luptatum zzril delenit augue duis dolore te.

1982 - 1987. Feugait nulla facilisi. Lorem ipsum dolor sit amet, consectetuer adipiscing elit, sed diam nonummy nibh euismod tincidunt ut laoreet dolore magna aliquam erat volutpat. Ut wisi enim ad minim veniam, quis nostrud exerci tation ullamcorper suscipit lobortis nisl ut aliquip ex ea commodo consequat.

1979 - 1982. Duis autem. Vel eum iriure dolor in hendrerit in vulputate velit esse molestie consequat, vel illum dolore eu feugiat nulla facilisis at vero eros et accumsan et iusto odio dignissim qui blandit praesent luptatum zzril delenit augue duis dolore te feugait nulla facilisi.

Education

Nam liber tempor cum soluta. 1978.
Nobis eleifend option congue nihil imperdiet. 1974.
Doming id quod mazim. 1973.
Lorem ipsum dolor sit amet. 1971.

Jeanne Q. Smith
123 Fourth St.
Dover, NH 56789

Position Lorem ipsum dolor sit amet, consectetuer adipiscing elit, sed diam nonummy nibh euismod tincidunt ut laoreet dolore magna aliquam.

Employment History 1990 - Present. Lerat volutpat. Ut wisi enim ad minim veniam, quis nostrud exerci tation ullamcorper suscipit lobortis nisl ut aliquip ex ea commodo consequat. Duis autem vel eum iriure dolor in.

1987 - 1990. Hendrerit in vulputate. Velit esse molestie consequat, vel illum dolore eu feugiat nulla facilisis at vero eros et accumsan et iusto odio dignissim qui blan dit praesent luptatum zzril delenit augue duis dolore te.

1982 - 1987. Feugait nulla facilisi. Lorem ipsum dolor sit amet, consectetuer adipiscing elit, sed diam nonum my nibh euis mod tincidunt ut laoreet dolore magna aliquam erat volutpat. Ut wisi enim ad minim veniam, quis nostrud exerci tation ullamcorper suscipit lobortis nisl ut aliquip ex ea commodo consequat.

1979 - 1982. Duis autem. Vel eum iriure dolor in hendre rit in vulputate velit esse molestie consequat, vel illum dolore eu feugiat nulla facilisis at vero eros et accumsan et iusto odio dignissim qui blandit praesent luptatum zzril delenit augue duis dolore te feugait nulla facilisi.

Education Nam liber tempor cum soluta. 1978.
Nobis eleifend option congue nihil imperdiet. 1974.
Doming id quod mazim. 1973.
Lorem ipsum dolor sit amet. 1971.

In the example at left, the lines of type are too long and the organizing information is difficult to locate.

The side heads in the example at right are easier to locate. There is also a more comfortable relationship between type size and line length.

202 Eliminate unnecessary words.

You seldom need to identify a résumé as a résumé. Thus, there is no reason to add a headline or title.

Likewise, address and telephone numbers are obvious and do not need to be identified as such.

Every time you eliminate unnecessary words, you gain more space to emphasize your unique achievements and accomplishments, increasing your chances of getting hired.

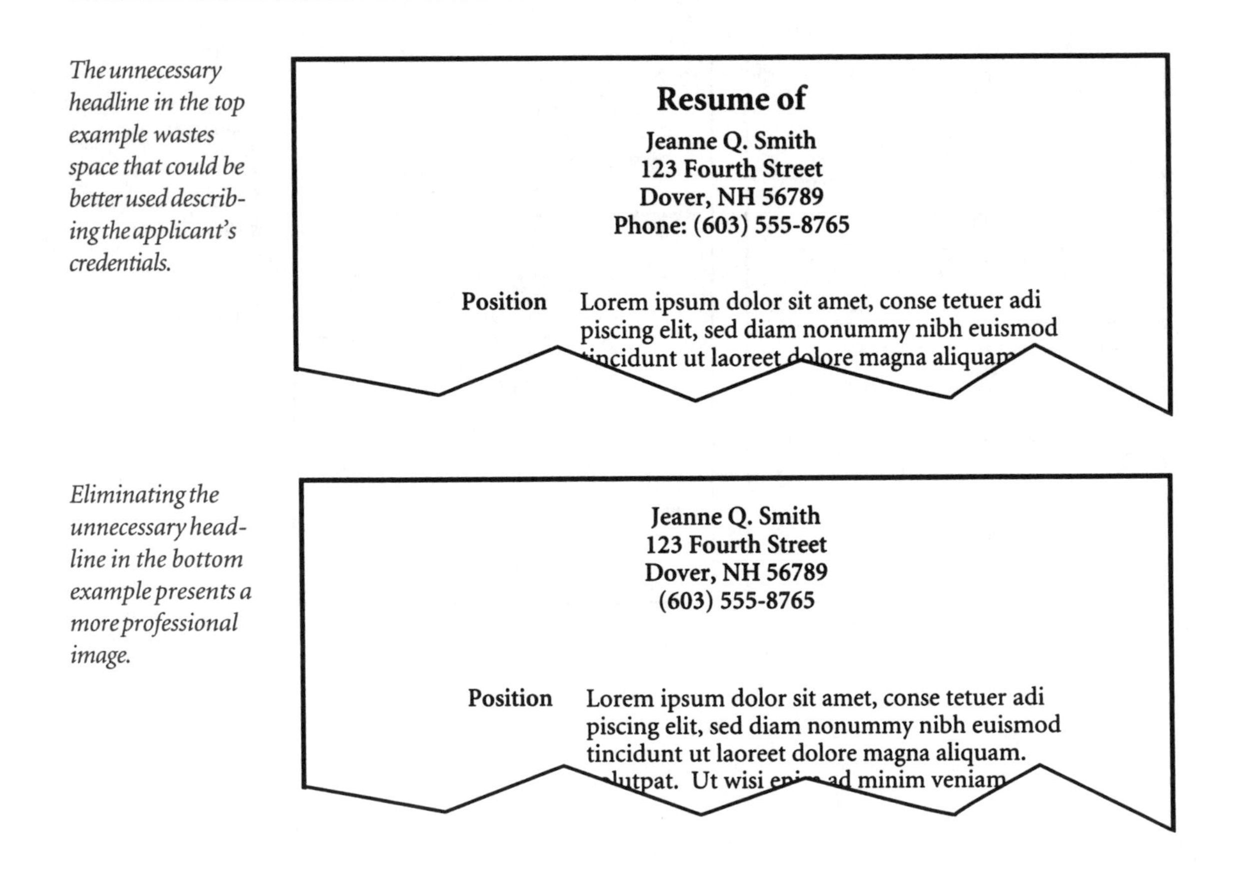

Resume of

Jeanne Q. Smith
123 Fourth Street
Dover, NH 56789
Phone: (603) 555-8765

Position Lorem ipsum dolor sit amet, conse tetuer adi piscing elit, sed diam nonummy nibh euismod tincidunt ut laoreet dolore magna aliquam

Jeanne Q. Smith
123 Fourth Street
Dover, NH 56789
(603) 555-8765

Position Lorem ipsum dolor sit amet, conse tetuer adi piscing elit, sed diam nonummy nibh euismod tincidunt ut laoreet dolore magna aliquam. lutpat. Ut wisi en[illegible] ad minim veniam

The unnecessary headline in the top example wastes space that could be better used describing the applicant's credentials.

Eliminating the unnecessary headline in the bottom example presents a more professional image.

Emphasize accomplishments not years. 203

Prospective employers are more interested in what you did than when you did it. Your accomplishments should attract the reader's eyes, not the dates of employment at various jobs. Prospective employers are interested in experience first, chronology second.

Thus, use typographic contrast and graphic accents to emphasize your most important accomplishments. The years when you did them can be less prominently mentioned in the text.

1981 - 1984	Fienjars, Inc., Manchester, NH. Program Support. Lorem ipsum dolor sit amet, consectetuer adipiscing elit, sed diam nonummy nibh euismod tincidunt ut laoreet dolore magna aliquam erat volutpat.
1984 - 1987	Smith Technologies, Derry, NH. Ut wisi enim ad minim veniam, quis nostrud exerci tation ullamcorper suscipit lobortis nisl ut aliquip ex ea commodo consequat.
1987 - 1992	Tri-State Electronics, Somerworth, NH. Duis autem vel ... dolor in ... vulputate ...

The top example wrongly focuses the prospective employer's attention on chronology rather than on accomplishments.

Youngest to achieve Triple-A Rating	Fienjars, Inc., Manchester, NH. 1981-1984. Program Support. Lorem ipsum dolor sit amet, consectetuer adipiscing elit, sed diam nonummy nibh euismod tincidunt ut laoreet dolore magna aliquam erat volutpat.
Reduced service calls 28%	Smith Technologies, Derry, NH. 1984 - 1987. Ut wisi enim ad minim veniam, quis nostrud exerci tation ullamcorper suscipit lobortis nisl ut aliquip ex ea commodo consequat.
Debug...	... Electronics ... rth, NH. 198...

The bottom example does a much better job of emphasizing past accomplishments.

204 Emphasize accomplishments not employers.

Prospective employers are more interested in what you did than where you did it. In most cases, especially when applying for jobs emphasizing initiative, perseverance, or quality, your accomplishments are more important than the names, addresses, and phone numbers of your employers.

If prospective employers are attracted by your accomplishments and feel you can contribute to their success, they will search out the details of your past employment history.

By placing emphasis on accomplishments rather than employer names and addresses, you can improve your chances of getting hired by quantifying your achievements in specific terms.

The bottom example does a more effective selling job because the reader's attention is focused on past accomplishments rather than information that will only be needed to check credentials.

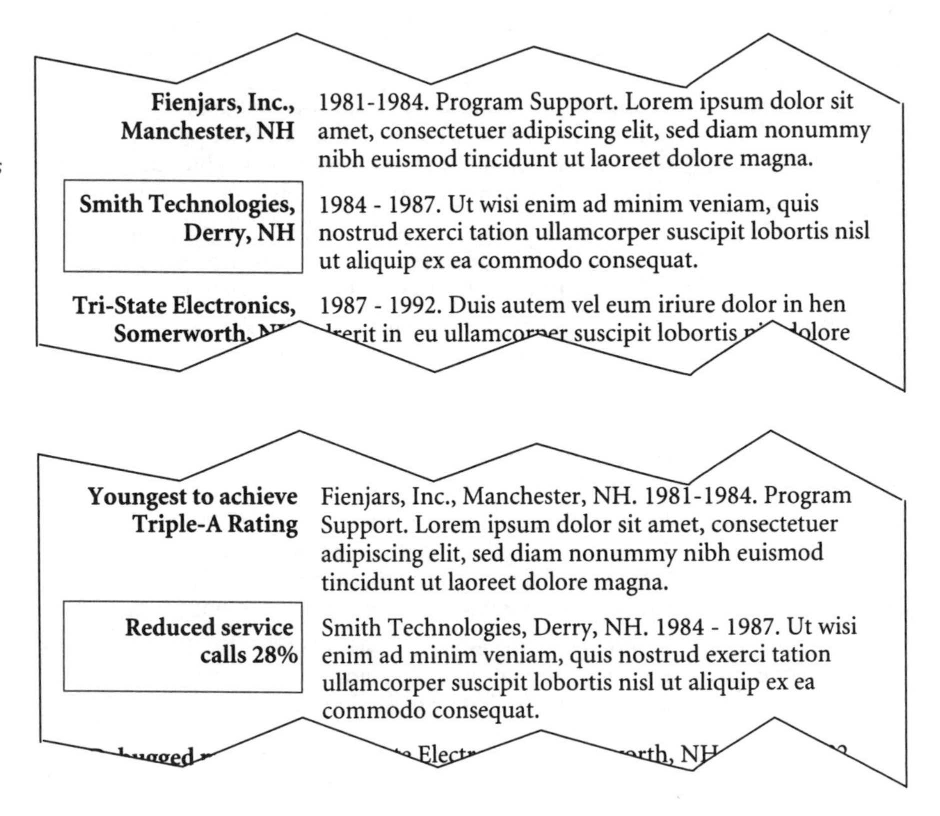

Appendix: Six Steps to Success

Step 1
Plan

Identify publication goals and necessary ingredients.

Start by writing out the goals of your publication and identifying audience needs and expectations. Use the questions in Points 1 and 4 as your guides. Your design skills will improve in quality and speed to the extent that you analyze your projects before beginning work.

At the same time, inventory the text and graphic elements to be included in your publication. A flyer to be hung on the walls of a Laundromat announcing a yard sale and read from three feet away requires a totally different approach than a proposal for funding a new space research project.

Design is information made obvious. Never let "creativity" get in the way of practicality and appropriateness.

Step 2
Experiment

Create reduced-size thumbnail drawings showing desired column arrangement and placement of headlines and visuals.

Review the samples in your "inspiration file" for publications containing elements you might want to include in your publication. Don't be afraid of plagiarism: by the time you have adapted these ideas to your own needs and made all your own refinements, the finished product will usually be very much yours.

Then, using one of the preprinted column grids as your guide, try out different arrangements of text and graphics using pencil and paper. Work as quickly as possible, avoiding the temptation to self-edit your ideas or work too precisely. Your goal at this point is to simply get a "feel" for alternative ways of arranging the text and graphics.

You'll find that your ideas flow better and that you can work faster when working with a pencil and paper than when working with a computer.

Step 3
Produce

Make appropriate typeface, type size, and type style decisions for each element of page architecture and save your choices as styles.

Once you've settled on a possible alternative, transfer your rough drawings to the computer. At this point, your publication begins to come alive as you replace "thick and thin squiggly lines" with actual typeface and type size choices.

When you are satisfied with your typeface decisions, save them as styles. Styles retain formatting information and make it easy to modify the appearance of your entire publication by simply editing the styles.

Use an image scanner to add visuals such as photographs, or indicate the placement of visuals and tables with square and rectangular boxes.

Step 4
Revise

Create and print the first version. Use the "Save As" command to try out different alternatives.

This is where the real work begins!

It is unlikely that the first version of your publication to emerge from your laser printer will be your final choice. When you see your publication at actual size, you usually can identify many areas of improvement. Typical improvements at this point include:

- Fine-tuning type size and line spacing
- Experimenting with letterspacing and word spacing justification limits
- Rewriting headlines so fewer words communicate the same ideas in less space

As you review your publication and the graphic accents and tools of emphasis employed, constantly ask yourself: "Is this word or graphic accent absolutely necessary?" As you approach the end of this step, your most important contribution will likely be that of removing elements you previously thought were essential.

Often, several printouts are necessary before you are satisfied with your working version.

Step 5
Review

When you are satisfied, analyze your document in terms of its coherence to your publication goals and audience expectations identified in Step 1. Ask yourself the following questions:

- How appropriate is your publication in terms of its *transparency* in delivering its intended message? Successful publications recede into the background, allowing their message to attract the reader's attention.
- Does your publication's design reflect the desired hierarchy of ideas?
- How successfully does your publication satisfy audience expectations?

Your publications will gain in impact to the extent that you critically analyze them in terms of their intended audience and function.

Step 6 Refine

Fine-tune and revise your work as many times as necessary, using the Preflight Checklist as your guide.

The final step may occupy as much as one-quarter of your total publication time, but the payoff comes in greatly improved communications.

Document fine-tuning involves such issues as

- Eliminating unwanted spacing within headlines and body copy – for example, default headline spacing and excess spacing following punctuation
- Reviewing hyphenation decisions to make sure that words are hyphenated according to their context and to eliminate "loose" and "tight" lines and unnecessary hyphens
- Proofreading to eliminate inappropriate spell-checker substitutions

The above six steps clearly indicate the importance of planning and iteration. Professional designers seldom get it right the first time. Rather, what separates a design professional from a design amateur is a willingness to take the time to plan before acting, an openness to experiment with alternative designs, and – most important – a disciplined commitment to getting the details right.

Your design skills will improve to the extent that you're willing to continually *plan, experiment, and revise.*

Glossary

Arm

Arm refers to the horizontal stroke found in the middle of uppercase A's and H's. The height, thickness, and slope of the arm play a very visible role in typeface design.

Ascender

Ascenders are typeface strokes contained in letters like b, d, l, and t that extend above the x-height of the typeface. Ascenders play an important role in reading as they contribute to each word's unique shape when set in lowercase type. Typefaces with a high x-height have shallow ascenders; typefaces with a low x-height have relatively high ascenders. Note: The cap height, or height of uppercase letters, may or may not be equal to the height of ascenders. *(See also cap height, x-height.)*

Asymmetrical

Designs characterized by unequal left-right balance, left-aligned or staggered headlines, columns of different widths, and significant differences in the sizes of photographs. *(See also symmetrical.)*

Axis

The axis of a letter refers to the point where the left- and right-hand strokes of letters meet, like the top of an uppercase A. An axis can be sharp, blunted, or sculptured.

Baseline

Baseline refers to the invisible line that a line of type rests on. The baseline is easily determined by looking at letters without descenders and is easily observed by looking at letters like x, i, and l. Notice that in some cases letters with rounded bottoms, like o's, extend below the baseline in order to maintain optical alignment with adjacent letters.

Black

Black refers to typeface weights created by using heavier or thicker strokes than those found in bold versions. Helvetica Black, for example, is a significantly heavier typeface design than Helvetica Bold. *(See also light, weight, ultra bold.)*

Bleed

A bleed refers to ink reproducing text, visuals, or graphic elements that extend to the physical page borders of a page, i.e. the trim size. Bleeds help make a page look larger than it really is, add motion to photographs, and avoid unwanted borders around background elements (like reversed newsletter nameplates). Bleeds increase printing costs because they require a larger paper size and trimming.

Blurb

Blurbs are sentences that elaborate on headlines. Blurbs are typically placed between the headline and the text it introduces. *(See also deck.)*

Bold

Bold type is used for emphasis. A bold typeface is composed of noticeably thicker strokes than roman, or regular text. Bold type occupies more horizontal space than roman text, reducing character count. *(See also character count, demi-bold, semi-bold.)*

Byline

Bylines are an element of page architecture identifying the author and, often, the author's qualifications or location (e.g. department or branch office). Bylines should appear below a headline and should be set in a typeface that contrasts with that of the adjacent headline or body copy.

Cap height

The cap height of a typeface refers to the height of uppercase letters. The cap height may be equal to the height of letters containing ascenders or may be either taller or shorter. *(See also ascender.)*

Character count

Character count refers to the number of characters that fit in a line of type set in a specific typeface and type size. Character count is influenced by the x-height of the typeface design.

Collage

A collage is a grouping of heavily cropped or silhouetted photographs of different sizes and shapes, arranged to form a single visual. *(See also frieze.)*

Color

In terms of type, color refers to the grayness of a page or text block. Typeface designs characterized by thick, uniform strokes create pages with a darker color than typeface designs based on thinner strokes and more open counters – or inside spaces.

Column

Column refers to the horizontal division of a page into spaces used to organize text graphics. Columns are the fundamental components in grids used to provide page frameworks. *(See also grid.)*

Condensed

Many typeface designs have been redrawn to accommodate a higher character count. True condensed typeface designs maintain the integrity of the original typeface design and avoid artificially increasing or reducing the widths of the horizontal and vertical strokes that make up each letter. Artificially condensed typeface designs are often identifiable by lighter vertical strokes. The x-height of a true condensed typeface is often higher than the original x-height, to enhance readability and prevent open spaces within the letters from closing in. *(See also character count, expanded, x-height.)*

Copy fitting

Copy fitting refers to determining the number of column inches a word processed manuscript will require when set into columns using specific typeface, type size, leading, and column width. Copy fitting also involves determining how many words will occupy every column inch set in a specified typeface, type size, leading, and column width. Copy fitting before writing helps avoid overwriting or underwriting.

Counter

Counter refers to open spaces within a character, such as the open spaces within the letters c and e. Counters contribute to your reader's ability to identify a typeface, as well as the grayness of a page or column of text. Pages set with a typeface characterized by large, open counters appear lighter than pages with smaller, closed counters.

Deck

A deck consists of one or more lines of text that elaborate on a headline and provide a transition from headline to body copy. Decks should be set in a type size midway between the headline and the body copy they introduce. Decks permit you to use shorter headlines without sacrificing information. *(See also blurb, kicker.)*

Decorative type

Decorative typeface designs are for words or phrases used to attract attention and create a desired emotional response. Decorative typefaces are rarely suitable for extended reading.

Demi-bold

Demi-bold refers to a typeface weight midway between roman, or regular, type and bold. A demi-bold weight adds emphasis without the overly dark appearance of a true bold. Demi-bold is similar to semi-bold. *(See also semi-bold.)*

Descender

Descenders are portions of the strokes, making up letters like g's, p's, and y's, that extend below the baseline of a line of type. Descenders play an important role in creating the unique outlines that readers use to identify words. *(See also ascender, baseline.)*

Dingbats

Dingbats are symbols used to introduce material in lists or separate paragraphs in a text block without paragraph indents or spacing. Zapf Dingbats is a popular collection of symbols designed by Herman Zapf.

Dot leader

Dot leaders are rows of dots used to connect categories of information, such as table of contents listings and page numbers, or food descriptions and prices in a menu.

Downrule

Vertical lines between columns are referred to as downrules. Use these lines only when absolutely necessary and not simply out of habit.

Duotone

Duotones are photographs printed in two colors. The second color is applied in a publication's second color or shades of gray. Duotones add impact to photographs by restoring detail otherwise lost.

Ellipsis

An ellipsis is a character consisting of three widely-spaced dots (. . .) used to indicate missing text. The advantage of using an ellipsis rather than three periods is that the ellipsis will not break between two lines and that dot spacing remains consistent.

Em dash

Use an em dash, rather than two hyphens, to set off parenthetical expressions. An em dash is a single line longer than two hyphens. The added length of the em dash emphasizes the parenthetical statement and prevents the two hyphens from splitting over two lines.

En dash

Use en dashes, rather than single hyphens in compound words. The extra length of the en dash makes the content clearer by eliminating confusion with hyphens used at ends of lines to indicate words split over two lines.

Expanded

Expanded refers to typeface designs that have been redrawn to create wider letters. Expanded typefaces can add impact to logos and titles. True expanded typefaces differ from scaled expanded typefaces in that the strokes that comprise the letters retain their original proportions and are not distorted. Expanded typefaces appear as separate listings on your font menu. *(See also condensed.)*

Extra bold

Extra bold refers to typeface weights one step beyond bold. Extra bold typefaces permit you to add more impact to headlines and subheads than with bold alone. *(See also semi-bold.)*

Eye

Term describing totally enclosed spaces within a letter, like in a lowercase a or e. Eyes play an important role in typeface recognition because of the foreground/background contrast they create. *(See also counter.)*

Folio

Folio information includes the publication's volume number and date of issue as well as the current page number. Folio information can also include the name of the publisher. *(See also masthead, nameplate.)*

Footer

Footer refers to text and graphic elements repeated at the bottom of each page. Footers can include borders and page numbers. *(See also header.)*

Frieze

A frieze is a group of photographs placed horizontally along the top of a page. It is often preferable to group photographs together in a frieze than to scatter them across the page. *(See also collage.)*

Geometric

Geometric typeface designs, like Avant Garde or Futura, are created out of circles and lines. They are usually characterized by even weight strokes. Although they can communicate a contemporary – or trendy – appearance, they are best used for display applications because they are difficult to read in long text blocks due to their lack of stress and other identifying characteristics which set each letter apart. *(See also Humanist, stress.)*

Greeking

Sentences consisting of random letters and words used to try out alternative layouts and illustrate the effect of various software commands. Greeking permits you to concentrate on the appearance, rather than the content, of a block of text.

Grid

A grid is a network of nonprinting horizontal and vertical lines that appear on your computer screen. Grids are used to align text and graphic elements precisely and to maintain consistent column spacing. Grid can also refer to a series of small photographs of identical size, placed close to each other, that creates the appearance of a single large photograph.

Grotesque

Grotesque refers to a category of straightforward sans serif typeface designs introduced during the 19th century. Grotesque designs are characterized by relatively high x-heights and moderate stress. The axis of the A is frequently squared. *(See also axis, Geometric, Humanist, sans serif, serif, stress.)*

Gutter

When referring to single pages, gutter refers to the space between columns. When applied to two-page spreads, gutter refers to the space between the right-hand margin of the left page and the left-hand margin of the right page. This space can be utilized when a single folded sheet of paper is used for both pages, as occurs in the center spread of a newsletter. With careful use of bleeds, you can also use this space with other pairs of pages, although it is difficult to maintain exact vertical alignment and to know exactly where the image area will be cut off.

Header

Headers refer to information placed at the top of the page. Header information typically repeats the title of the publication and the name and number of the current chapter. In newsletters, headers can include page numbers and the date of the issue. In dictionaries and encyclopedias, headers include a synopsis of the material covered on the page. *(See also footer.)*

Humanist

Typeface designs based on human handwriting, as contrasted to designs based on geometric shapes like circles and squares. Humanist typefaces typically reflect a diagonal stress, which reflects the changing stroke width created by a wide brush held in the hands. *(See also Geometric, Grotesque.)*

Icon

Symbol used to replace words, typically employed to help readers quickly identify warnings or associated information.

Initial caps

Initial caps are oversize letters used to draw the reader's eye to the first paragraph in a story. Initial caps can be raised (in which case they create white space between the paragraph and the previous paragraph); dropped (when they cut into the paragraph); or adjacent (when they are placed in the white space to the left of the paragraph).

Italic

Italic refers to typeface designs which have been redrawn to closely resemble human handwriting. In a true italic typeface, not only do the letters appear at an angle, but the shapes of the letters also are different than the roman, or regular, version. Italic typefaces occupy less space than roman type, which is one of the reasons Aldus Manutius, the originator of italic type, created it during the Italian Renaissance. *(See also oblique.)*

Jumpline

A jumpline is the page architecture element that identifies the page on which an article is continued. Jumplines can also be used to indicate the pages articles are continued from. Jumplines should be set in a contrasting typeface so they are not read as part of the article.

Kerning

Kerning refers to increasing or reducing letterspacing between selected pairs of letters. Kerning becomes more important as type size increases. Negative kerning involves reducing letterspacing. Positive kerning involves increasing letterspacing. Certain pairs of letters are more likely to require negative kerning than others, especially combinations of overhanging uppercase letters (like T, W, and Y) and short, lowercase letters (like a, o, and i). Positive kerning is necessary with certain pairs of sans serif typefaces to increase their legibility, such as increasing the spacing between l's in "million" set in Avant Garde. *(See also tracking.)*

Kerning pair

Most typeface designs come with reduced spacing for a limited number of letter pairs. Some typeface publishers, however, ship their typeface designs with up to 1,000 predefined kerning pairs, including letter pairs with increased spacing. In addition, many software programs enable you to create custom kerning tables. These are either stand-alone programs or additions to dedicated page layout programs. Such programs save you time by allowing you to define, in advance, desired letterspacing for specified letter pairs in certain typefaces and certain type sizes. Whenever you set headlines or subheads in a certain typeface and type size, the program properly spaces the letters automatically. *(See also kerning, tracking.)*

Kicker

A kicker is a short phrase introducing a headline, usually placed above the headline in a smaller type size. Kickers often help readers relate a headline to a category – for instance, "Personnel" or "Upcoming events" – or provide a conversational introduction to the headline. *(See also blurb, deck.)*

Leading

Leading refers to vertical spacing between lines of type. Leading is as important as type size in determining text readability. The term originated in the days of metal type, when strips of lead were used to separate lines of type. Leading, like type size, is measured in points. There are approximately 72 points per inch. The amount of leading required is based on the associated typeface, type size, and line length (or column width).

Ligatures

Ligatures are letter combinations that can be accessed and printed as a single character. Ligatures look more professional than separate letters, save space, and avoid unwanted hyphenation at line endings. The most common ligatures are combinations of ff, fi, fl, ffi, and ffl. Many typeface designs include a limited number of ligatures. A wider selection of ligatures is also available from a typeface's alternate character sets and Expert sets.

Light

Light refers to typeface design variations composed of very thin strokes. Although rarely used for body copy, light typefaces provide an additional method with which you can "voice" your publication because they permit you to include more white space in pages containing large headlines. Light typefaces are ideal for text used as graphics, such as oversize chapter numbers at the beginning of a chapter. *(See also black, bold, extra bold, ultra bold.)*

Lining numbers

Lining numbers are the normal numbers that come with a typeface. Lining numbers extend the full height of the uppercase letters in a typeface design. This is in contrast to Old Style Figures which have descenders and are often only as tall as the x-height of an alphabet. Use lining numbers in headlines, spreadsheets, and tables, as contrasted to Old Style Figures which are ideal for use in running text. Old Style Figures are either included in a typeface's Expert set or appear as a separate font listing in your software program's font menu. *(See also Old Style Figures.)*

Loose line

A loose line describes a visually distracting line of justified text containing unusually wide gaps between the words. Loose lines typically occur in short lines that are not hyphenated or that contain two proper nouns (which shouldn't be hyphenated). Often, the best way to eliminate loose lines is to rewrite or transpose words in a previous line, or to modify your software program's maximum word-spacing specification. *(See also tight line.)*

Masthead

The masthead is a newsletter part containing publication information such as the publisher's name, address, and telephone number; frequency of publication; subscription costs; and the names and positions of the editor and others associated with producing the newsletter. *(See also nameplate.)*

Modern

Modern typeface designs, actually introduced during the 1800s, are characterized by greater stress – or differences in thickness between horizontal and vertical strokes – than Old Style or Transitional designs. The direction of the stress is vertical, rather than diagonal. Modern typefaces are often characterized by very long, thin serifs. Examples include Bodoni, Ellington, and Waldbaum. At large sizes, Modern typefaces can communicate elegance, but are often difficult to read in extended text blocks. *(See also Old Style, stress, Transitional.)*

Monospace

Monospace refers to typeface designs in which all letters occupy the same amount of space, regardless of the space needed to reproduce it. Thus, a monospaced i is alloted the same space as a monospaced m or w. Monospaced characteristics are found on typewriters. A few monospaced typeface designs are available for computer use, where their design makes it easier to align numbers in spreadsheets. *(See also proportional spacing.)*

Mug shot

Newsletter slang term for small headshots, or photographs containing just the head of an individual, typically someone being interviewed or recently promoted. Mug shots are also used as part of the introduction to editorials.

Nameplate

A newsletter nameplate is the publication title and associated information set in a distinctive typeface, often highlighted by graphic accents like horizontal rules or reversed or tinted backgrounds. The nameplate typically contains a subtitle or motto which identifies the editorial point of view or intended audiences, as well as the volume and issue date and the publisher's name. *(See also masthead.)*

Narrow

Narrow typefaces are mathematically condensed designs, in contrast to typefaces specifically designed to occupy less space than normal designs. Narrow typefaces are typically distorted, compromising elements of the original typeface design. *(See also condensed.)*

Oblique

Oblique is a typographic term describing typeface designs placed at an angle, as opposed to italic type which has been redrawn to appear more like handwriting. An oblique typeface retains the proportions and strokes of the original letters and simply reflects the changed angle of the letters on the page. *(See also italic.)*

Old Style

Old Style is a typeface design closely resembling handwriting, characterized by diagonal stress, abrupt changes in stroke thickness and medium x-heights. Popular Old Style typefaces include Caslon and Garamond. *(See also Geometric, Humanist, Modern, Transitional.)*

Old Style Figures

Old Style Figures are a typeface option containing numbers designed to be used in body copy text. They are scaled to the x-height of the typeface and frequently contain descenders.

Old Style Figures avoid the visual disruption caused by the height of lining numbers. Old Style Figures are typically included in a typeface design's optional Expert set or as separate typeface design option appearing as a separate font listing in your program's font menu. *(See also lining numbers.)*

Ornaments

Many typeface designs include special Ornament fonts. These consist of characters that you can use to create distinctive borders. You can also use ornaments as end-of-story symbols, or to separate paragraphs placed as a single large text block without either first-line indents or extra space between paragraphs.

Orphan

An orphan consists of letters left over from a word hyphenated from a previous line, or a phrase less than one-third the length of the line, isolated at the top of a column or page. *(See also widow.)*

Pica

A pica is the fundamental unit of measurement used in graphics. There are approximately six picas to an inch. Picas are primarily used for horizontal measurements. *(See also point.)*

Point

Type size is measured in points. There are 72 points to an inch. Points are also used to subdivide picas. Thus, a column width might be indicated as 12 picas, 6 points. There are 12 points to a pica. *(See also pica.)*

Posterization

Posterization is a technique that you can use to add impact to photographs by dropping out the middle, or gray tones. With gray tones eliminated, the photographs begin to approach highly stylized line art. This can add interest by creating an impressionistic or highly stylized image.

Primary colors

Primary colors are the colors red, yellow, and blue – the colors which, when added together, create white. *(See also secondary colors.)*

Proportional spacing

Most computer typeface designs are proportionally spaced; that is, each letter occupies a differing amount of space. Thin letters like i's occupy less space than thick letters like m's or w's. This is in contrast to monospaced, or typewritten characters where each letter occupies the same amount of space in a line. Proportionally spaced type saves space and creates easier-to-read type by allowing word shapes to emerge more visibly. *(See also monospace.)*

Pull-quotes

Pull-quotes are short phrases or sentences extracted from the body copy of a story and set in a contrasting typeface. Pull-quotes succeed to the extent that they succinctly summarize the content of a story in a simple, easily read, and – at best – memorable way. You should include pull-quotes for both aesthetic and functional reasons. Pull-quotes help break up long text blocks, as well as offer readers an additional opportunity to enter your story and begin reading.

Resolution

Resolution refers to printer clarity or the amount of detail that a printer can reproduce. Most laser printers operate at 300 dots per inch. High-resolution printers can create letters and numbers at 400, 600, 800, or 1,000 dots per inch. High-resolution typesetters can create letters at 1,250 or 2,470 dots per inch. High-resolution printing eliminates the unnatural thickening of serifs and filling in of details that often occurs at 300 dots per inch. In addition, high-resolution printing eliminates the granularity, or large dots, characteristic of gray screens.

Rivers

Rivers are distracting vertical or diagonal white shapes running through columns of justified text. Rivers are created by the unintentional alignment of oversize gaps between words. Rivers are frequently created when two spaces are inserted following end-of-sentence periods.

Rule

Rules are horizontal, vertical, or diagonal lines used to add emphasis to a headline or subhead, or to provide a visual barrier to indicate closure of one topic and introduction of another. Rules can be thick or thin, printed in shades of gray, or printed in a second color.

Run-in

Run-ins are subheads set in the body copy. They usually represent the lowest level in the subhead hierarchy. Run-ins are typically set at the same size as the body copy, but are frequently set in a different type style – often bold or italic. They can also be set in a contrasting typeface.

Sans serif

A primary design characteristic and classification tool, sans serif ("without serif") typeface designs are unadorned by the horizontal strokes which aid letter identification and provide letter-to-letter transitions for the reader's eyes. Sans serif typefaces present a simple, unadorned contemporary appearance. Their primary characteristic is legibility (the quality which sets one letter off from another) at the expense of readability (the ease with which readers can read long text blocks). *(See also serif.)*

Script

Script typeface designs are designed to mimic handwritten words. Script typefaces are typically best used for short, formal applications, like invitations or diplomas. Extended text passages set in script typefaces are difficult to read.

Secondary colors

Secondary colors are created by mixing the primary colors, creating orange, green, and purple. These offer more opportunities for creative expression. *(See also primary colors.)*

Semi-bold

Typeface design midway in weight between roman, or regular, and bold. Semi-bold typeface designs, which appear as separate font listings on your font menu, allow you to add emphasis without the often unwanted "shouting" added by the use of a full bold style. *(See also bold, demi-bold, extra bold, weight.)*

Serif

Serifs are small, horizontal strokes that typeface designers add to letters to enhance readability by providing letter-to-letter transitions and helping emphasize the shapes of the individual words. Serifs can be prominent or unobtrusive; sharp, rounded, or squared; and of either uniform or varying thickness. *(See also sans serif.)*

Sidebar

Sidebars are short passages extracted from an article that focus on a single aspect of the longer text block. Sidebars are placed within or next to the longer feature; they are introduced by their own headline, subordinate in size to the primary headline. Sidebars are frequently surrounded by boxes or placed against a screened background.

Sink

A sink is a consistent amount of white space added at the top of each text column. This space creates page-to-page unity and provides space for headlines or visuals. Also called a "drop."

Small caps

Small caps are uppercase letters, shorter than regular uppercase letters, that are used within headlines or body copy. There are two types of small caps: scaled or true. Scaled small caps are created by your software program. Although you can sometimes specify their height, it is usually midway between a typeface's x-height and the height of its uppercase letters. True Small Caps are specially designed fonts that are designed to equal the x-height of the typeface. *(See also True Small Caps.)*

Sparkle

Sparkle applies to pages set in a "busy" typeface design that attracts unnecessary attention to itself, interfering with the reader's comprehension of the message. Sparkle often results when Modern typefaces, characterized by prominent serifs and a great amount of stress, are used for body copy. *(See also Modern, texture.)*

Spread

Although most computer screens show a single page at a time, most readers simultaneously encounter the left- and right-hand pages of a publication together. A spread refers to the left- and right-hand pages when viewed as a single unit.

Stress

Stress refers to the proportional difference in stroke thickness between the thickest and thinnest parts of a letter. Stress also refers to the direction of the changes, as well as the abruptness of the transition from thick to thin. Typefaces with no stress are composed of strokes of uniform thickness, as contrasted to typefaces with a moderate amount of difference or high-stress faces with a great amount of difference. Modern typefaces are characterized by a great deal of dramatic, vertical stress; Transitional typefaces are characterized by moderate, diagonal stress. *(See also Geometric, Humanistic, Old Style, Modern, Transitional.)*

Stroke

Strokes refer to the horizontal and vertical lines which make up individual typeface characters. The strokes of a letter can be thick or thin. Strokes can be the same thickness or change in thickness depending on their horizontal or vertical orientation. *(See also stress.)*

Styles

Styles are files containing formatting options for the various elements of page architecture. Once created, styles maintain consistency and save great amounts of time. Styles can contain the following character and paragraph formatting options (among others): typeface, type size, type style, line spacing, alignment, tracking, color, paragraph indent, and hyphenation. You can share styles between documents and edit them. When edited, the changes will "ripple through" the document, reformatting every occurrence of the text associated with the style.

Swash character

Many typeface designs include alternative characters that can add visual interest to a title, logo, or newsletter nameplate. Not intended for use in general body copy, swash characters include uppercase A's, Q's, and R's with strokes that extend far to the left or right of the main body of the letter, tucking under adjacent letters.

Swipe file

Slang for "inspiration" files which professional graphic artists often create, containing examples of good-looking printed pieces which catch their eye. Their intention in saving the pieces is not to copy these pieces, but to analyze them and learn what makes them look good. Artists often consult these files at the start of a project in order to get the creative juices going. Printed pieces can also be used to ascertain client likes and dislikes.

Symmetrical

Symmetrical refers to pages or two-page spreads characterized by left-right balance. Symmetry is a goal of conservative or classical designs in which text and visuals are centered and of relatively uniform sizes. *(See also asymmetrical.)*

Templates

Templates are "empty" documents containing previously established page layout and formatting options. Templates typically include page borders, column placement, page numbering, and styles containing character and paragraph formatting options. Templates permit you to assemble documents on the framework of previously created documents, avoiding the need to "reinvent the wheel" each time you begin a new issue of your newsletter or training document. Many software programs include a selection of professionally created templates. You can also purchase templates from third parties or create your own on the basis of existing documents. Most software programs prevent you from inadvertently modifying previously created templates; others request that you verify your intention to modify the template. *(See also styles.)*

Text offset

Text offset refers to the amount of white space between text and adjacent visuals or graphic accents. By defining a desired text offset, you can automatically maintain consistent spacing between subheads and horizontal rules or graphics inserted within or between columns of text.

Texture

Texture refers to the "weave," or consistency of letter and word spacing throughout a text block. Good typography is characterized by consistent texture from line to line and page to page. Bad typography is characterized by alternating "loose" and "tight" lines. *(See also loose line, tight line.)*

Tight line

When setting type in justified columns, "tight" lines occur when the line contains several short words and word spacing is squeezed to the minimum amount possible. "Tight" lines are especially bothersome when they immediately follow "loose" lines, which have unusually wide spaces between words. The cure is to overrule your software program's hyphenation choices or to increase the minimum acceptable word spacing specification. *(See also loose line.)*

Tracking

Tracking refers to software commands that permit you to alter letterspacing over words, phrases, or extended text blocks. Tracking permits you to increase or decrease letterspacing uniformly for every letter pair in the selected text. Tracking also enables you to tighten up headline and body copy letterspacing for a more professional appearance, or increase letterspacing for words set in uppercase or small caps. *(See also kerning.)*

Transitional

Transitional typeface designs are characterized by moderate amounts of vertical stress and rounded serifs. Times Roman is perhaps the most popular Transitional typeface. *(See also Geometric, Humanist, Modern, Old Style, stress.)*

True Small Caps

True Small Caps are typeface designs characterized by uppercase letters scaled to the x-height of the normal alphabet. They are most commonly found in serif typefaces. True Small Caps differ from small caps created on-the-fly by software programs in that they are exactly the x-height of the typeface, and the strokes have the same thickness as the original typeface. (Scaled small caps have noticeably thinner strokes.) True Small Caps appear as separate listings in the font menu. *(See also x-height.)*

Ultra bold

Ultra bold typefaces are typeface design variations containing noticeably thicker strokes than found in the typeface's bold or extra bold style options. Ultra bold typeface designs are best used for headlines and logos. *(See also bold, extra bold.)*

Weight

Weight describes the thickness of the horizontal and vertical strokes that make up each letter and number in a single font. Most typeface designs are available in a variety of weights, ranging from light or thin, to heavy or black. The strokes of light typefaces are noticeably thinner than heavy, or black typeface designs. Think of weight as a measure of how much ink is needed to reproduce the letter. *(See also black, demi-bold, light, semi-bold, stress, ultra bold.)*

Widow

A widow consists of letters left over from a hyphenated word, or a word or group of words less than one-third the length of the line, isolated by themselves at the bottom of a column or page. *(See also orphan.)*

X-height

The x-height of a typeface refers to an imaginary line along the tops of lowercase letters lacking ascenders – such as a, e, i, o, u, as well as the bowls of letters like b and d. The x-height of a typeface plays a more important role in determining how large the type appears on the page than its size. Typefaces with a small x-height appear significantly smaller than high x-height typefaces set the same size. *(See also ascender, descender.)*

Bibliography

A Manual of Comparative Typography: The PANOSE System

Bauermeister, Benjamin. New York: Van Nostrand Rhinehold, 1988. Contains the most concise description of typeface architecture plus the way most characters of the alphabet are modeled on a few basic letterforms.

Better Type

Binns, Betty. New York: Watson-Guptil, 1989. A large, highly visual treatment of the way type can be manipulated through changing letter, line, word, and paragraph spacing.

The Elements of Typographic Style

Bringhurst, Robert. Point Roberts, WA: Hartley & Marks, 1992. The elegant treatment of the architecture and use of type is a delight to hold, admire, or read.

Grid Systems and Formats Sourcebook: Ready-To-Use Materials for Print, Projected and Electronic Media

Burden, Ernest. New York: Van Nostrand Reinhold: 1992. An exhaustive look at the many ways multicolumn grids can be employed to organize text and graphics for a variety of projects.

The Electronic Type Catalog

Byers, Steve. New York: Bantam/ITC Books, 1992. This large-format volume contains both large and small samples of the major typeface designs. It's unique in that bold and italic variations are displayed along with regular roman designs.

Typographic Design: Form & Communication

Carter, Bob, Ben Day, Philip Meggs. New York: Van Nostrand Rhinehold, 1985. Contains numerous examples of the way type influences the effectiveness of the printed page.

Basic Typography: A Design Manual

Craig, James. New York: Watson-Guptil, 1990. A textbook approach to type.

Design with Type

Dair, Carl. Toronto: University of Toronto Press, 1989. A reprint of a short, but highly influential, pioneering study of type, emphasizing the psychology of reading.

The Designer's Guide to Creating Corporate I.D. Systems: For companies of all types and sizes

DeNeve, Rose. Cincinnati: North Light Books, 1992. Great education for designers and clients alike; a sequential walk through the various steps involved and issues raised.

Desktop Publisher's Easy Type Guide: the 150 Most Important Typefaces

Dewsnap, Don. Rockport, MA: Rockport Publishers, 1992. Large, horizontal format concentrates on displaying the major typeface designs accompanied by a short annotation of suggested usages.

How to Get Great Type Out of Your Computer

Felici, James. Cincinnati: North Light Books, 1990. Numerous short and to-the-point tips, ranging from the aesthetic to the practical, e.g. "how to prepare manuscripts for typesetting."

Essay on Typography

Gill, Eric. Boston: David R. Godine, 1988. (Reprint of a 1936 essay with a new introduction by Christopher Skelton.) At times outdated, this short volume, which originally appeared in 1931, nonetheless offers an opportunity to hear a master typographer discuss rules, many of which remain valid today.

The Verbum Book of Digital Typography

Gosney, Michael, Linnea Dayton, Jennifer Ball. San Mateo, CA: M&T Books, 1991. Contains numerous examples of how type can be manipulated with drawing and illustration programs.

The PostScript Font Handbook: A Directory of Type 1 Fonts

Grosvenor, Jonathan, Kaye Morrison, Alexandra Pim. Reading, MA: Addison-Wesley, 1992. A highly useful addition to anyone's library; contains examples of just about every typeface design offered by the major typeface vendors and a short historical introduction.

The ABC's of Type

Haley, Alan. New York: Van Nostrand Rhinehold, 1990. Informed essays on the origins and proper usage of the major typeface designs.

Typographic Milestones

Haley, Alan. New York: Van Nostrand Rhinehold, 1992. Required reading for anyone interested in the frequently confusing and often tumultuous field of type design.

Mapping Hypertext

Horn, Robert E. Lexington, MA: Lexinton Press, 1989. A provocative look at the future of information delivery.

Anatomy of a Typeface

Lawson, Alexander. Boston: David R. Godine, 1990. The "new classic" volume on type design, so good you may want to purchase the hardbound version instead of the more readily found softbound edition.

Letterhead and Logo Designs 2

Rockport, MA: Rockport Publishers, 1992. Inspirational samples from around the world.

News by Design: A Survival Guide for Newspapers

Lockwood, Robert. Denver: Quark Press, 1992. Focuses on the increasingly visual nature of print communications with numerous before and after examples of newspaper redesigns.

Designer's Mix & Match Type

Pape, Ian. New York: Design Press, 1992. A very tactile book; spiral bound, each page is horizontally cut into four sections. As a result, you can compare any combination of headline, subhead, body copy, and footnote sized types.

The Complete Typographer

Perfect, Christopher. Englewood Cliffs, NJ: Prentice Hall, 1992. The most satisfying type specimen book to date. Each section opens with detailed descriptions of a few of the category's most important typeface designs followed by full upper- and lowercase alphabet samples of other designs.

Typography Now: The Next Wave

Poynor, Rick and Edward Booth-Cliborn. Cincinnati: North Light Books, 1991. A look at the latest trends in avant-garde typography and layout which offers a new level of reader involvement in the communication process.

47 Printing Headaches (And How To Avoid Them)

Sanders, Linda. Cincinnati: North Light Books, 1991. Practical and well-informed, this book can save you hundreds, even thousands, of dollars.

Making a Good Layout: A hands-on guide to understanding and using basic principles of design and layout

Siebert, Lori and Lisa Ballard. Cincinnati: North Light Books, 1992. An organized combination of text and examples. Short and to the point.

Stop Stealing Sheep & Find Out How Type Works

Spiekermann, Erik and E.M. Ginger. Mountain View, CA: Adobe Press, 1993. Recommended to anyone who wants to "think" instead of just "read." Relates the language of type to the language of words, photography, and everyday visual design.

How to Design and Use Layout

Swan, Alan. Cincinnati: North Light Books, 1987. Numerous examples of type in use.

The Form of the Book

Tschichold, Jan. Point Roberts, WA: Hartley & Marks, 1992. A "return to the classics" book by the typographer most associated with contemporary typography and page layout.

Treasury of Alphabets and Lettering

Tschichold, Jan. New York: Design Press, 1992. Updated reprint of a book that originally appeared in 1952 and contains numerous concise statements worthy of repetition today.

Type in Use

White, Alexander. New York: Design Press, 1992. Teaches by example; contains over 300 examples of typography gathered from samples which range from slick, polished magazines to corporate internal publications. Its 11 chapters are organized into the major elements of page architecture: headlines, subheads, body copy, captions, and so forth.

Editing by Design

White, Jan V. New York: R.R.Bowker, 1983. The classic volume which introduced the era of "functional, rather than decorative" design.

Color for the Electronic Age: What every desktop publisher needs to know about using color effectively in charts, graphs, typography, and pictures

White, Jan V. New York: Xerox Press, 1990. Illustrated examples of the right and wrong ways to use color.

The Mac Is Not a Typewriter

Williams, Robin. Berkeley: Peachpit Press, 1992. This slim volume shows how to achieve correct punctuation using a variety of software for Macintoshes.

The PC Is Not a Typewriter

Williams, Robin. Berkeley: Peachpit Press, 1992. A slim volume that shows how to achieve correct punctuation for users of Windows 3.1 software.

Publications

Aldus Magazine

(Bimonthly) Aldus Corporation, 411 First Avenue South, Seattle, WA 98104-2871. Expands your creative horizons by helping you translate the ideas in this book to software programs like Aldus PageMaker, Freehand, and Persuasion. Its tips and techniques save you time so you can spend more time fine-tuning your documents.

Before and After: How to Design Cool Stuff

(Bimonthly) PageLab, 1850 Sierra Gardens Drive, Suite 30, Roseville, CA 95661. 916-784-3800. Each issue shows numerous advanced techniques made easy through step-by-step guidance.

Font and Function

(Quarterly) Adobe Systems, PO Box 7900, Mountain View, CA 94039-7900. Adobe System's catalog of available typefaces, focusing on their latest designs.

In-House Graphics

(Monthly) United Communications, 11300 Rockville Pike, Suite 1100, Rockville, MD 20852-3030. Required reading for anyone working in a corporate environment. Covers both theory and practical issues. A highlight is its yearly compensation and responsibility review based on reader surveys.

Newsletter Design

(Monthly) Newsletter Clearing House, PO Box 311, Rhinebeck, NY 12572. Each issue contains detailed critiques of numerous newsletters; an excellent starting point for improving your own designs.

Reference Guide: The Complete Font Software Resource, Version 4.0

Commack, NY: Precision Type, 1993. Extensively cross-referenced listing and specimens of every major typeface design from every major software publisher.

Publish: The Art and Technology of Information Design

(Monthly) 501 Second Street, San Francisco, CA 94107. The original publication in its field, balancing the needs of newcomers as well as sophisticated users. Required reading for those who want to push the envelope of technology to its limit.

The Page

(Ten times/year) PO Box 14493, Chicago, IL 60614. A professional designer's outspoken and pragmatic analysis of the latest hardware and software and their real-world applications. Balances design and hardware/software issues for both Apple Macintosh and Windows issues.

U&LC

(Quarterly) International Typeface Corporation, 866 Second Avenue, New York, NY 10017. Designed to teach by example, features historical studies of familiar typeface designs, articles featuring individual letters, and samples of the latest typeface designs.

X-Height

c/o FontHaus, Inc., 1375 Kings Highway, Fairfield, CT 06430. An informed collection of design and function articles certain to please any type lover.

Index

Colophon

The ONE-MINUTE DESIGNER *was typeset primarily in Adobe Minion and Frutiger.*

Minion was chosen because of its availability in a variety of weights and widths. Minion also contains True Small Caps and Old Style Figures.

Point numbers are Minion Display at 60 points. Headlines are set in Minion Black, 18 points with 18-point leading.

Text is set in 11 on 12 with a one-pica hyphenation zone. Annotations are set in Minion italics, 10 on 12.

Unless otherwise indicated, Minion and Frutiger are used in the examples.

The ONE-MINUTE DESIGNER was created on a five-column grid with a one-pica gap between columns. Software included PageMaker 4.0 and Adobe Illustrator 4.0 running under Microsoft Windows 3.1. Additional software included Microsoft Excel 3.0, Micrographx ABC FlowCharter, and Graphics Works. Hardware includes a Dell 486-DX50 and a Hewlett-Packard II-P scanner.

Pages were proofed on Hewlett-Packard LaserJet II, IIID, and IV printers equipped with LaserJet WinJet 800 and WinJet 1200 accelerator and resolution improvement hardware and software. A Linotronic 330 was used for final output.